God's Armies

God's Armies

CRUSADE AND JIHAD:
ORIGINS, HISTORY, AFTERMATH

Malcolm Lambert

PEGASUS BOOKS
NEW YORK LONDON

GOD'S ARMIES

Pegasus Books Ltd
148 West 37th Street, 13th Fl.
New York, NY 10018

Copyright 2016 © by Malcolm Lambert

First Pegasus Books paperback edition October 2017
First Pegasus Books hardcover edition October 2016

ISBN: 978-1-68177-531-9

10 9 8 7 6 5 4 3 2 1

Printed in the United States of America
Distributed by W. W. Norton & Company, Inc.

This book is dedicated to the memory of Leo Liepmann, co-founder of Oxfam and at one time our landlord in Oxford. Jewish in origin, Quaker in belief, Professor of Economics at Breslau, he left Germany in 1933, as soon as Hitler came to power, carrying with him a giant bottle of aspirins which I remember admiring in his kitchen.

CONTENTS

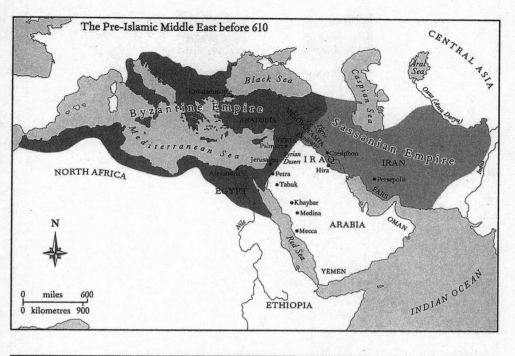

The Pre-Islamic Middle East before 610

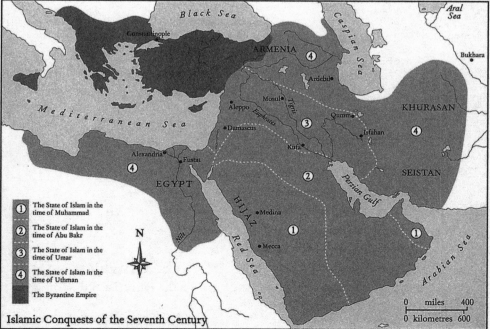

The State of Islam in the time of Muhammad

The State of Islam in the time of Abu Bakr

The State of Islam in the time of Umar

The State of Islam in the time of Uthman

The Byzantine Empire

Islamic Conquests of the Seventh Century

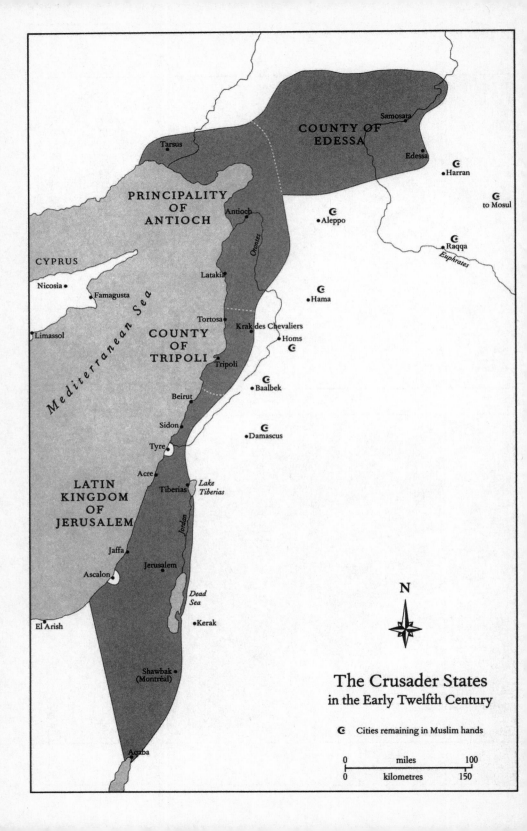

COUNTY OF
EDESSA

Samosata

Tarsus

Edessa

Harran

PRINCIPALITY
OF
ANTIOCH

Antioch

Aleppo

to Mosul

Orontes

Raqqa

Euphrates

CYPRUS

Latakia

Nicosia

Famagusta

Mediterranean Sea

COUNTY
OF
TRIPOLI

Tortosa

Krak des Chevaliers

Hama

Homs

Limassol

Tripoli

Baalbek

Beirut

Sidon

Damascus

Tyre

Acre

Tiberias

Lake Tiberias

LATIN
KINGDOM
OF
JERUSALEM

Jordan

Jaffa

Jerusalem

Ascalon

Dead Sea

El Arish

Kerak

N

Shawbak
(Montréal)

The Crusader States
in the Early Twelfth Century

☾ Cities remaining in Muslim hands

Aqaba

| 0 | miles | 100 |
| 0 | kilometres | 150 |

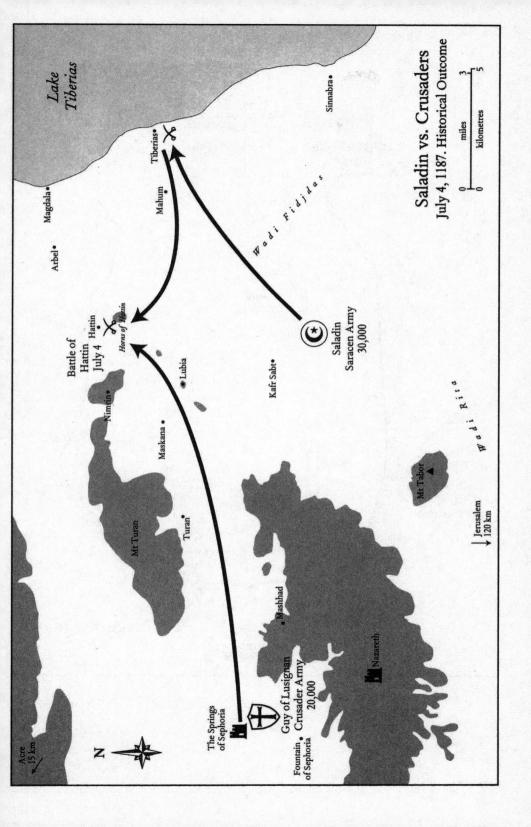

Saladin vs. Crusaders
July 4, 1187. Historical Outcome

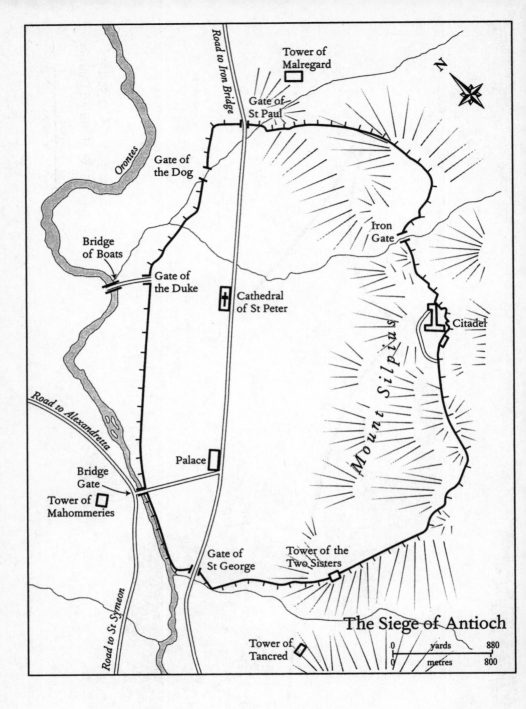

Road to Iron Bridge

Tower of
Malregard

Gate of
St Paul

Orontes

Gate of
the Dog

Iron
Gate

Bridge
of Boats

Gate of
the Duke

Cathedral
of St Peter

Citadel

Mount Silpius

Road to Alexandretta

Palace

Bridge
Gate

Tower of
Mahommeries

Gate of
St George

Tower of the
Two Sisters

Road to St Symeon

The Siege of Antioch

Tower of
Tancred

| 0 | yards | 880 |
| 0 | metres | 800 |

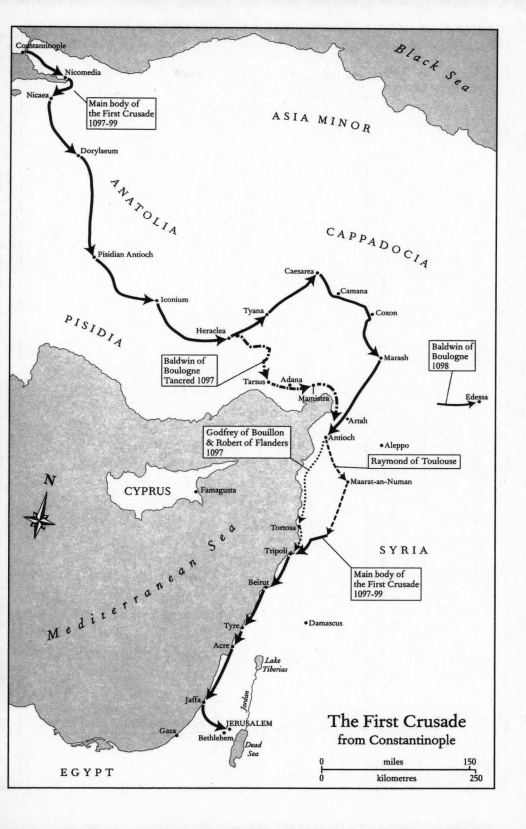

Constantinople

Black Sea

Nicomedia

Nicaea

Main body of
the First Crusade
1097-99

ASIA MINOR

Dorylaeum

A N A T O L I A

CAPPADOCIA

Caesarea

Camana

Pisidian Antioch

Coxon

P I S I D I A

Iconium

Tyana

Marash

Baldwin of
Boulogne
1098

Heraclea

Baldwin of
Boulogne
Tancred 1097

Tarsus

Adana

Mamistra

Edessa

Artah

Antioch

Aleppo

Godfrey of Bouillon
& Robert of Flanders
1097

CYPRUS

Famagusta

Raymond of Toulouse

Maarat-an-Numan

Tortosa

Tripoli

S Y R I A

Main body of
the First Crusade
1097-99

Beirut

M e d i t e r r a n e a n   S e a

Tyre

Damascus

Acre

Lake
Tiberias

Jaffa

Jordan

Gaza

JERUSALEM

Bethlehem

Dead
Sea

The First Crusade
from Constantinople

E G Y P T

| 0 | | miles | | 150 |
| 0 | | kilometres | | 250 |

A Simplified Family Tree of the Prophet and the Caliphal Dynasties

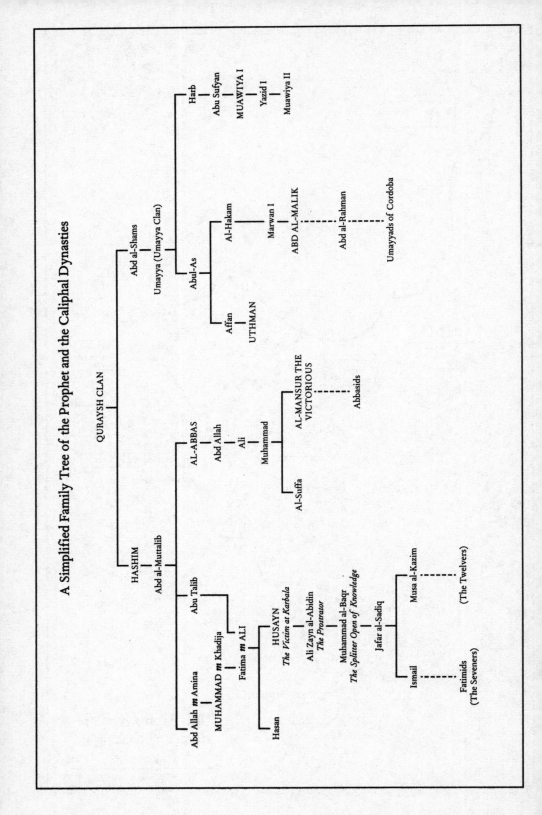

The Genealogy of the Kings of Jerusalem

Godfrey of Bouillon (d. 1100), Advocate of the Holy Sepulchre, died without issue, as did his brother King Baldwin I (d. 1118)

Baldwin II (d. 1131) *m* Morphia of Melitene (d. between 1126 and 1128)

Iveta, Abbess of Bethany (d. 1178)

Fulk V of Anjou King of Jerusalem (d. 1143) *m* Melisende (d. 1161)

Alice (d. 1151) *m* Bohemond of Antioch (d. 1130)

Hodierna (d. c. 1165) *m* Raymond II of Tripoli (d. 1152)

Constance (d. before 1174) *m* Reynald of Châtillon (d. 1187)

Raymond of Poitiers (d. 1149)

Baldwin (d. before 1176)

Maria (d. 1182) *m* Manuel Comnenus (d. 1180)

Bohemond III (d. 1201)

Eschiva II of Galilee (d. after 1187) *m* Raymond III of Tripoli (d. c. 1187)

Agnes of Courtenay (divorced 1163) (d. c. 1186) *m* Amalric (d. 1174) *m* Maria Comnena (d. 1217)

William of Montferrat (d. 1177) *m* Sibylla (d. 1190) *m* Guy of Lusignan (d. 1194)

Baldwin IV, the Leper (d. 1185)

Baldwin V (d. 1186)

Isabella (d. 1205)

m Humphrey IV of Toron (d. 1198)
m Conrad of Montferrat (d. 1192)
m Henry II, count of Champagne (d. 1197)
m Aimery of Lusignan (d. 1205)

INTRODUCTION

Emmanuel Sivan* drew me into writing this book. I chanced to come across his work at Bristol University, made it the theme of a contribution to a symposium of the Medieval Society and was thereafter intrigued.

Sivan approached crusading history from a less familiar angle, using Arabic poems and chronicles to show how the First Crusade, by capturing Jerusalem in 1099 from the Muslims, permanently altered its importance as a pilgrim's objective for the Islamic world. Mecca and the *Kaba* should be visited once in a lifetime, is the Prophet's command to believers. Medina is the site to which Muhammad fled to avoid persecution and likely death and holds his tomb. It is second to Mecca. Jerusalem, the site of Mount Moriah and of the Night Journey of the Prophet, was also a place of pilgrimage, but it ranked third and had fallen away in importance. The crusade changed everything: Jerusalem became a vital objective. Poets, preachers and Muslim leaders called for *jihad*, war for the defence of Islam to recover Jerusalem. It became the most divided city in the world, sacred to three religions: Christianity, Judaism and Islam. However, Sivan was too good a historian not to note that the changes he described took time. Muslims at first saw the capture of Jerusalem as a temporary phenomenon

---

*E. Sivan, *L'Islam et la croisade: Idéologie et propagande dans les réactions Musulmanes aux croisades* (Paris, 1968).

and were distracted by plague and their own dissensions. There was much abuse and self-interest behind early talk of jihad.

Sivan changed my view in another way. He taught me how important Nur al-Din was, the true master of Saladin and a broader thinker, who developed from being a self-seeking warlord to a true *jihadi* and a protagonist of moral rearmament within Islam to win God's favour for the recovery of Jerusalem. He was a propagandist of great style, who commissioned a pulpit to be put into the al-Aqsa mosque when the city fell to Muslim troops. But he also spoke for *jihad* to recover purity of faith, to establish Sunni orthodoxy against what he saw as the heresy of Shiism. This, I came to realise, was the more important objective for him, leading him to commission an architecture reflecting Sunnism and to sponsor a script for the Quran replacing the traditional Kufic, designed to eliminate obscurities in textual readings which aided Shiite missionaries.

Saladin acted for Nur al-Din and was a former mercenary who made his way from a humble position by sheer talent and achieved two vital objectives: Jerusalem and the elimination of the Fatimids as a power holding Cairo. There is no doubt which mattered more to Nur al-Din, and he lived to see it, as the *khutba* – the prayer for the ruler – ceased to be spoken for the Fatimid caliph in Cairo. Saladin it was in 1187 who took Jerusalem and installed Nur al-Din's *minbar*, the specially constructed pulpit, in the al-Aqsa mosque after his death.

The conflict between Sunni and Shiites remains the deepest source of division within Islam, as was painfully apparent in 2015 with the emergence of the Isil group. My first chapter surveys the period 610–61, which is vital for understanding how the conflict originated and is appropriately studied by a medievalist.

Crusades as a field of study has moved rapidly in recent decades and has been written up by fine historians. Islamic history also has had excellent historians, and both the United States and Britain have made major contributions but it has not been so well publicised. This has encouraged me to give space to the Islamic side, and to devote my second chapter to give a glimpse of the complexity of belief and aspiration in the formative years before the eleventh century and to illustrate the deepening divisions in

Islam. Information can only illuminate on both sides. Public opinion in the West has too often been inclined to see Islam as one unified force, often in its most radical form. This is a grave distortion, and I hope to explain something of the variety of forms that Islam takes and the possibilities it offers of healing and reconciliation with Christianity. On the other side, a leading Western theologian on a mission for the Blair Foundation in Iran found that scholars there were surprised and interested to learn of the great variety of opinions within contemporary Christianity.

After I had embarked on writing, my last inspiration came from Thames and Hudson's splendidly illustrated account of the making of a new *minbar* to replace Nur al-Din's original within the al-Aqsa mosque, destroyed by a deranged Australian arsonist in 1968. It has made me realise what a vital contribution has been made both by the Hashemite rulers of Jordan and HRH Charles, Prince of Wales,* rescuing traditional Islamic workmanship from near extinction, drawing from Turkey the vital walnut and giving the impetus to as exact a reproduction as is possible, recreating the ancient technique, which dispenses with glue, holding in balance patterned wood and inlays of ebony and ivory. The Prince's School of Traditional Arts brings together skilled workers without distinction of belief, in accordance with his wish to act as Defender of Faiths. I was especially moved by the passages on sacred geometry, the illustration from Chartres Cathedral and the argument that the religions of the world have a major part to play in the combating of crude materialism.

A last note: in keeping with the notion that Christians and Muslims worship the same God, I have substituted God for Allah, as far as I am able, in the quotations.

---

*For a broader explanation of the Prince of Wales's views on materialism, see his book *Harmony: A New Way of Looking at our World*, written with T. Juniper and I. Skelly (London, 2010).

THE ORIGINS OF ISLAM

To the Arab world of the seventh century, the coming of Islam was a major shock. Traditionally idol-worshipping and polytheistic, this was a society which believed in a kind of slot-machine use of deities – of which there were many, each responsible for some of the functions of daily life. Sacrifices to these deities, it was hoped, would produce the results desired. These nomadic desert dwellers inhabited a largely arid peninsula, living by their flocks and herds and, above all, by the camel, which was pre-eminent for raiding, provisioning and trading because of its capacity for speed and for travelling two weeks without water. Possession of, or access to, oases made these people's hardy life possible. The dull routine of pastoral life was enlivened by the excitement of raiding, driving off animals, fighting over sources of water and grazing rights, avenging deaths of clan members. In this harsh environment the burying alive of unwanted female infants was customary. Poetry celebrating heroic warriors, their victories and their deaths was greatly valued. The Bedouin used magic to propitiate demons (*jinn*) and worshipped ancestors, sacred stones and the stars. It was an anarchic society, whose tribes were constantly splitting, so kinship ties were vital for community cohesion and law enforcement.

Beyond the desert, the *haram*, the pagan sanctuary, gave opportunities for common worship and economic exchange, and was a refuge from fighting. Pagan society linked their idols and temples to security of trade and to local commercial transactions, setting aside feuds and allowing for seasons in which trade would be undisturbed by violence. Fighting was never allowed in the temple area.

Muslim historians described this desert world and its assumptions as the *jahiliyya*, the 'time of ignorance', from which they were delivered by Muhammad, the Prophet of God. To this pagan society a new way of thinking, which passionately preached monotheism and believed the world of idols was wholly wrong, came as a threat, especially since this new preaching came from one of their number. Muhammad was an orphan member of the Hashemites, a lesser clan within the Quraysh ruling aristocracy of Mecca, who had made his way in the world and had risen to become a successful camel trader, a task which automatically demanded literacy. He made a happy companionate marriage with the rich Quraysh widow Khadija, fifteen years his senior, whose business he managed.

The Revelations of God which Muhammad believed were transmitted by the Archangel Gabriel came to him in about 610, as he was meditating in a mountain cave at Hira overlooking the town of Mecca. The Revelations, which continued at intervals throughout Muhammad's life and which were memorised by his followers or recorded on palm fronds and camel shoulder bones, made up the Quran – literally, 'that which is recited' – and to this day the recitation of the Quran remains a prime duty of the believer. The power of Muhammad's preaching and his charismatic personality began to win converts within Mecca, known as the Companions. They were especially dear to him, being the first followers to join him in times of adversity.

Mecca, on the desert lands of the Hijaz in Western Arabia, was ill equipped for any agriculture because of its poor water supply, but it had become the leading pagan pilgrimage centre of the region, with a massive assemblage of idols and tribal gods in an open temple in the main square. This attracted merchants, making it a commercial centre for trade, largely in raw materials, using camel caravans travelling to the north. Truces associated with the annual pagan pilgrimage gave opportunity for bargaining and for settling disputes. As Muhammad spoke openly of his Revelations, he found the aristocracy of Mecca turning against him, fearful of the effects on their trade of his denunciations of idols and anxious for the fate of their ancestors as he described the torments of scorching fires in hell for all who worshipped idols. Some converts felt such a pressure on them that in about 615 they left for Abyssinia, also known as Ethiopia, where they were given protection by the Christian ruler, Negus. Other converts tended to come from those who were not leaders in trade or from slaves, responding to Muhammad's teaching about care of the poor and his rejection of the avarice of the ruling aristocracy.

One exception was Abu Bakr, a wealthy Quraysh and pragmatic fellow camel trader, who sacrificed his fortune to help Muhammad in his mission and to compensate other followers who lacked resources. He suffered damage by adhering to Muhammad's teaching. It was a personal comfort to Muhammad that Khadija believed in his Revelations and was an unfailing supporter until her death. Among the wives whom he married after Khadija's death, Abu Bakr's daughter Aisha was his favourite, having the greatest influence on him as well as a willingness to speak independently.

Muhammad's cousin Ali, a devoted early supporter married to Fatima, daughter of the marriage to Khadija, was a hero in the tradition of pre-Islamic Arabia, admired for his poetic gifts and reckless valour. He was in a sense the son which Muhammad never had, for with Khadija he only had daughters, their two sons dying in infancy. Ali occupied a special place in Islamic history because of his undeviating integrity: both his strength and his weakness.

In 619 Muhammad's uncle and clan leader, al-Abbas, died. Although he never became a Muslim himself, he had defended Muhammad from enemies, and his death exposed the Prophet, for that was what he had become, to the danger of sharp counteraction by Quraysh kinsmen determined to put a stop to the continuing Revelations and the effects they might have on their commercial power.

The bitter disputes of the two major pagan clans in Medina, an oasis town a little over 200 miles north of Mecca, had issued in a disastrous battle in which many men had been killed. In about 620 a deputation called on Muhammad to ask if he would become an independent arbiter to ensure that there would be no recurrence. After negotiation he agreed. The decision, enshrined in a formal agreement between Muhammad and the people of Medina, provided a potential haven for Muhammad and his followers when they were persecuted in Mecca.

Muhammad in Medina

When Abu Bakr and Ali uncovered a plot by the Quraysh to assassinate Muhammad, preparations to move to Medina were implemented. In 622 about seventy of his followers were sent to the town in small batches so as not to arouse suspicion. Medina was a settlement with wells, some agriculture, silver and gold mines and with basalt volcanic rock on three sides, making it highly defensible. While Abu Bakr and Muhammad slipped away and hid in a cave overnight before making their way by little-known paths to Medina, Ali took the risk of sleeping in Muhammad's bed, infuriating the assassins and narrowly escaping death. This emigration, the *hijra*, forms the starting-point for the Islamic calendar. Diplomatically, according to tradition, Muhammad let his camel choose the spot where he would stay in the long line of fortified farms and water sources which made up Medina.

In Medina, Muhammad and the Companions gained freedom of worship but had to fight against the Meccans as the Quraysh sought to eliminate them. The Revelations in the Quran from the Meccan period urge the believers to show patience and forbearance under suffering and deter them from any retaliation. In the Medinan period they are urged to take direct military action to defend themselves and their beliefs against attacks which could well have extinguished the young religion, while at the same time many detailed instructions are given for the practice of faith in daily living. In effect a theocratic mini-state was being called into life.

In all, only twenty-four verses in the whole of the Quran mention *jihad* (literally, 'striving'), and most frequently they have a spiritual meaning, inspiring the hearer to a total commitment of possessions and mind to obedience to God. *Jihad,* striving in the way of God, however, in the Medinan period for the elite leadership often had the meaning of fighting for the faith – albeit with careful restrictions on when and how this should be done. Warriors from the desert, accustomed as they were to fighting, took up arms willingly, while the example of Muhammad's actions and the words of the Quran inspired the leaders who took charge of the early Muslim armies.

Muhammad used his preaching power to make converts in Arabia, being prepared to endure hostility, even missile-throwing, and sending out letters to clan leaders and rulers – even, according to tradition, to the Christian Byzantine leader, the emperor Heraclius – calling on them all to recognise his divinely inspired teaching. He attacked the Quraysh by launching fighters against camel caravans, on which their prosperity was based, successfully assaulting them at the well of Badr in 624, overcoming a much superior Meccan force and gaining wealth to sustain Medina. In the aftermath of their defeat at Badr he became aware of the unwilling-ness of Jewish clans in Medina to accept his leadership and dispatched one of the clans to exile at the oasis of Khaybar, north of Medina, confiscating their goods. The Meccans reacted with subtlety to defeat at Badr and in 624–5* sent an army to the hill of Uhud, whence they were able to raid Medina and damage crops while not endangering their cavalry, among its trees and defences. Muhammad accepted the challenge and went out to fight but was injured. Meanwhile, the Jewish clans remained neutral, and Muhammad began to see that he could not win security in Medina for himself and the faith as long as they remained; another clan was sent into exile to Khaybar. Finally in 627 his army faced its most serious challenge, from the Quraysh. At the battle of the Trench the Prophet made his own military decision, ordering the digging of a trench at the north side of Medina, the one point where there were no rock formations to ward off cavalry attack. His decision led to a Meccan defeat and also to a final reck-oning for the last Jewish clan, the Banu Qurayza, whom he believed to be treasonable. For the battle of the Trench, Jews from Khaybar had joined

---

*Islamic dating is based on the lunar year and cannot always be reconciled with the Western traditional solar year of 365 days; hence the convention of linking two Western years for some Islamic dates.

forces with the Quraysh army. It was the last straw. Muhammad accepted the decision of an intermediary that the clan should be eliminated, the men being beheaded and the women and children sent into slavery. The *qibla*, the direction of prayer, which had been Jerusalem, was changed to become Mecca. Pagans had accepted Muhammad, Jewish opposition had been eliminated and a way of life set out, with the duties for the faithful that are the Five Pillars of Islam: the profession of faith in one God, prayer, almsgiving, fasting and pilgrimage. Medina, and the decisions made there were thus formative for the Muslim future. An *umma*, the community of faith based on the conduct of Muhammad and the teachings of the Quran, had come into being. The term subsequently applied to all Muslim believers in the world.

In the aftermath of the suppression of Khaybar, Muhammad developed his teaching on the role of the *dhimmis*, the Peoples of the Book, principally the Jews and Christians, who had sacred scriptures of their own. They were misguided in Muhammad's teaching: Jesus, for example, was a prophet to be venerated but never worshipped as God and is depicted as sorrowing in heaven at the grievous misunderstanding of his role by the Christians. Still, the *dhimmis* were to be distinguished from the polytheist pagans and their rights were to be respected. They should pay a special tax, the *jizya*, not an unduly arduous sum and not imposed on the poor. Over time it might well act as an inducement for them to convert to Islam, although it was expected that they would in any case come to understand the superiority of the Muslim faith. Muhammad's teaching was the culmination of all previous prophecies and intimations of God's will, while Judaism and Christianity represented stages on the way to the full and final revelation proclaimed to the world by Muhammad.

The Quran has no unified message about the treatment of unbelievers, whether they were pagans or *dhimmis*. Muhammad emerged as a fighting prophet from the persecutions he and his followers suffered in Mecca, battling for the life of his community against his Meccan opponents and against the Byzantine Christians who came belatedly to recognise the challenge Islam presented to them. In the Quran he is consoled with the example of Moses who fought external enemies more powerful than he was, repressed idolaters among his followers, was protected by God and is mentioned more frequently in the text than any other personality from the Hebrew Scriptures. On the other hand, there is a bewildering variety of views expressed on *jihad*. In the Sword text – *sura* 9, 15, much cited by militarists – the Quran, after citing repeated breaches of agreements by pagans, goes on: 'When the sacred months have lapsed, then slay the polytheists [...] seize them and encircle them.' Exasperated by this abuse of agreements, it is proclaimed that the tradition in the pre-Islamic world of the last of the four months being kept free from warfare should in this instance be ignored and war declared. Nevertheless, there is provision for a withdrawal by the polytheists. The text goes on: 'But if they repent, then let them go on their way.'

The Quran provides for asylum to be given to polytheists who ask for it, even if they decline to come over to the Faith (*sura* 9, 6). They are treated as ignorant, not able fully to understand and needing protection from attack by their fellow polytheists. Muhammad had a paternalist concern for *dhimmis*. *Sura* 22, 39–40, gives permission for believers to fight when they have been expelled from their homes solely because of their monotheist Muslim beliefs, but goes on to note that resistance to such oppressors should not mean that they attack *dhimmis* as well and expresses concern for their welfare and their places of worship, 'monasteries, churches, synagogues'; and another *sura* is concerned that Jews follow the requirements of the Torah and Christians the Gospels. He was not an uninhibited warrior: *sura* 2, 216, prescribes fighting and speaks of a 'dislike' for it, and *jihad* in other passages speaks of a patient forbearance under oppression as worthy of praise. A recent authoritative analysis of the Quran has concluded that under the heading of *jihad,* literally 'striving', there are more references to peaceful striving (against evil passions) than there are to armed combat!*

---

*A. Afsaruddin, *Striving in the Path of God: Jihad and Martyrdom in Islamic Thought* (Oxford, 2013). This is a work of high scholarship to which I am indebted for reflections, Quranic quotations and the Muslim response to the Twin Towers atrocity (see Chapter 12); see also her introduction, note 3, on the dating of the Quranic text.

Calm confidence and trust in God's power and the forces of angels He commands in the face of hostile unbelievers is enjoined in *sura* 8 of the Quran and no doubt reflects Muhammad's injunctions to his followers at Medina. Booty was the gift of God and the sign of favour, but there should be no excessive plundering and no self-enriching: the austerity of the desert should prevail, and the needs of the poor and the common cause should be paramount.

The victory for Medina and the faith at the battle of the Trench created an impasse. The Quraysh of Mecca could not eliminate the menace of Medina and its Muslim focus, and their trade was being damaged. On the other hand, Muhammad needed the support of the powerful men of Mecca if he was to make his universal appeal to all humanity. He set about making a deal with Mecca and at the well of Hudaybiyya in 628 achieved a compromise peace, with Ali acting as his secretary. There was to be a truce for ten years, and Muhammad with a small body of followers was to make a mini-pilgrimage, an *umra*, to the sacred enclosure at Mecca. Idols indeed were still there, but Muhammad understood that its sacredness sprang from Abraham and Ishmael, believers in one God, and only subsequently had been polluted by idol worshippers, who could not wholly remove its sacredness. So he was allowed to go on pilgrimage, and it was agreed that for three days Meccans would withdraw and leave him and his followers to enter the city.

Muhammad's mixture of diplomacy and war against the Quraysh of Mecca brought its fruit. In much of Arabia victories and conversions brought submission or alliance to the new Islamic power. The Yemen, which by a quirk of climate had its own agriculture and had been controlled by a Persian governor and garrison, suddenly found its troops withdrawn because of an emergency in the Persian heartland and thought it wise to listen to Muslim missionaries and accept Islam. A similar situation prevailed in Oman and Bahrain.

There was a clash with the Christian power of Byzantium in 629 as Muhammad's adopted son, the freed slave Zayd ibn Haritha, was dispatched to raid well beyond Arabia following the murder of a Muslim envoy in Syria. Zayd had reckoned with hostile tribesmen, whom he could expect to beat, but the Emperor Heraclius had got wind of the new power of Islam and sent his own professional troops to stiffen the tribesmen. At Mutah, at the southern end of the Dead Sea, Zayd's forces suffered a heavy defeat and he was killed. It was a blow, albeit mitigated by a second expedition, which was not targeted by Byzantine troops and which restored an Islamic claim on the edge of Syria.

Some Quraysh were not satisfied with the deal at Hudaybiyya and conspired against it. The Prophet took military action, heading an army of 10,000 that seemingly took Mecca by surprise; resisting calls for vengeance, he contented himself with a few executions of apostates and of singers who had satirised him. A high point of his life was his entry with Ali to the sacred enclosure in January 630, breaking the idols, leaving the Black Stone, the volcanic rock associated with Abraham, as a sacred object to be acknowledged on the *hajj* as pilgrims circled the *Kaba* (plate 2). Townspeople now abandoned their idols and Mecca became a stronghold of Islamic belief. Almost at once Muhammad's new supremacy was challenged by a multitude of Bedouin tribes led by men from Taif, the wealthy resort to which Muhammad had come during the Meccan years to spread his message, only to find himself contemptuously rejected. They were said to be 30,000 strong. At Hunayn he defeated them, immensely raising his prestige in Mecca and forcing the submission of Taif. They too had their idols broken and some of their inhabitants, the Thagafi, turned into valuable supporters of Islam. He continued to spread Islamic belief and influence, leading an expedition to Tabuk, 350 miles north-west of Medina, and taking the opportunity to make alliances with tribes near the gulf of Aqaba. Not all were willing to follow him, and a *sura* of the Quran refers to those who put comfort before their obligations, calling them hypocrites who profess belief but avoid actions.

As Muhammad made his pilgrimage to Mecca in the last year of his life with his wives and leading supporters, questions arose for his followers: how was the Muslim community, the *umma*, to be kept in being when Muhammad was gone? He had conveyed the voice of God to his world; was this prophetic power to be continued after death? As a leader, he had been a diplomat, statesman and commander in war, and had begun to transform the Arabian peninsula. How was his legacy in practical matters to be carried on?

It was clear that Muhammad was ill. He was about sixty-two and was no longer able to walk, so he was forced to ride round the sites on a camel instead, acting ritually to remove from each one all of its pagan associations. The modern *hajj* follows Muhammad's movements on this Last Pilgrimage in a stylised manner. The prescribed white clothing worn by men as the pilgrims circle seven times anti-clockwise round the *Kaba* and carry out the rest of the ritual duties, fulfils the Prophet's wish for austerity and eliminates all distinctions of wealth or class made manifest by clothing. The women circle round with the men on equal terms, totally covered but with face and hands exposed.

In a dialogue with the crowd accompanying him Muhammad gave what came to be remembered as his Farewell Sermon, believed to have been delivered on the Plain of Arafat. In it he stressed the need for fidelity to his message, the ethical requirements of belief, the rejection of usury, the proper relations of husband and wife, the treatment of slaves and the universal character of Islam with the words 'An Arab is superior to a non-Arab in nothing but devotion!' His position at the end of the pilgrimage was unassailable and unique. But what was to be done when he died?

On his way back to Medina there was a long pause at the oasis Ghadir Khumm, the pool in the Ghadir valley, as the caravan rested and took in water. The company swept a place for Muhammad under two palm trees from which he led prayers, entered into a dialogue with the people, then took Ali by the hand and conferred authority on him. It is not clear exactly what this authority was. Some sources do not mention Ghadir Khumm at all, while others suggest that Muhammad was conferring authority solely over Ali's own clan within the Quraysh. Another view that has been held by the Sunnis is that Ali had made an error of judgement over booty on the expedition which had created indignation among men who felt they had been cheated. Muhammad in this interpretation was using his authority to support Ali against these dissenters. The partisans (*Shia*) of Ali came to believe, by contrast, that the Prophet was conferring all his own authority on Ali.

The company moved on to end the journey at Medina in March. As he was weak, Muhammad asked Abu Bakr to take his place and lead prayers, and for some this was the sign that he wished Abu Bakr to be his successor. But the fact that anxieties over the succession were moving his followers in his last days is shown in the Episode of Pen and Paper, in which he called for writing materials, saying, 'I may write for you something after which you will not be led into error'. Confusion ensued. In the end nothing was written down, but many accepted a point forcibly made by Umar (also known as Omar), that Muhammad had already given his Revelations in the Quran. Umar had been an early Companion, close to the Prophet; an ex-wrestler, he was marked by strength and great powers of decision, and became the second caliph after the Prophet's death.

Muhammad ended his life in Aisha's hut in Medina. Partisans of Ali believed that the most intimate links between the two men were demonstrated when Ali washed the Prophet's body and wrapped it for burial in the hut where he died. However, it is perhaps significant that Muhammad's body remained in Aisha's hut for several days, quite against the conventions of burial away from habitation. It is not clear why this happened: did the Prophet's followers expect some miraculous event, a final judgement or a Resurrection? There is good reason to suppose that Muhammad's belief in an imminent Last Judgement gave an urgency to his preaching and military activities designed to bring the benefits of true monotheism to as many as possible before the End came. Aisha had evidently moved away to sleep with another of the wives. Three days later she was astonished to hear the noise of picks as a night-time burial took place under the floor of her hut. The Prophet lies there to this day, the site now enclosed in a mosque.

The Caliphate

Elsewhere in Medina a committee mainly of Emigrants from Mecca (that is, former Companions) assembled. Their prime concern was for the military and organisational tasks necessary to ensure the continuance of the developing Islamic state at Medina. The successor came from their own number rather than from the Helpers – those followers from Medina who had backed Muhammad inside his adopted place of residence – who had also put forward a candidate. They all needed a man of action but did not rule out a spiritual role for a successor, or *khalifa* (hence the term 'caliph').

Abu Bakr was a natural choice, with his great knowledge of the tribes and leaders of the Arabian peninsula through his experience of camel caravans (which could only be cost-effective if there was agreement with local powers along the route); and to end any dispute he was forcefully supported by Umar. In the interests of unity, the Medinan clans fell in with the decision, and on the morning following Muhammad's death, while Ali was tending to the Prophet's body, Abu Bakr climbed into the *minbar*, the pulpit in the mosque, and led the prayers. Reared in the tradition of personal austerity and accessibility of the Prophet, he then spoke to emphasise the duty he had undertaken to do justice, to secure the rights of the weak and to demand obedience only so long as he obeyed God and His messenger. He adopted the title Commander of the Faithful, emphasising the military side of the caliphate.

For the sake of the unity and the continuance of Islam, everyone acquiesced in Abu Bakr's elevation. Ali did not congratulate him, but neither did he press his case for recognition. Dissent slumbered.

Abu Bakr's Caliphate (632–4)

Abu Bakr was a man of action. Against some opposition he laid down that steps should be taken against tribal leaders who had stopped paying the charitable tax after the death of the Prophet, arguing that the contract was with Muhammad personally and that on his death the tax had lapsed. It was not, they argued, that they were abandoning the faith of the Prophet, but the tax should be given up. Abu Bakr knew the fissiparous nature of Arab tribal society and that, if he allowed this, the confederation in Arabia built up by Muhammad would at once unravel. He insisted that in all matters the Prophet's wishes must be fulfilled and, against some opposition, that Syria should continue to be a target for attack.

Abu Bakr set about harnessing the energies of the desert warriors. The peoples of the Arabian desert, who scratched a bare living from their flocks and herds, saw raiding and fighting rival tribes as a vital part of their lives and an essential remedy against the boredom of pastoral life. *Jihad*, understood as fighting, gave them action in an honourable cause – spreading the faith. Abu Bakr used his knowledge of the tribes of the peninsula to play one group off against another and avoid a battle when possible, but for major action he used Khalid ibn al-Walid, a latecomer to the faith who had fought against the Prophet at the battle of Uhud in 625 and who was regarded in some quarters as an opportunist. He turned out to be an inspired military leader. To him Abu Bakr entrusted the hard task of subduing the Beni Hanifa of the Yamamah lands east of Medina. They had a prophet of their own, who, in Arabic tradition, suggested that he would accept Muhammad as a prophet in Mecca and Medina, provided he was left as a prophet for the Beni Hanifa. But in Islam there could only be one Prophet and one Revelation. The slaughter of Companions and new Muslims as well as the Beni Hanifa that took place in the orchards known as the 'garden of death' was terrible, but Islam prevailed. It was a key action in what became known as the apostasy (*ridda*) campaigns of Abu Bakr.

Muhammad and Abu Bakr were heirs to the decline of two empires – that of Iran, based on the fertile lands of the Tigris and Euphrates, and that of Byzantium. The Persians in Iran were deadly enemies of Byzantium and had driven into Palestine to attack and capture Jerusalem in 614 and seize the True Cross. This was one of the greatest of all Christian relics, recovered by St Helena in the fourth century. With skill and energy the Byzantine emperor Heraclius (610–41) overcame the Sassanian dynasty and destroyed Iran's empire. He returned in triumph to Jerusalem bearing the True Cross, which he had taken from the Persians in a series of battles, and after entering the city in March 630 returned the relic to the Sepulchre, an event still commemorated in the liturgy of the Greek Orthodox Church. The triumph was the prelude to disaster, however, as the two major powers had exhausted themselves, creating a power vacuum and unwittingly opening the way to the new power of Muhammad and his followers.

Abu Bakr allowed his commanders to gain vital military experience as his expeditions pressed on to gain the wine, oil and grain of fertile lands known to him from his camel caravan days. Early in 634 one of those commanders, the wily Amr ibn al-As, defeated a small Byzantine force at Dathin, near Gaza. This alerted Byzantium to the arrival of a new enemy, confirmed as Abu Bakr's men captured Bostra, in southern Syria, south of Hauran, and laid siege to Damascus. To his successor Abu Bakr left the task of meeting the Byzantine backlash and carrying conquest farther north and west.

Abu Bakr's achievements were considerable, as he prevented the Islamic empire created by the Prophet from disintegrating, kept armies in being, sustained the attack on Syria and made Arabia a Muslim peninsula. His death took place in Medina in the summer of 634; he was buried with the Prophet. The designation of Umar as his successor was a formality and raised no controversy.

Caliph Umar (634–44)

Under Umar, who directed campaigns from Medina or a nearby training camp and did not move except to participate in the *hajj*, the full use of the dynamic driving force of the *jihad* made immense inroads into Palestine and Syria, leading city after city which had been Byzantine to accept a Muslim takeover. They preferred being compelled to pay the *jizya* rather than continue meeting the heavy burdens of taxation from the distant Byzantine government; moreover, doctrinal pressure from Constantinople to accept the Byzantine Trinitarian doctrine was particularly hard for the Coptic Monophysites, with their dissident views on the nature of Christ. Chronicles of the Empire, written in Syriac and Aramaic, give us clues to the reasons for Byzantine failure and Islamic success. They see the conquests as punishment for their sins, only to be overcome by prayers and good conduct. They had no will to fight.

Realising the threat now presented to his rule by the Muslims, Heraclius took station in Antioch in 636 and in southern Syria assembled a large army which was supplemented by many Arab forces – including, for example, the Ghazznavid dynasty, who had long been committed allies – in order to crush the new power once and for all.

Umar kept cool and assembled the largest Muslim army he could muster, denuding other danger points of men and pressing into service even the shakiest and least trained. Muslims came out of the cities so as to meet battle on terrain where they could best use their cavalry and, under Khalid's fine leadership, dashed in and out from the desert to the Byzantine position, harassing the enemy by the Yarmuk, a tributary of the River Jordan off the Sea of Tiberias which ran through deep ravines in the area of the Golan Heights. The Byzantines faced supply difficulties; their commander had expected the Arabs facing him to fade away in time or that he would be able to bribe them into submission, but what he actually faced was a new unity of faith. When battle was joined in October, it was hard fought for six days until Khalid manoeuvred his opponents on to a mass of ravines and skilfully pressed them towards a bottleneck over a Roman bridge. It was a rare event, in which the new resolution of Islamic warriors, battlefield manoeuvring by them to avoid the counter-skills of the Byzantine cavalry and a rumour of defection by Christian Arabs all played a part in producing utter and complete catastrophe for the Byzantines. Hardly any prisoners were taken, and Heraclius in Antioch, hearing of the disaster, recognised that his position was irremediable. He retreated to Anatolia and thence home to Constantinople.

Arab valour and cavalry skills now turned against the faded and exhausted power of Iran ruled by the Sassanians, an ancient warrior aristocracy rigidly based on descent. It was remote from its gentry class and still more from the Aramaeans, the farmers who brought to them the fruits of their work from the fertile lands between the Tigris and Euphrates and who were not well treated by the aristocracy. In consequence the Sassanians had few loyal followers who would defend them and their state. The state religion was Zoroastrianism, based on country temples and served by a state-supported priesthood, who did not seek popular support. There were many Christians and Jews. In battle the aristocracy practised a cautious defensive tactic, relying on fortifications and palisades, and were unable to match the Arab cavalry.

Khalid continued the existing policy of subduing all Arab tribes and, receiving help from a local dissident leader, made terms with Christians (mainly Nestorians) at the small city of Hira on the Euphrates obtaining tribute. After Khalid went on to attack Homs, a new attack was staged under Umar's direction, but unfortunately under an inferior leader from Taif and by weaker troops taken from the Helpers of Medina. At the battle of the Bridge in 634, overawed by the elephants in the Persian army, they suffered a major defeat. Umar responded by assembling another army, making Abi Waqqas, a fiery early Companion from the Quraysh, its general. In 636 he went on to inflict a major defeat on the Persians at Qadisiyya, lying on the edge of the desert lands and at the beginning of fruitful agricultural territory. (This is the starting-point in modern times for pilgrims travelling from Iraq along the desert road to Mecca.) Qadisiyya's fame echoes in all subsequent Iraqi popular history, to which Saddam Hussein bore witness when he issued 'Qadisiyya bonds' to finance his war against Iran. The Persians had overwhelming numerical superiority, but Umar's forces prevailed against them because of their cavalry skills and archery.

The victory made so strong an impression that other leading Persians in the lands beyond Qadisiyya, thinking they would escape death, offered the Arab troops means of crossing the web of waterways in the Fertile Crescent. Unexpected help to the Arab cause both in Syria and in Iran came from devastating visitations of the plague. This principally affected those who lived in the cities where the rats, whose fleas spread the disease, were congregated. It was not devoid of effect on Islam, as Umar had to replace some of his governors in Syria, but on the whole the plague favoured the Muslim attackers. Then the drive continued into Khuzistan, taking the legendary city of Susa with its tomb of Daniel and finally, after the death of Umar, reached the Zagros mountains.

The Fall of Jerusalem, 638

The defeat at Yarmuk in 636 was a great turning point: it sealed the fate of Jerusalem. Disorder and disruption had cut off the routes whereby provisions had traditionally reached the city and, as pathetic remnants of the defeated Byzantine army made their way back to Anatolia, it was clear that there would never again be a reliable field army to defend the city against enemy attacks.

Sophronius, the patriarch of Jerusalem, scholarly, eloquent, devoted to the city to which he had addressed Greek poems, ruled on behalf of the Byzantine emperor. He exhorted the garrison and prayed, hoping against hope that somehow an intervention might take place to rescue his city, but he was aware that the defenders' numbers were being reduced and that his people were hungry. Moreover, the Western Church of the Dark Ages was preoccupied with its own problems of Germanic barbarians. No help could be expected from them.

Those who now besieged Jerusalem were in fact desert cavalrymen, ill equipped for such warfare, and Jerusalem had good walls; nevertheless there was a steady attrition of the garrison as a result of missiles thrown by the enemy and from losses which followed sorties made to disrupt the besiegers. In the spring of 638 Sophronius made his decision and conveyed his wish to surrender to the highest authority in Islam, Umar the caliph, and his wish was met. Sophronius asked for respect of the rights of Christians and Jews, which was granted.

Stories of the surrender were various and laden with symbolism, contrasting the simplicity and poverty of the Muslims with the wealth of Sophronius, a churchman from a tradition which believed in honouring God through beautiful and expensive objects. Umar was the authentic example of the austerity which the Prophet had sought, and imposed ferocious discipline on his followers. He travelled with a whip, which he was ready to use, and it was known that when he found his own son drunk he subjected him to eighty lashes, which killed him. Umar had only two garments – one for the winter and one for the summer – and was accustomed to sleeping on the desert floor in his worn clothing; he may have thrown a white cloth over himself in honour of the pilgrimage. In one tradition Sophronius wore his bejewelled vestments; in another he wore black in mourning.

Together, patriarch and caliph entered the city. Sophronius escorted Umar to the Church of the Holy Sepulchre and invited him to pray with him there, to which the caliph responded by pointing out that, if he chose to accept, his successors would treat it as an invitation to make it a mosque. Instead Umar unrolled his prayer mat and responded to the *muezzin* outside the Sepulchre, on a site where indeed a mosque was later built. Then he passed on to be shown the Temple Mount, the giant rectangular platform dug into the bedrock for the Temple created by Herod the Great and destroyed by the Romans. Massive blocks and rubble remained, as the extraordinary structure was too substantial to be totally eliminated. When the Emperor Constantine had made Christianity the religion of the Empire, the Christians left the rubble on the site, recalling the words of Jesus in the thirteenth chapter of St Mark's Gospel, prophesying the fate awaiting Jerusalem: 'Not one stone will be left upon another; every one will be thrown down.' It was a form of triumphalism, announcing the victory of Christianity over both Judaism and Roman paganism.

In the classic story of the Muslim capture of the city, Umar, seeing the ruinous remains of the Temple Mount, exclaimed against the desecration, scooped up some debris in the hem of his clothing and threw it into the Kidron valley. It was a compelling symbolic gesture, followed by his cavalrymen using all manner of containers, clothing, baskets, shields and pots to clear the surface.

Eventually the Temple Mount was fully cleared, exposing what they believed to be the site of the sacrifice which Abraham in Jewish tradition was ready to make of his son Isaac at Mount Moriah. This site, early Muslims believed, lay at the end of the Temple Mount and carried a footprint on the bare rock, said by many Muslims to be that of Muhammad. The area was subsequently roofed over and celebrated by the great shrine of the Dome of the Rock. When clearance was finally made, it became the Haram al-Sharif, the Noble Sanctuary of the Muslims.

The last act of the caliph was to decree the building of a mosque at the southern end of the Mount, at the opposite end from Abraham's abortive sacrifice. It was called the al-Aqsa mosque, the Farthest Mosque, since it was the most westerly place of worship known to the Arabs. We know from the Christian visitor Arculf some three decades later, that it was a very simply improvised structure with planks and beams over ruins; but he said it could hold three thousand people.

The Temple Mount had great significance for the Muslims because it was the setting for the Night Journey of the Prophet, described in *sura* 17 of the Quran:

Glory to God
Who did take his servant
For a journey by Night
From the Sacred Mosque
To the Farthest Mosque
Whose precincts We did
Bless – in order that We
Might show him some
Of our Signs: for he
Is the One who heareth
And seeth (all things).*

The Sacred Mosque was the mosque at Mecca, surrounding the *Kaba*. It was held that, while Muhammad was meditating there, he was conducted, in a vision, by the Archangel Gabriel to Jerusalem where he conferred with Adam and Abraham and all the prophets – Jesus, Joseph and Moses – before being taken up on Buraq, the winged steed with a woman's face, to enter the higher heaven.

Another wave of conquest captured Egypt and did so in an extraordinarily short time. Amr ibn al-As, already successful at Dathin and a participant at the battle of Yarmuk, went on from taking Gaza to attack Egypt, with the blessing of Umar but very much on his own initiative and with a much smaller army than the Byzantines. By tradition Umar had second thoughts and wrote to Amr telling him to draw back if he had not already passed the frontier: guessing what would be in the letter, Amr avoided opening it till he had passed el-Arish, on the coastal road. Reinforced by additional troops under another early Muslim hero, Zubayr ibn al-Awam,

---

*From *The Holy Qur'an*, trans. Abdullah Yusuf Ali (Birmingham, 1934; repr. 2000), sura 17, v.1, p. 768.

he seized Alexandria. Resistance had been weakened as a result of the mal-treatment of the Coptic Church by the bullying Byzantine patriarch Cyrus, who originated from the Caucasus and knew nothing of Egypt. Cyrus was intent on forcing Heraclius's favoured doctrine of Monothelitism down the throats of the Monophysite Copts, who formed a majority in the country, and on doing so by brute force, using imprisonment and torture. But Egypt had also been affected by plague, which had diminished its pop-ulation: probably there were insufficient troops to guard the great walls of Alexandria.

From his move past el-Arish in late December 639 to an agreed surren-der late in 641 and a final settlement in 642, Amr captured the bread-basket of the Byzantine Empire in just over two years. Umar, however, had the last word, as he required Amr and his supporters to create a garrison town at Fustat, which became the nucleus of old Cairo. Umar feared Muslims might be overwhelmed by the much greater numbers of non-Muslims or be seduced from Muslim belief by the Greek heritage in Alexandria. Tol-erant terms were made for Christians, allowing freedom of worship, and the Copts rejoiced at being free from tyranny. Benjamin, the Coptic patri-arch, whose brother had been tortured and killed under Cyrus, lived peacefully to a great age and was treated with honour by Amr.

Umar, who proved to be the most dynamic and, indeed, terrifying of all the early caliphs, built on Abu Bakr's achievement. Both were deploying disciplined armies, as desert warriors responded to *jihad* as individuals and therefore composed armies that were not tribal. Nor were they moving with wives and families in mass migration. Their traditional valour and fighting skill were being harnessed by a leadership from towns rather than the desert. Umar continued recruitment, boldly deployed large armies where needed, and made one other decision of prime importance when he insisted on rewarding successful warriors with pensions rather than land. His *diwan* system gave pensions on graduated scales according to the time when the recipients converted to Islam. It prevented Muslims from taking the land and creating appanages.

In succession, Syrian cities fell to Muslim troops as the inhabitants were aware that there would be no more landward support after Yarmuk; coastal settlements such as Tripoli and Caesarea retained a measure of independence longer, being supplied by Byzantine sea power, but succumbed in the end. The rigidities of Umar's outlook led to a somewhat artificial preference for the Emigrants over the Helpers. He would recognise talent where he found it, but gave preference in command to those who joined the Prophet earliest, and this inevitably caused irritation amongst the Helpers. He is reported later in life to have recognised the greater wisdom of his predecessor Abu Bakr, based on long business experience, in selecting men by virtue of their character rather than origin.

Umar was a dour misogynist and tradition assigns to him a baleful role in the institution of the *niqab*. In desert conditions natural functions had to be carried out in the open, outside settlements; this was potentially embarrassing to women, and total covering of face and body would preserve their anonymity. Nonetheless an intervention by Umar in the Prophet's lifetime seems to have reached beyond the demands of privacy in special circumstances to a demand for the covering of face and body outside the home at all times. Unprompted, the Prophet himself might well have remained much less rigorous: he loved women and children and was in private life a genial host, but the appearance of Umar always cast a chill on his noisy, cheerful family gatherings. Muhammad regulated family life, ending female infanticide, raising woman's status from that of a chattel available to several men in volatile relationships in pre-Islamic desert society, and demanding consideration of the individual woman's interests and property rights.

Umar's utter lack of any wish for personal power and enrichment, his devotion to the memory of the Prophet and his teaching, his accessibility and his untiring energy in planning and directing affairs and sending off armies served the new power in the Near East immeasurably. He was the greatest master of conquests. To the north of Arabia the former Byzantine power cracked and dissolved under his attacks. Until his death, Umar maintained his iron control and looked to solve the future security problems represented by the disparity between the overall numbers of Muslim conquerors – perhaps no more than 50,000 in all – and the much greater number of non-Muslims that inhabited the conquered lands. Muslim leaders were welcoming to rival troops who surrendered and were happy to use them in their armies. Still, the disparity between the numbers was overwhelming and Umar set about mitigating its dangers by a policy of establishing garrison towns and sending out scouts to choose suitable sites. Gathered together, Muslim troops and their dependants could support each other and provide strongpoints from which to ride out and suppress rebellions. Such a strongpoint should have good communications to Medina, be well watered and have sufficient agriculture but should also lie on the edge of desert territory, where the core of Muslim armies with their camels were at home. Kufa, on the banks of the Euphrates close to Hira, fitted these requirements and was formally laid out with roads and adequate space, but with the proviso that no house should have more than three apartments and none should be too high. Umar's austerity, his military sense and his desire for equality among believers shine out from these arrangements. A similar decision was made when the former Sassanian capital at Ctesiphon was found to be unhealthy and Muslims transferred to a garrison town created at Basra. It was the last major achievement of Umar. He was as good as his word and lived with great simplicity in Medina without guards and gatekeepers, attending the mosque, shopping, talking informally. One day in 644 a Persian slave approached him with a grievance; receiving an answer he found unsatisfactory, he stabbed Umar in the mosque the next day and then killed himself.

Caliph Uthman (644–56)

As Umar lay dying, he gave a committee of six of the earliest Companions, including Ali, the right to decide who should succeed him. Over three days they deliberated in the mosque at Medina. One of the group being away, the remaining five came to their decision under a chairman, who renounced his own chances of succession. At a critical moment he put a question to the others, asking if the successful candidate would accept the decisions of the two previous caliphs, Abu Bakr and Umar. Abu Bakr, though eclectic in outlook, was Companion first and foremost, while Umar also kept a strong preference for Companions over Helpers. It was, Ali's supporters felt, a loaded question, for Ali, with his sense for the equality and simplicity of Islam, would not have been willing to accept a predominance of Quraysh, early Companions though they were. He would have wished to balance them with more of the Helpers who had been converts at Medina. So he stood aside and the choice fell on the oldest man present, the 70 year old Uthman of the clan of the Umayya, a senior branch of the Quraysh. He was a wealthy businessman of the highest talent, an early convert who had put his money at Muhammad's disposal for a multitude of tasks: buttressing the Prophet's position in Medina, digging wells, aiding the poor, building – but not fighting. He was never going to be acceptable to veteran warriors of the years of expansion.

Nevertheless, under his rule conquests continued and he listened to pleas for his generals to neutralise Cyprus and to build a Muslim navy. He made Jeddah a port to serve Mecca. Under his rule Cyprus was finally conquered outright in 653, and at the battle of the Masts in 655 Uthman's men defeated the Byzantine navy. He showed practical engineering skills, widening the area of the Meccan centre of worship and creating embankments in Medina to stop flooding. He ordered an agreed version of the Quran to be compiled, to eliminate all conflicts between texts. It was another aspect of the drive for centralisation. Reciters of the Quran grumbled, but Ali himself praised Uthman's work without stint.

What went wrong? Uthman was surely one of the great caliphs, yet his reign ended in catastrophe. Tradition has it that troubles began with the loss of the Prophet's signet ring in 651 as, with his habitual attention to detail, Uthman leaned over to point at a fault in stonework to workmen deepening a well in Medina: the signet ring fell from his finger into the depths, never to be recovered. And while it is true that his first six years were successful, the remaining six were not. He was determined to build a financial system to hold together the new massive Islamic Empire, overturning the loose, informal arrangements of Umar's day and the late caliph's insistence on austerity and equality in wealth. Without Umar understanding what was happening, state lands of the Sassanians had been taken and their wealth quietly enjoyed by the early fighters settled in Kufa: this was unsatisfactory to Uthman, who believed that surpluses should be forwarded to Medina and used for the whole Islamic community under a general accounting system, with lists being kept of those who were entitled to the *diwan*. Tax administrators were given a role independent of provisional governors, and a new post was created – that of supervisor of markets – which became routine in Muslim towns. A key position was given to a young cousin, Marwan.

In Egypt, Amr the conqueror, it seems, had not forwarded revenues to Medina but used them to reward the conquerors who had fought and suffered with him. Uthman acted briskly and dismissed Amr, replacing him with an appointment of his own, Abdullah ibn Abi Sarh, with the duty of forwarding revenues to Medina. When the Greeks of Alexandria rose in revolt and were aided by a Byzantine naval force, Uthman reappointed Amr to fight them off, which he did, damaging Alexandria to make sure there could be no repeat attack. Uthman then showed his steel by leaving Amr as governor-general in Fustat but insisting that his man should be in charge of finance. Amr's protests were disregarded, and he was again removed from office, making him an enemy. Uthman arranged for Abi Sarh to lead troops into North Africa in the hope that military prestige would ease his unpopularity, a move that culminated in victory over a Byzantine army at Sbeitla. That was all very well, but centralisation continued to create indignation, and a crisis arose in 656.

Settlers in Kufa resented the requirement that funds from confiscated Sassanian lands should be sent to Medina, and an early Companion who protested about what was happening was beaten up in the mosque in Medina. Umar's preference for the first Companions – the Emigrants from Mecca – against the Helpers had been disliked, and Uthman began redressing this. He was happy with a traditional clan leadership in the provinces, again setting aside Umar's arrangements. Financial pressures emerged as, in Muhammad's ruling, when slave concubines gave birth, they were automatically freed and had to be given support in terms of finance and food. In Kufa dissidents rejected a governor appointed by Uthman and marched on Medina to protest under the leadership of Malik al-Ashtar, a respected former leader in the conquest of Iraq. In Egypt, after Amr's dismissal, his early followers were irritated at interference with their enjoyment of the rewards of conquest and the policies of Uthman's appointee. Although Uthman had some vociferous support, notably from a controversial figure from Damascus, Muawiya, a capable organiser of the Muslim settlement in the former Byzantine cities in Syria, it was not enough. An Egyptian protest party set out for Medina and was met by Caliph Uthman, who spoke reassuringly to them but made the mistake of sending a letter to his man, Abi Sahr, telling him to punish the rebels when they got back. The fat was in the fire when knowledge of this emerged, and the Egyptians returned to Medina in anger.

Uthman was remarkably blind to the irritation caused by his naked appointment of relatives to office and his own wealth and ostentation. The austerity of Muhammad himself, who believed that wealth should always be devoted to the common good, and especially the poor, had gone by the board and Uthman built himself a fine palace on the edge of Medina, welcoming ambassadors and treating himself and his visitors to finely cooked food. Elsewhere grand residences were built by various magnates. When Uthman denounced rebels in the mosque, they attacked him with stones. Uthman's house came under siege and the besiegers were further inflamed by the news that Muawiya was hurrying from Damascus to rescue him. Ali, knowing that Uthman's house had no well, contrived to send an agent through the siege with goatskins of water. Uthman remained unmoved by demands for his departure, saying that the position of the caliph had been conferred on him and was not negotiable. He was killed with the Quran in front of him and blood dripping on its pages while his young wife had two fingers sliced off as she defended his body. Uthman insisted that no Muslim blood should be shed for him and came to be seen as a martyr.

Caliph Ali (656–61)

Ali now appeared as the only possible candidate and so at last became caliph, but in the worst possible circumstances. The population had been so divided and disturbed that Medina had become untenable, and Ali had to fear a backlash from the Quraysh, aware of his own predilection for the

Helpers. He left for the garrison of Kufa to gather support. Aisha had long been an opponent of Ali and she was backed by al-Zubayr, an early Muslim supporter who had married another daughter of Abu Bakr, and by another notable supporter, Talha ibn Ubayd Allah – both members of the committee who had elected Uthman in 644. They went to seek support in the garrison town of Basra, but gained little. At the battle of the Camel, fought nearby in November 656 – so called because it swirled round the camel on which Aisha had stationed herself – the two former electors were killed and Aisha dispatched to seclusion in Medina. Ali made his own appointments, displacing those against him, but he faced a major opponent in Muawiya, of Uthman's dynasty, who had a duty as his relative to avenge his murder. The young widow who had lost fingers at the death scene sent Muawiya the bloodstained shirt from the body of her husband, begging him to avenge his death. A man of peace, Ali, of course, had had no share in Uthman's death, but among his supporters in Kufa was Malik al-Ashtar, who had led the Kufan protest delegation to Medina. He had not killed Uthman but still carried a heavy responsibility for the siege in Medina as a result of which Uthman was murdered. Muawiya stood firm on his duty as clan leader to avenge Uthman's death and would not accept Ali as caliph until he had done so. As always, Ali stood for spiritual leadership above quarrels over family disputes and taxation, for equality among all believers and strict justice. But he had had to stand for office at a time which took him away from the Prophet's town of Medina, the long-established base for campaigning, and forced him to immerse himself in complex Kufan politics to seek supporters.

There was now civil war within Islam. Ali felt compelled to oppose Muawiya, but he was also forced into a confrontation with the sect of the Kharijites – literally, 'those who go out'. The term originated with the sect's enemies, who felt that they had left Islam: i.e., abandoned all the norms of the Islamic community. Kharijites believed in an excessively rigid adherence to the Quran, had egalitarian views on the religious leaders of Islam and insisted on equal distribution of booty from the great conquests. Ali had much in common with them and persuaded many to drop their opposition. But there remained crosspatch extremists over-fond of fighting. At Nahrawan in Iraq, as some took to brigandage, he had to attack and kill them, so damaging his reputation.

Ali assembled his army at Kufa and marched north along the Euphrates to Siffin, a point near the frontier of Syria and Iraq, to confront Muawiya's forces. The armies stood over against each other; there were skirmishes, individual duels, a long stand-off and, finally, a full-scale battle, in which Ali's side were winning when a section of the Syrian cavalry came forward with leaves from the Quran on their lances. With this gesture the battle stopped and Ali accepted arbitration. But the arbiters were not in reality neutral and Ali's cause began to unravel. The surviving Kharijites, impatient with the politicking, rejected Ali's compromises, believing that he could not be the true caliph if he was accepting arbitration. 'Only God has the right to decide', they said. They yearned for the simplicities of Muhammad's lifetime but, again, some turned to brigandage. Ali's army had to react, and in another battle many were killed.

In 661 came full-scale tragedy. Kharijites decided to kill the leaders of the disputing parties but failed in the attack on Amr, who persisted in advancing his rights, and Muawiya. Only Ali, characteristically open and unprotected in the mosque at Kufa, fell to the assassin's knife. His son renounced all claim to succession to the Prophet's powers. With a general weariness of dissent and a fear that Islam's enemies would take advantage of disunity, it was decided that Muawiya should take the caliphate. The Umayyads had won after all. But there was widespread distaste for Muawiya and because of this only the first four caliphs – Abu Bakr, Umar, Uthman and Ali – were given the title of the Rightly Guided Caliphs. To the supporters of Ali, the Shiites, the whole idea of such a listing was complete nonsense. For them, there had only ever been one true caliph, Ali, unjustly forced out of his rightful inheritance designated by the Prophet at Ghadir Khumm and betrayed by deceitful manoeuvres.

2

THE SEARCH FOR THE JUST SOCIETY

Caliph Muawiya (661–80)

The new caliph ruled in the style of an Arab patriarch, with *hilm*, shrewdness, moderation, calm: managing, dealing, defusing crises, respecting wealth but avoiding the preferences for family which had been the undoing of Caliph Uthman. His relatives were left in wealthy seclusion. He was at pains to reconcile Kufa and Basra to the dominance of his power base in Damascus and his widespread support in Syria. To this end he employed individual Thagafi, from the elite in Taifa, the summer resort of wealthy Meccans, which in the early years had repudiated Muhammad's Revelations and which came late to the acceptance of Islam. They were entirely independent of the deep tensions within Iraq. One of them, forgiven by the Prophet for a murder committed before he became a believer and by Caliph Umar for adultery after he had accepted the Faith, turned out to be an ideal manager for restive Kufans, overlooking minor transgressions and securing additional income for them from a site in the Zagros mountains. Later on another Thagafi, Zayid ibn Abihi, who had been a stout supporter of Ali, turned round, accepted Muawiya, became his blood brother and was appointed as a kind of informal viceroy to the caliph for both Kufa and Basra. Zayid concluded that those he ruled would become restless if not given prospects of war, booty and land, and with the assent of the caliph he dispatched many thousands of settlers to the oasis town of Merv, then lightly garrisoned, and beyond Merv into Khurasan. He made the region his own, with the greatest concentration of Muslim inhabitants anywhere outside Arabia.

Muawiya, too, thought it unwise to reject the attractions of war and conquest, and launched expeditions against Rhodes and Crete, extracting tribute from the Byzantines. Constantinople was kept under pressure as year by year his son Yazid blockaded the city, although the strength of the Byzantine navy prevented him from taking it. In the administering of his territories Muawiya continued to use Byzantine Christians working in Greek and the existing coinage remained legal tender. It was business as usual.

Muawiya was no idealist. He could justly claim to have acted as Muhammad's secretary, but his thought-world was alien to the Prophet's. The zeal for giving up riches and devoting resources to the care of the poor and to the central purposes of Islam in the style of Abu Bakr and Umar was an approach he did not share. He sought acknowledgement of his son Yazid's right to rule after him and plainly intended to create a hereditary caliphate. The question had to be asked: what would become of the *shura*, the consideration of suitability for the task facing future caliphs, if the arbitrary chances of hereditary succession took over? There was disquiet over this, especially among the Helpers in Medina, as Muawiya set about developing farmland in the vicinity of the city solely to boost caliphal revenues.

The Second Civil War, 680–92

After Muawiya's death and the succession of his son, who duly reigned as Yazid I (680–83), the peace was broken. When Ali's second son, al-Husayn, who had been living in seclusion in Medina, heard of Yazid's succession, he took his followers to travel across the desert towards Kufa, the former stronghold of Ali's supporters. They never got there. Muawiya's faithful viceroy, Zayid, had been succeeded by his son Ubayd Allah, who blocked their way forward, kept them in the desert, where they suffered from thirst, then massacred them, women and children included, at Karbala, north-east of Kufa, on 10 October 680, a date and place never forgotten by the Shiites.

They erected a mosque there, and continue to commemorate the suffering of al-Husayn every year on the date of his death. The Kufans did not move to support al-Husayn, so, if he had hoped to raise an insurrection against Yazid, he failed.

Ali's supporters elsewhere and subsequent Shiites saw it very differently. Al-Husayn, they believed, deliberately intended to sacrifice himself in order to raise the consciousness of all Muslim believers to Muhammad's right and just order, which had been abandoned by Muawiya and Yazid. He was a martyr in a sense familiar to Christians: a passive, suffering victim of persecution. In his view Caliph Yazid I was taking Islam back to the cruelties and arbitrary behaviour of the Arabian desert in the *jahiliyya*, the time of ignorance before the Prophet. Political and military action alone would not do, for they would only end in toleration of a corrupt and debased caliphate. So al-Husayn gave himself, his devoted followers and his family up to a sacrificial death.

Al-Husayn's pitiful end moved the Muslim world generally and not just Ali's supporters, for al-Husayn had been in the household of the Prophet and had been dandled on his knee. A defenceless idealist had been done to death and reaction to his end stimulated opposition to the caliphate as a flawed institution. It also stirred up further disquiet over the adoption of the hereditary principle. Yazid was well liked personally, showed competence and might well have been a good caliph, but was swept into a maelstrom of conflict. In Mecca, ibn al-Zubayr, the son of the recalcitrant elector who had been defeated and killed by Ali at the battle of the Camel in 656, emerged as an opponent of the hereditary caliphate, insisting that the choice of a new caliph should be made from the ranks of the Quraysh; the elite of Mecca naturally backed him. The people of Medina, angry over their treatment at the hands of Muawiya, were also recalcitrant, refused mediation, drove out Umayyads and were finally suppressed by a Syrian army in the battle of the Harra in 683. Medina was sacked. Then Yazid I died of natural causes in his desert encampment, followed in a short time by his son.

There was no obvious candidate to succeed, and in the crisis for the Umayyad caliphate the dynasts turned to Marwan, an aged and reticent nephew of Uthman who had long lived quietly in Medina and had moved to Syria only because of the clash in his city. He was induced to reign as Caliph Marwan I (684–5). Under him yet another internecine battle took place as rival clans from southern and northern Arabia struggled for mastery, with heavy loss of life at the battle of Marj Rahit in the summer of 684. Marwan died after a year and his son Abd al-Malik succeeded him as caliph: young, energetic, clear-sighted and one of the great figures of Islamic history.

There was a slow diminution of troubles. A revolt by Ali's supporters in Kufa failed. Kharijites again emerged and were suppressed. Abd al-Malik in person led an army to take the submission of Kufa in 691 and in the following year, having cut off ibn al-Zubayr from his allies, sent troops to destroy his power base in Mecca, a melancholy episode for all believers in which Mecca was fired and the black stone at the *Kaba* broken into three: thereafter it had to be held together by silver threads. Agitation brought to light a long-standing clash between the interests of the traditional Arab chiefs and the *mawali*, new converts to the faith, who came over to the Muslims and ceased to pay the tax of the *jizya*. No doubt it was a compliment to the vitality of belief that they wished to become Muslims, but there were major financial drawbacks in the loss of the buffer *jizya* tax, and the chiefs preferred to leave *dhimmis* in a conveniently subordinate position. Karbala, the battle of the Harra, Marj Rahit, the sacking of Medina, fire in Mecca and damage to the *Kaba* ... this formidable list made the second civil war more grievous than the first, which had lasted from 655 to 661.

The talents of Abd al-Malik, his long reign and the will for peace after conflict ensured that the future lay with a hereditary caliphate: there would be no reversion to the choice of individual caliphs serving only for a lifetime. Abd al-Malik believed that Muawiya's form of rule, which avoided the use of family ties in government, was not effective and proceeded to govern with the aid of members of his family, considering that the force of family loyalty, which gave caliphs security, was too great to be disregarded. For good or ill, this became the pattern for a hereditary caliphate. Mecca and Medina were both damaged and Damascus was now the undisputed caliphal capital. The *hajj* would continue without question, and repairs to the sacred sites would be made, but the days of political power based on the holy cities of the Hijaz were over. Abd al-Malik had at his service an excellent fighting general in the Thagafi al-Hajjaj ibn Yusuf and made full use of him in establishing what was, in effect, an imperialist caliphate. Separatism in Kufa and Basra was to end, and a Syrian garrison was put into a new site between them at Wasit. Iraq was to remain subordinate to Syria. Investment was made in irrigation schemes and land reclamation but only for the benefit of the Syrian caliphate, not for local Muslims.

Another decision marked a sharp reaction against Muawiya's *laissez-faire* approach, in which Arabic had not been requisite in government and in consequence Byzantine Christians had been free to use Greek for their Muslim masters just as they had done for their own emperors. Abd al-Malik made Arabic the language of bureaucracy and court culture. Similarly, Arabic superseded Aramaic and Pahlavi, so everyone would now have to carry out their duties in Arabic. Coins in Byzantine style ceased to be used and were replaced by coins with Arabic inscriptions, including the anti-Trinitarian text from *sura* 112 of the Quran: in short, it became a caliphal coinage. A unity was established between the language of the Quran, of scholarship and that of the common people, in contrast to the West, where Latin continued to be the language of scholarship and of administration alone.

The Dome of the Rock is Abd al-Malik's work. A masterpiece of Islamic architecture and a triumphal statement of Muslim command of Jerusalem, it dominates the skyline to this day, placed so as to overshadow the Christian sacred structures below.* Only a caliph with control of massive reserves of money could have commissioned a building of this size and complexity. It is a shrine designed to give solemn commemoration to the site of Mount Moriah and the abortive sacrifice of Abraham. Pilgrims were to pass through its corridors, appreciating the vistas of light,

---

* The Church of the Sepulchre and the Byzantine Emperor Justinian's church of the Mother of God, the Nea, built in 543 and now vanished but recovered in outline by archaeologists.

designed with ingenious use of the octagon and showing a high skill in geometry.

Within, the magnificent mosaics of Byzantine craftsmen convey both crowns and jewels, symbols of power, and paradisal imagery of fruit and flowers, anticipating an ultimate Islamic Garden of Eden. The years of disturbance before Abd al-Malik had led Muslims to a high expectation of an imminent Last Judgement and all were conscious of the fact that Jerusalem was the site destined for this event. Extracts from the Quran make plain that Islam had superseded the other monotheisms of Judaism and Christianity. Space is given to Muhammad and his work of intercession for sinful humanity and there are denunciations of Christian belief that God can have a son, but these are put quietly. Jesus was a prophet and his work is praised, but that work is now past and completed. The next and final stage was the intercessory work of Muhammad.

The Limits of Conquest: North Africa and Spain

Under the Umayyads, Islamic conquest reached its term. Abd al-Malik sent 40,000 men to take the North African coastline back from the Byzantines, whose troubles eased his army's progress. Abd al-Malik's brother, governor of Egypt, took a hand after Abd al-Malik's forces had reached what is now the frontier between Tunisia and Algeria and appointed his own man, Musa ibn Nusayr, the son of a slave captured in the glory days of the early caliphate and one of the great battlefield commanders, to carry the conquest forward. He had considerable success in exploiting the divisions between the wild Berber tribesmen in the mountains and converting a corps of warriors from their ranks who took Tangier, crossed to the mainland and began to plunder the treasures of southern Spain. Musa took over with a largely Arab army and subdued the Christian Visigoths, troubled by a succession dispute after the death of King Wizita, pushing the remnants of their leadership back to a position guarded by fortresses on the edge of the Pyrenees on a line south of the Cantabrian mountains. It was the prelude to 800 years of Muslim occupation in the Iberian peninsula. The limits of conquest reached in 716 fell effectively within the reign of Abd al-Malik's son and successor, Caliph al-Walid I (705–15), although there were later raids into southern France.

Iran, India, Transoxania

On the eastern side of the Islamic Empire, the limits of conquest were also reached under the Umayyads, with the exception of Transoxania. Caliph Umar had initiated the conquest of Iran by sending out an army to bring Sassanian rule to an end. The last Sassanian king, Yadzgard III, sought to revive his dynasty after it had been racked by internal disputes. His troops fought for him at the little town of Nihavand in 642 and at Istikhar, capital of the Fars region, where heroic resistance led to massacre, plunder of its riches and destruction of Zoroastrian fire-temples. More often, however, local rulers who had lost allegiance to the dynasty made terms and paid tribute as Umar's army pressed on by the southern route through the Zagros mountains to the Sassanian heartlands. At the fortress of Merv, Yadzgard was refused entry; he met his end in destitution at the farthest limit of his lands, in Khurasan. Sassanian institutions collapsed, yet, paradoxically, Persian language and culture survived. Belief in Islam prevailed, but as there was only limited garrisoning at this stage, local rulers kept a measure of independence, keeping Arabic for the Quran and for intellectual life but not surrendering spoken Persian and the literature which flowed from it. Later Arab expeditions seeking a full-blown conquest came up against problems of terrain and climate within Iran and southern Afghanistan and lost momentum.

In the far south-east, just as in the Iberian peninsula, the limits of conquest were reached in the caliphate of al-Walid I. Conquests in India, occasioned by a punitive expedition followed by an act of piracy, were commissioned by Abd al-Malik's general al-Hajjaj and carried through by the latter's cousin Muhammad ibn Qasim, who crossed the Indus river, braving elephants in the enemy army and showing toleration to alien religions: he discreetly decided to treat as honorary *dhimmis* both the Buddhists and the Hindus. Brave soldiering, use of a siege weapon and the capable exercising of command carried the Muslim attackers through.

Al-Hajjaj died in 714, and his cousin, a statesman as much as a military man, fell victim to the change of regime on al-Walid's death, after which he was dismissed and died in prison.

On the north-eastern frontier Khurasan and its numerous settlers formed an army ready to press forward and take land across the Oxus. But this proved more difficult than might have been expected. There were riches to be gained, but in a first phase soldiers only raided, returning to winter quarters. Al-Hajjaj believed he had found a good instrument of policy in a certain Qutayba, who came from a little-known tribe, with no strong local commitments. Qutayba took tribute from rulers beyond the Oxus but proved to be harsh and oppressive; he alienated his troops and was assassinated. Tribute-taking was all he achieved and, after Qutayba's death, campaigners found that Turkish nomads in the region were resilient and resourceful opponents. Plunder came back across the river, but it was only in 750 that small garrisons were finally installed in Bukhara and Samarqand. There was a late, ill-recorded clash with the Chinese by an Arab force deep in Central Asia at Talas in 751, which resulted in a defeat for the Chinese emperor's army. The Arabs and the Chinese never fought again, and the Arabs did not advance to make conquests along the Silk Road. The Tang dynasty's internal problems prevented a Chinese counter-attack, but it is believed that the capture of artisans at the battle introduced the Islamic world to the use of paper – a momentous event.

The weakness of opponents aided the great expansion of Islamic rule. The fighting between the Byzantine Empire and Sassanian Persia caused grave losses on both sides, leaving them totally unprepared for the intervention of a new power from Arabia. Plague, we may strongly suspect, reduced populations and made it hard for survivors to man defences effectively and engage new enemies: the interest of Muslims in capturing slaves in great numbers points to a widespread shortage of manpower. Centralisation of command by both Byzantium and the Sassanians had the paradoxical effect of undermining their powers of resistance: once central leadership failed, local militias and small-scale powers were no longer ready to act in their place.

The desert bred warriors. The literature of Arabia celebrated the solitary, tough and courageous hero. Given the justification of *jihad* for the raiding which had long been a solace and release from the dullness of an age-old pastoral routine, excellent armies were created, salaried in consequence of wise early decisions by Abu Bakr and Umar rather than receiving land grants in reward, and inspired by belief in the righteousness of their cause. There was no mass migration; families could follow afterwards and settle in towns. Bedouin were accustomed to live hard and accept a low diet and in consequence early armies did not need a supply train and acquired an extraordinary mobility. They were consoled in death by the rewards of paradise and in success by rich booty. The result was to raise armies with a remarkably high, battle-winning morale. Caliphs were open-minded about promoting outsiders as generals: Khalid, the former opponent of Muhammad at the battle of Uhud, who won the victory at Yarmuk; the slave's son Musa ibn Nusayr, the conqueror of al-Andalus; the youthful Thaqafi Muhammad ibn Qasim, with his precocious military and diplomatic skills.

But caliphs were ungrateful: Khalid ended in disgrace; Musa ibn Nusayr, ordered away from the lands of conquest, was imprisoned and died; the same fate befell Muhammad ibn Qasim. Tragic as the fates of these men were, they demonstrated the power of the caliphate to control what happened in its vast territories and to ensure that no successful general could build up an independent domain for himself. Neither the Byzantines nor the Sassanians were so open to promoting talent irrespective of origin and they were much more vulnerable to usurpation of power by generals.

Rule by Muslims after the trauma of conquest was by no means burdensome, allowing many to continue to lead their lives much as before. Amr's little army which took Egypt respected the Monophysite Christians. An illuminating example from al-Andalus is the treaty made in 713 by a son of Musa ibn Nusayr with a Visigothic nobleman which guaranteed his territorial rights, his churches and his freedom of worship in return for payment of tribute in money and in kind. Cases differed, and personal relationships mattered, but there are grounds for thinking that a generous understanding of *jizya* and the role of monotheists eased the way to acceptance of Muslim rule.

Often it was easier to accept Islamic rule rather than to fight against it, and over time certain broad likenesses between the monotheisms – Islam itself, Judaism and Christianity –facilitated a process of conversion which extended over a long period of time but ended by bringing into being the Muslim Near East familiar to us today. As with the Quran, the Jews had Hebrew Scriptures, the Christians their Bible, and names familiar to the older monotheisms – Abraham, Moses and Jesus – reappeared in different guises. Both Islam and Judaism rejected the eating of pork. A dominant Islamic culture established itself, was recognised and respected and attracted recruits, all aided by peaceful contacts not well recorded in Arabic sources which were concerned in the traditional style with narratives of campaigns and warrior heroes.

The ending of the second civil war and the long and successful rule of Abd al-Malik which followed made plain that a hereditary caliphate was set to become the norm in Islamic lands. The wealth of the caliphs and their powers of patronage affected interpretation of the Quran, stimulating scholars to put forward militarist at the expense of peacemaking interpretations and to insist on the duty of all able-bodied Muslims to obey a call to war issued by the caliph. Scholars who served the caliphate in this way will have been aware of the pressures exerted on the broad Islamic lands by external enemies and the effects of restive populations within the frontiers.

A body of scholars working independently, often of holy life and limited resources, writing commentaries on the Quran – a *tafsir* literature long overlooked by researchers – contested the views expressed in the caliphal tradition, emphasising that peaceful persuasion and forbearance were just as important as the call to warfare in the cause of Islam in the text of the Quran and made plain that verses on this had been discounted and overridden by the militarists. As well as this literature, the *hadith*, the body of traditions about the life and teaching of Muhammad, gives us clues on how the militarist school of interpretation grew more prominent over time.

Jihad has often been cited as if it was a term standing on its own and meaning, simply, 'holy war'. This does not do justice to the Quranic text. With very rare exceptions, it is linked to the phrase 'in the path of God':

thus, 'striving in the path of God', with multiple meanings. If the striving is associated with the term *qital*, 'war', then there can be no doubt that it means armed combat; if, on the other hand, it is associated with the term *sabr*, 'patient forbearance', then it refers not to physical combat at all but to a number of peaceful possibilities. Different scholars in the peaceful tradition have different emphases and views have solidified over time. Some found justification in the words of the Quran; others favoured peaceful persuasion; others chose patient endurance under oppression; and finally the majority came to see it as, above all, the combat with the evil passions of the soul. These scholars tended to speak of a lesser and a greater *jihad*. The lesser *jihad* was hedged with restrictions and its incidence as an obligation to armed combat was, in their view, a relatively rare event. The greater *jihad*, which could never be abandoned and was incumbent on all the faithful throughout life, was the inner struggle with demons – the egotistical, evil passions in the soul.

The rivals developed opposed doctrines of martyrdom. Hawks and doves among the scholars battled over the search for priorities among the varied texts of the Quran. Militarists pushed for a technique of abrogation by which decisions were made on the priority of certain texts which suited their purposes as against others which did not. The doves rejected this outright.

When the hawks had their way, a martyrdom in war issued in potent battlefield symbolism. Traditionally, the body of the devout Muslim was washed before being wrapped for burial, while by contrast the body of a soldier who died fighting in a righteous cause was left unwashed in the bloody garments in which he met his death. He needed no prayers and his supporters could dispense with the normal ritual accompanying death. The blood was, as it were, his ticket to instant paradise. Doves would have none of this. For them the devout believer fasting, strenuously engaging in prayer over and above the set times imposed on all, using resources in obedience to God's will, who died in bed and not on the battlefield, was a martyr quite as much as the military martyr.

Debate, thus initiated at the time of the Umayyad caliphate, had a long future.

The Abbasid Caliphate (750–1258)

Over time Merv had become a boom town, awash with booty obtained from raiding across the Oxus river, an area of great riches and great poverty. It was cosmopolitan in that new settlers and merchants intermarried with Persians and were influenced not only by their culture but also by the aristocratic pride of the Sassanians and their strong sense of independence. Khurasan was equally prosperous and independent. But the poor and observant Muslims in both places felt neglected by Umayyad caliphs, who were twenty days' journey away, and by their unsympathetic local governors. Thus the massive Muslim settlements in and around Khurasan were a prime source of unrest. They were not alone. Syrian troops had crushed the Kufans, but there were still embers of rebellion, and in about 720 one Kufan, disguised as a wandering perfume seller, made contact with the head of the Meccan clan of Abbasids, a meeting which led to the rise of a new dynasty.

The view took hold that only a return to the family of Muhammad would right things and enable a return to the simplicity of the Prophet and of the earliest caliphs. The Abbasid family came to believe that they could fill the gap and bring in better times. They interpreted descent loosely, as in direct line the Abbasids were descendants not of the Prophet but of al-Abbas, Muhammad's uncle, who had not accepted Islam; but they stressed descent from Muhammad's ancestor Hisham, and that at the time seems to have satisfied opinion.

In Khurasan the remarkable Abu Muslim became an energetic missionary for the Abbasid cause. He bore an assumed name and it was rumoured that he was the son of a Kurdish slave girl but the obscurity of his origin as well as his message appealed to the weak and poor of the area, enabling him to recruit effectively. He had great military skill, raising an army to defy the Umayyads.

At first sight, despite the achievements of Abu Muslim, the odds seemed to be stacked against an Abbasid seizure of the caliphate because of the attachments of loyalty and self-interest of the governors and tribal chiefs in the Muslim world farther to the west of Khurasan. However, discreet pressure and inducements won a proportion of these crucial personalities to the new cause, and in the mosque at Kufa in October 749 leading men gave their hand and their loyalty to an acceptable Abbasid candidate, who reigned as Caliph al-Suffa. In 750 at the River Zab, outside Mosul, an Abbasid force, blooded by much fighting against the Turks at the far eastern end of Islamic lands and relying on their technique of a spear wall against cavalry, defeated the Umayyads and ended their reign.

The first, gently reticent, Abbasid caliph, al-Suffa, died in 754 and was succeeded by his brother, al-Mansur the Victorious (754–75). He was the true creator of the Abbasid caliphal dynasty and not a warrior but a masterful, brilliant administrator with a touch of genius. There was never any doubt about his own piety. He banned alcohol: the distinguished doctor who treated him was, as a Christian and a *dhimmi*, not bound to teetotalism, but at the caliph's table he had to be content with Tigris water, which he tactfully pronounced to be as good as wine. Music was prohibited as un-Islamic and, when a eunuch in the palace thinking he was out of earshot played his mandolin to a slave girl, he found the caliph's wrath descend on him, as his mandolin was broken over his head and he was sold into slavery.

Mansur's miserliness was legendary, so the conspicuous, wasteful expenditure of Uthman or the Umayyads generally was emphatically avoided. He kept the tradition of the early caliphs and sat regularly receiving in person the petitions of his subjects and acting on them. He had the gift of eloquence; his presiding over Friday prayers was no formality, as his audience packed in to hear him and was moved week by week by the cadences of his exhortations. But for the wishes of the minority within Islam who had grown restive with the Umayyads he had no sympathy at all.

He ran his vast lands with imperialist efficiency, devoting hours each day to intelligence reports from confidential agents far and near, independent of Islamic judges, the *qadis*, and governors, on whom they gave vital information. Food prices were also reported, for he knew how sensitive they were as indicators of unrest. It was a spider's web of control, ensuring smooth payment of taxes, an absence of rebellion and, in correlation with taxpaying, the maintenance of a standing army of Khurasanis to defend caliphal interests. Mansur was aware that his imperialism would disquiet those who had made the Abbasid revolution and he kept a keen eye on the Alids — that is, the direct descendants of Ali and Fatima — and on Ali's supporters generally.

In 762 Mansur decided to create a new capital at Baghdad. Skilled irrigation works made the lands between the Tigris and the Euphrates very fertile and the most lucrative taxpaying territories in all the Islamic world. It was sensible to place a new capital here, away from Damascus and its Umayyad associations. In his hard-headed way Mansur understood that a brand-new site would be much the cheapest option: a virgin site with open lands to reward followers. Caliphs attracted officials and merchants and big populations, so Mansur chose a site with easy access to food supplies and goods. Land use could be planned and mosques, palaces and barracks built as desired. Over time it became a focus for learned men, a seedbed for poets, historians, administrators and translators, and important for the West as its scholars recovered classical learning and made a channel for conveying it to other scholars in western lands. A round city went up, with millions of bricks laid at the lowest possible costs through hard bargaining with contractors, and with gates leading to Syria, Khurasan, Basra and Kufa. The walls kept the caliph secure and provided barracks for the Khurasani, not always popular in other parts of the Islamic world but protectors for the caliph, his treasures and his bureaucrats.

Mansur died on the *hajj*. His successor, Caliph al-Mahdi (775–85), was also away from the caliphal palace and heard the news from his wife that his father had left a key with her to a storeroom below the palace that was only to be opened in the event of his death. He hastened back in happy anticipation of treasure but on entering the great underground chamber was appalled to find lines of Alid corpses of all ages, mummified in the dry air of Mesopotamia, with a label in each ear bearing name and genealogy. He buried them in haste and secrecy, but the episode cast a shadow on his own hopes of reconciliation with the Shiites.

The Rise of Prophetic Shiism and Abbasid Decadence

Husayn's son Ali Zaynu l'Abidin (died *c*.713) lived in seclusion at Medina and was known as the Prostrator because of his devotion to prayers and his calloused forehead. He had few followers but quietly and steadily mourned his father's death and was harassed but not killed. It was his son Muhammad al-Baqr (died *c*.733), the 'splitter open' of knowledge, who took the major step, transforming the Shiite movement by disseminating the doctrine of *taqiyya*, or quietism, absolving all his followers from the need to declare their Shiite beliefs in a hostile Muslim world. The doctrine preserved, however, the vital line of prophetic teachers, the hidden imams, on whom the spiritual welfare of all believers in the end depended because of their gift of understanding the concealed meanings of the Quran, given to them by God. He was backed by his son and together they changed the attitudes of many Shiites. They gave a special new Shiite meaning to the term 'imam', which for the majority of Muslims had meant a prayer leader. These Shiites now became the possessors of esoteric knowledge. The number of hidden imams came to be settled – al-Baqr described himself as the fifth imam in the line of hereditary descent from the first Ali himself, who had been followed as number two by Hasan, who was poisoned, then as number three the martyr of Karbala, Husayn, and as number four al-Baqr's father, the Prostrator. Al-Baqr's son Jafar al-Sadiq took his father's teaching farther and developed the doctrine of *nass*, or designation, whereby one Shiite imam decides on the rightful succession.

Shiism had a natural appeal to the poor and the outsiders of whom there were many in Baghdad, another boom town in which the extremes of poverty and wealth existed side by side. The consequence was that over time, as Mansur the Victorious made Baghdad his capital and the seat of the authority of the Abbasids with its soldiers and guards, it came to contain within its walls and in the poor districts outside them an unknown number of quietist Shiites opposed to the caliphate. The movement split when al-Baqr's younger brother Zayd rejected quietism and taught that the only imams who should be followed were those who were ready to fight for their beliefs. His own rebellion was crushed in 740, but miscellaneous groups of fighting Zaydites continued to exist.

The caliphate of Harun al-Rashid (786–809) marked a high point in Abbasid history, yet still had disquieting features. Harun, who corresponded with Charlemagne,* maintained a full treasury. He was an assiduous observer of the *hajj* and kept the tradition of the *jihad* by doing something that had become unusual: personally leading a campaign against the old enemy, Byzantium. In Baghdad he presided over a brilliant court which gave a place to historians, Islamic scholars and administrators of high calibre and poets who were showered with golden dirhams. Fed by the fertile territories of Jazira and Sawad, the capital grew to a great size but attracted a multitude of the landless and impoverished Shiites, camping out in mosques and baths and living in shanty towns outside the gracious circle of Mansur's Round City. An arbitrary autocracy was revealed when Harun turned savagely on the Barmakid dynasty, faithful adherents who had brought him to power, and he failed to solve the perennial problem of Khurasan. He died there, and his death was followed by a damaging civil war between two of his sons in competition for the succession to the caliphate, leading to the execution of one of them, al-Amin, after a military failure. It was an event which although not instigated by the victorious brother al-Mamun (813–33), nevertheless tarnished the repute of the Abbasids and did not put an end to internecine strife: the war marked a stage in the downhill spiral of the caliphate. Disturbances created by the succession dispute had a life of their own. Revenues and caliphal control were lost.

After a failed attempt to bring in a pliable Alid candidate for the caliphate, al-Mamun turned to a doctrinal issue in the hope of defusing Shiism and gave his backing to Mutazilism. *Mutazila* means 'withdrawal' and denotes scholars and their supporters who chose to withdraw from the long-lasting clash between Shiites supporting the martyr Ali's claim to a prophetic power derived from Muhammad himself and the rival school of thought which believed that a working authority in Islam lay with caliphs, commanders of the faithful with practical and military tasks, ruling on the basis of the Quran and *hadith*. Mutazilites proposed a middle way, designed

---

*King of the Franks in 768 and Holy Roman Emperor in 800.

to take some of the force away from Shiites and their claim of a prophetic power by giving doctrinal authority to the caliphate. The Quran, they argued, had been created in time and consequently, in the course of time, could be modified by an appropriate authority dealing with problems that could not have been envisaged by the Prophet – and what better authority could there be than the caliph himself? The teaching of the Mutazilites had been in the field for some time, based as it was on the reading of Greek philosophy and a taste for rationalist analysis, but hitherto it had had no official backing. In 827 al-Mamun declared belief in the doctrine of the creation of the Quran to be an article of faith, made it a touchstone of loyalty which should be accepted by all who held office under the caliph and instituted the *mihna* to inquire into the beliefs of his subjects. Torture and imprisonment could be inflicted on those who denied the doctrine.

Al-Mamun's action failed, partly because of a widespread hostility to the caliph's advisers, partly because of the brave stand made by Traditionists against Mutazilism. Ahmed ibn Hanbal (780–855), who became an icon of the Traditionists, was a scholar with all the qualifications for attracting the respect of Muslims because of his austere and simple life, lack of possessions or political connections. He denounced human reason as frail and subject to the depredations of Satan, insisting that only the words and actions of the Prophet in the Quran and *hadith* could be the true guide for Islam. Imprisoned and tortured, he would not yield and remained forgiving to the caliph under whom he had suffered. He prevailed and, though successive caliphs attempted to follow al-Mamun's line, under al-Mutawakkil (847–62) Mutazilism was given up, the Quran was declared to be eternal and reconciliation with Shiites emphatically abandoned. Ali was cursed from the *minbar*, Shiite shrines were destroyed including Husayn's shrine at Karbala which was demolished and ploughed over.

Meanwhile, the Mutazilism controversy had had an effect on Abbasid attitudes towards Baghdad, the capital they had created. Al-Mamun's successor, his half-brother al-Mutasim (833–42), was a fighting general who made an impression by capturing Amorium from the Byzantines. Aware that the Khurasanis had ceased to provide a faithful caliphal army, he hit on the expedient of recruiting Turkish soldiers to make an army totally dependent on him and followed up this Turkish expedient by moving the capital from Baghdad. Tensions there had been ratcheted up by the battle between Mutazilites and supporters of Hanbal and the practical-minded al-Mutasim thought he would be better off by giving up Baghdad altogether and getting a new home for himself and his Turks.

It all turned out badly. For his palace and his barracks he chose Samarra, on the banks of the Tigris, 80 miles north of Baghdad. The site was cheap, an immense array of buildings could be erected and the Turks kept under the eye of the caliph and yet it soon proved to be a bad choice, for the soil was poor and there was no secure nor substantial water supply. Determination made the site work for a time but left a dangerous dependence on a small number of military commanders. The Turks themselves had alien traditions and began to get out of hand after al-Mutasim's day. Al-Mutawakkil moved the capital yet again to a site north of Samarra. Still the situation grew worse and the Turks murdered a caliph in 861. Anarchy followed and, though there was some revival in the tenth century, the traditional Abbasid structure never recovered: central control was lost, volatile successor states appeared and there was a breakdown of the once great empire. The major blow occurred in the reign of al-Muqtadir (908–32), when the irrigation systems, on which the fertility of Mesopotamia depended, broke down. So much war and internecine dispute meant that no one kept up the sophisticated and intricate control of waterways that produced the rich abundance of the region. Petty military manoeuvres between rival generals in 937 led to the use of flooding as a weapon and caused the breaching of the Nahrawan canal, vital for water diffusion in the Baghdad region. The new centres of Muslim power became Egypt and Iran.

The Growth of Sufism

Sufism, just emerging under the Umayyads as a reaction against their worldliness, was another expression of the perennial wish to go back to the values of the desert; it began in a desire for personal poverty and asceticism, purging the soul of its base desires so as to enter into a deeper personal relation to God. The name Sufi derived from the Arabic *suf*, referring to the coarse woollen garments worn by the poor but voluntarily assumed by enthusiasts wishing to go beyond the observances of Islam to find their way to God.

The caliphate stood for the *sunna*, the path, the way of interpretation of the Quran backed by the *hadith*, the tradition of the sayings and doings of the Prophet. *Hadith* has a multitude of traditions, with contradictions, and requires the wisdom of scholars to debate and find ways forward. They are, above all, juristic discussions. A body of devout Muslims, satisfied with these ways and with the associated religious practices, formed a majority. The external minority, whose dissatisfaction lay at the starting-point of the Abbasid revolution, were still in existence and found an outlet in a developing Sufism, unhappy with the grievous personal disputes among the Abbasids and the raw militarism of the Turkish mercenaries. They found support in the Quran and in some *hadith* in such phrases as that in *sura* 2 verse 115, 'Wherever you turn, there is the face of God', and the *hadith* where God is cited as saying 'My mercy takes precedence over my wrath'. From the asceticism and zeal for poverty in the Sufism of the early Umayyad age there was a progression towards a more organised practice of meditation and mortification designed to eliminate selfish, lower desires, approaching more closely to God in this life. The stress lay on contemplation and cultivation of the soul. A third stage involved the selection of a master to instruct his pupils, who would often impose major acts of humiliation, such as serving for many days in a kitchen. The love of God was the supreme aim. Collective activities involved repeating the names of God; music and poetry and gatherings created a collective experience and, in due time, special training centres.

Sufism ran easily to hagiography and in the tenth century acquired a martyr in al-Hallaj, executed in 922 largely for political reasons after a long career in Baghdad uttering bizarre, paradoxical statements and gathering pupils. His demise showed an extraordinary willingness to forgive his enemies and endure great suffering in a slow, botched execution. At a popular level, Sufi shrines for dead masters acquired a following among the masses. It was a spontaneous movement, sometimes divided, falling victim to charlatans yet acquiring a momentum through the troubles of the Abbasid caliphate. Numbers were few and its greatest days were yet to come; yet it influenced Islamic society, its leaders and its soldiers, and was a continued witness to the frustrated yearning for the just Islamic society.

A Split in Shiism: The Twelvers and the Seveners

A dispute over the succession to the imamate led to a split in the Shiite movement and a subsequent powerful new challenge to the Sunnis and their caliphate. Jafar al-Sadiq, who had done much to buttress the quietist tradition in Shiism, expected to hand on his office, designating his eldest son, Ismail, as his successor. But Ismail died, and doubt arose as to whether a designation could be withdrawn or transferred to another candidate. A majority believed that it could and so al-Sadiq's younger son, Musa al-Kazim, became for this Shiite tradition the seventh imam. The line continued from father to son until the demise of the twelfth imam, Muhammad al-Mahdi, who either died or disappeared in about 878. It was at first believed that God had hidden the imam for the time being and that agents on earth were able to receive guidance from him, but when the fourth such agent died in 940, it was concluded that this twelfth imam had passed into the Greater Occultation to come back at God's will to prepare the world for the End of Time and Judgement. These Shiites became known as the Twelvers.

Remembering and still sorrowing for the sufferings of Ali, Husayn and the visible Shiite imams, the Twelvers accepted that they could do nothing to undo injustices and return Islam to the Reform days of Muhammad. They accepted the injustices of the Sunni caliphate and the abuses all around, which they could not alter, and consolidated their movement, bringing together different classes in southern Iraq and Iran and encouraging their scholars to establish laws and codes of conduct for Shiites. The great conquests had left Sassanian influence in the mountain strongholds of Iran. Their tradition of autocracy infiltrated Shiism, leading ultimately through the Safavid dynasty in the sixteenth century to the present-day acceptance of Shiism as the state religion in Iran.

The dissidents, who would not accept the designation of Musa al-Kazim as valid, believed that Ismail as eldest son had been the imam and had rightly designated his son Muhammad ibn Ismail to be the seventh imam. The followers of this Shiite tradition are in consequence known as the Seveners. They believed that a line of imams, who were the true leaders and teachers of the whole Muslim world, had followed on from Muhammad ibn Ismail and that, although it was inconvenient to name them publicly, their time to be openly revealed would come. An underground movement of the Seveners developed, skilfully directed with a core of trained *dais*, or missionaries, working incognito and gathering groups and hearers who responded to the appeal of secrecy and to the attraction of being introduced to esoteric doctrines hidden from the conventional teachers and secular rulers of Sunnism. Claimant imams took on assumed names to put hostile Abbasid agents off their track. 'Lieutenants' of imams, occupying a Trustee role, appeared, and there seems to have been some use of a notion of 'spiritual parenthood' to get over problems in establishing a strict father-to-son descent from Ali and Fatima as was required in Shiite belief. *Dais* appealed to listeners with their notion that the Quran had hidden meanings which they alone could elucidate. The disorder and confusion created by the decay of the Abbasid caliphate encouraged Muslims, distressed at this, to welcome news of an imamate to deliver them and to give them a better understanding of the Quran's teaching. The spread of their listeners was remarkable as they travelled as far as India and roused circles of hearers in Yemen, North Africa, Iran, southern Iraq, eastern Arabia and Syria.

The Fatimid Caliphate

A breakthrough occurred when a leading personality, Ubaydallah al-Mahdi (873–934), who had made a reputation in Syria, was forced out and transferred his attention to North Africa, where he established an army. Kutuma Berbers from the Kabyle mountains in Tunisia broke cover and announced that he was the long-hoped-for imam and caliph in person – in effect, a caliph with unique powers. A shaky genealogy, derided by Sunnis, did not undermine him and with his Berber supporters he expelled the Aghlabid governors of Tunisia in 909 and beat opposition from the iron radicals, the Kharijites. He successfully established a caliphate and held sway until his death in 934; the movement became known as the Fatimids, after Muhammad's daughter Fatima.

All was not plain sailing for the new dynasty. Fatimids came up against another intensely Shiite group which had also broken cover, the Qarmatians, who had rebelled against the Abbasids in the 890s. They had created a mini-state in north-eastern Arabia, had success among desert Bedouin and for a time established a presence in northern Syria; they fought Abbasid armies, survived defeat and challenged the Fatimids in North Africa. There were dramatic episodes. In 930 the Qarmatians attacked the *hajj* and killed pilgrims. It is not clear why they did this, as they were not opposed to the great pilgrimage: they may only have wished to extract tribute from Abbasids. Further shock was created when they stole the black stone of the *Kaba* from Mecca and took it to Bahrain; it was only returned in 951. Their militancy in the end died away. There was much confusion in this epoch, in which Bedouin tribes held sway over cities and leaders struggled for power, often damaging settled agricultural land. But they never accepted the claims of Ubaydallah al-Mahdi and for a time competed for Egypt.

Ubaydallah sought no major changes from those who accepted his rule in North Africa, relying on his mountain Berbers, whom he made into a paid militia, and on slaves recruited over a wide area, thus creating a loyal military force. He was well aware that he held sway over a considerable Sunni population and was content to obtain from them a passive acceptance of Fatimid rule. An elite held to Shiism and there were *qadis*, judges, to establish codes of conduct; a governing elite had to accept Ismaili principles, but there was no pressure to make converts. Ubaydallah was aware of the importance of the sea and established a port at Mahdia. But advances into Egypt failed in his time.

The decisive step was taken in the reign of a later Fatimid caliph, al-Muizz (953–975), under the leadership of Jawhar al-Siqilla, probably a Greek former slave of notable military talent, who took a massive force of Berber horsemen to Egypt in 969, timing an attack when Egypt was suffering from famine and was ready to welcome a stabilising force. The tolerant regime of Ubaydallah's time prevailed and there were no massive dispossessions. *Qadis* of the previous regime were left in place. The system enabled the Fatimid caliphs to make use of Jews and Christians in administration. But the *khutba*, Friday prayer, was now to be in the name of the Fatimid caliph, and here a vital transformation was made.

The actions taken by Jawhar were important for the future: the founding of the navy which was vital for the control of Egypt also carried Sicily into the Fatimid sphere, and the creation of Cairo as a capital. Cairo was purely the administrative capital and designed to give the new ruler security. It housed Jawhar's own Berber troops, a vital praetorian guard, and had wide roads for ease of travel. Its separation from the main market areas avoided clashes with other ethnic groups. Its two great palaces impressed ambassadors and visitors and made a fitting setting for elaborate ceremonial, appropriate for a caliph who claimed world authority and held all the powers of an imam. Mosques served different purposes. Most notable was the al-Azhar mosque, designed to be the centre for worship in the Ismaili tradition and for instruction in the faith. The state owned land and gained revenues from markets. Nubian gold and the fertility of the Nile delta brought in revenues to support building and decoration, brought pay for standing armies and supported the *dais* still spreading the Ismaili message. Gardens separated Cairo from Fustat, which was a centre for population and economic activity.

There was little Sunnis could expect to do because of the degradation of the natural Sunni leadership, the Abbasid caliphs in Baghdad, who reached a low point when they were in effect taken over by a loosely Shiite group, the Buyids, who in response to a power vacuum came over the mountains of Iran. They were warriors, mainly in pursuit of governmental grants to satisfy their troops, too little interested in doctrine to displace the Sunni caliphs altogether; rather, they were plunderers who damaged agriculture and put Sunni caliphs into and out of office as they pleased. These Abbasid caliphs led pampered lives in their palaces in Baghdad, while outside there was ruin. An objective surveying of the scene at the start of the eleventh century would have been justified in anticipating a full victory for the cause of the Shiites across the Muslim world. Divided they may have been, but their numbers were considerable. Iran, influenced by the Sassanians, had become a strongpoint for the Twelvers. Qarmatians had established mini-kingdoms; the fighting Shiites had adherents. Persian Buyids dominated a shrunken Sunni Abbasid caliphate and Fatimids had created a caliphate for themselves, had conquered Egypt and so gained the resources to continue to send out missionaries.

The Sunni Response

Change came with the death of the dominant Buyid, Baha al-Dwala, who had borrowed grand titles from the Sassanian dynasty and treated the Abbasid caliphs as puppets, confining them to a religious role. But even a puppet caliph could turn and, taking advantage of the death of Baha al-Dwala in 1012, the Abbasid caliph al-Qadir (991–1031) for the first time sought to declare the Sunni doctrinal position. As we have seen, over the centuries disputes over the caliphate had arrayed rival armies against each other, had issued in battles and killings and had had devastating effects on the descendants of Ali and Fatima – yet a full definition of the implications of Sunnism as a rival to the Shiites had never been given. In the eleventh century al-Qadir in Baghdad, long shorn of real power and lacking an army to enforce his will, saw an opportunity.

There was no popular feeling in favour of the feeble Abbasids, but nonetheless there was a growing preference for them as a shield against shrill Shiites. Even the Buyids reacted against the claims of the Fatimids, and al-Qadir was emboldened to attack them and to cast doubt on the genealogical claims which underpinned them. The death of Baha al-Dwala in 1012 opened new opportunities, which al-Qadir was happy to take. It was the beginning of a process of defining Sunnism. In 1018 al-Qadir condemned Shiism and Mutazilism, requiring orthodox believers to venerate the Companions of the Prophet and the first four caliphs. This meant rejecting the Shiite claim that Ali had been the true choice of Muhammad as his successor and had been unjustly deprived of his position by the early caliphs.

Al-Qadir broke with tradition by making his own decision on the succession, appointing his son; he then went further in 1029 when he issued a decree which rejected the belief that the Quran was created, once put forward by the caliph al-Mamun in the ninth century, implying a doctrinal role for Abbasid caliphs such as himself. Al-Qadir also rejected allegorical interpretation of the Quran, the stock-in-trade of Shiite missionaries. Sunnism based itself on the Quran and the *hadith*, the sayings and doings of the Prophet, a firm set of rulings by which Sunnism was defined. The two sides were now formally and doctrinally arrayed against each other.

Buyids lost their power and became a spent force. Another rival power in Iran, Mahmud of Ghazna, exercising his authority from 998 to 1030, gave his support to al-Qadir, claiming that the Shiites were heretics. Al-Qadir's son, supporting his father, helped to give more emotional force to the Sunni cause by creating shrines in their interest and suppressing those of the Shiites. Abbasid caliphs still had no land and no army but in two reigns they had asserted a claim to religious decision-making and created a definition of Sunnism.

The Seljuq Turks

Yet the event which more than anything else stemmed the tide flowing in favour of Shiism was the irruption into the Islamic world of nomads from the Central Asian steppe. Famine was the spur. Desperate for new territory to feed their flocks and themselves, they came with their tents and their beasts into the farthest frontiers established by the great Muslim conquests in Khurasan and Transoxania and flowed across the Islamic world. Turkish-speaking and carrying with them no mental baggage, like distinguished nomads before and after their day – such as the Arabs from the Hijaz with their folk memories of *jahiliyya* before Muhammad, the Mongols with their cults which puzzled Franciscan missionaries or the Ottomans carrying with them their stories of folk heroes – Seljuqs of the eleventh century had no significant history or cultural traditions. They were, so to speak, a blank slate on which Sunni convictions could be written. Merchants, missionaries and raiders of the Sunni persuasion converted them out on the frontiers, giving them the zeal of new believers. They fractured the political systems of the eleventh century. From the eastern frontiers they moved southwards into Iran, Iraq, Syria and Anatolia, barely under the control of the Seljuq dynasty from which they took their name, who did what they could to prevent opportunistic herders from damaging agricultural land. A leader from the family, Tughril Beg (1040–63) entered Baghdad peacefully with the aid of an existing Turkish presence in the area and expelled the last of the Buyids; the caliph gave Tughril Beg the title of 'sultan', which literally means 'power'. Raiding by the Seljuqs began to affect Anatolia, just as the Byzantine Empire was suffering a malaise due to excessive expansion, heavy taxation and over-reliance on mercenaries.

An attempt by the fighting Emperor Romanus IV Diogenes to challenge the nomad enemy and restore imperial authority made matters worse. He set out to a chosen battle site far on the frontier at Manzikert, north of Lake Van, where he met Alp Arslan, one of the great leaders of the Turks and nephew of Tughril Beg. Romanus miscalculated. His army lacked cohesion, he suffered desertions and his personal guard was overwhelmed. Alp Arslan had no hostile intentions on the Empire and was moving with his cavalry in the Sunni interest to attack the Shiite Fatimid power in Egypt. He gave merciful terms to Romanus, but this did nothing for the defeated leader, who was blinded and then removed from power by aristocratic opponents on the Byzantine side. There followed a ten-year civil war between these rival aristocrats who, as they battled over the leading cities of Anatolia, made use of the Seljuqs as their agents. The consequence was that a series of Byzantine strongpoints fell into the hands of a small number of Turks who, being nomads with the steppe peoples' mastery of the horse and skills in mounted archery but with no particular capacity for siege warfare, would not normally have captured these cities. When one aristocratic leader, Alexius Comnenus, emerged as victor and in 1081 became emperor, he faced a lost Byzantine heartland in Anatolia. From the Islamic side, al-Ghazzali, the classic Sufi writer and one of the masters of Islamic thought, who did more than anyone else to give respect to the Sufi movement, was inclined to regard the nomad intervention philosophically, although he felt its drawbacks, seeing it as an inevitable part of the Sunni rise while he was in the service of Nizam al-Mulk.*

In summary, the Seljuq intervention in the eleventh century brought unexpected vitality to Sunnism. Seljuq power led to the setting up of *madrasas* to give security to scholars and act as training places for *qadis*. The struggle against Shiites was far from over, but a new phase of the conflict had opened.

---

* See below p. 81.

3

THE DOG THAT
DID NOT BARK

In 996 an eleven-year-old boy was playing in a tree in Bilbais in the Nile delta, where his father, the caliph al-Aziz, had been assembling troops and ships. The eunuch Barjawan, chief of the palace treasures, persuaded him to come down and told him that his father had just died, put on his head a jewelled turban and addressed the boy with the classic formula 'Greetings to the Commander of the Faithful'. He took the title al-Hakim bi-amr Allah.

Over the years he learned from Barjawan of the absolute powers of the Fatimid caliph who, in Shiite doctrine, had divine inspiration in all he did. By the time he was fifteen he had realised that, for all the outward respect Barjawan showed him, the eunuch was an inveterate intriguer who was steadily marginalising him. Al-Hakim's revenge was swift. He ordered a servant to knife Barjawan to death. An edict from the head of chancery explained that Barjawan had once pleased the commander but, with a quotation from the Quran about God being 'most knowing and most watchful' with his servants, went on to say, 'when the fellow went bad, he inflicted on him punishment'. This execution of Barjawan initiated a long sequence of terror with many executions, often for arbitrary reasons, some far-reaching edicts and persecution of the Peoples of the Book, the *dhimmis*, Christians and Jews.

He terrified his people. Very few who held highest office under him survived: sooner or later he ordered their execution, sometimes for offences such as embezzlement, sometimes for no apparent reason – thus killing men who had given devoted service, yet often showing unusual generosity after their deaths in grants to their children. He could display the classic virtues of an Islamic leader: generosity and care for mosques and for learning, being accessible to petitioners, whatever their rank, manumitting many slaves and making generous charitable grants. He founded a House of Wisdom to make books available and to give stipends to scholars – yet he killed three professors who lived on these stipends. He loved astronomy but drove away astrologers. Over and over again real achievements were smeared by attacks of paranoia.

A major strand of al-Hakim's policy was his attempt to make traditional regulations effective and to enforce Fatimid principles. The empire he inherited had indeed wide bounds, but at the same time it embraced a ramshackle religious structure, especially in Egypt where Fatimid caliphs had loosely imposed their doctrines and practices on many Sunnis, and even relied on Christians and Jews for some key offices. As he took more and more responsibility from 1004 onwards, al-Hakim began issuing edicts, either traditionally Islamic or specifically Fatimid, looking back to Ali and the beginnings of the early Shiite conflicts. Two dietary regulations look simply eccentric at first sight. They are indeed minuscule and extremist, but make sense for Shiites. He prohibited the use of *mulukhiyya*, a herb used to flavour soups: it was a favourite herb of Muhammad's wife, Aisha, the opponent of Ali. A modern visitor to Egypt, where it is widely used today, regards it as the one sound decision of al-Hakim. He banned a certain kind of watercress for the same reason. He acted fiercely against the use of alcohol, ordering jars of honey to be thrown into the Nile because they might be used to make mead. He destroyed grapes and prohibited the drinking of *fuqqa*, a fizzy, light beer – the Coca-Cola of the eleventh century – a drink disliked by Ali.

Paranoia was fed by an uneasy awareness of the Egyptian disregard of the Quranic prohibition of alcohol. Al-Hakim's physician, a Christian, who treated him for melancholia, drowned in 1007 as he plunged into a pond in order to sober up after heavy drinking, but was too far gone to take off his clothing and perished in the water. This could not be hushed up. It transpired that he was a member of a nocturnal drinking club, which included the caliph's commander-in-chief and his chief justice who were in the habit of enjoying themselves secretly, together with Sunnis, Christians and Ismailis. Al-Hakim was not going to tolerate this and, despite delays and apparent forgiveness, he executed them both.

Waves of legislation alarmed the populace. The Cursing of the Emigrants, a Shiite slogan directed against those Companions of the Prophet who were the first three caliphs before Ali, was by his order displayed in mosques and on walls. Then quite suddenly the measure was cancelled, and it was ordered that the Cursings should be taken down.

Women were progressively exposed to very harsh restrictions, initially, it seems, sparked off by eccentric episodes in which the caliph took to riding about at night in Cairo and encouraged citizens to light up the streets. Seeing men and women getting drunk in public, he decreed that women were not to be allowed to go out in the evening. Later, restrictions were tightened: they were no longer allowed to go and reside in tents by family tombs on days of visitation of the dead. Finally in 1014 all women, bar the very young and the very old, were prohibited from going out at all. Shoemakers who made women's shoes were prohibited from doing so and consequently were ruined. Near the end of his reign, the town of Fustat was burned and the populace devastated, perhaps because they had disobeyed al-Hakim's edicts or attacked his reputation.

He reversed the religious toleration of his father. The Epiphany procession with lights, attended by Muslims as well as Christians, was banned; Christians and Jews were put under pressure and forced to wear badges in public. At one stage crosses were confiscated and publicly burned. Later, Christians, no longer allowed to ride horses, were forced to wear massive wooden crosses round their necks when in public. Jews were made to wear a badge, possibly depicting a calf wrongfully worshipped by Israelites in the days of Moses. Synagogues and churches were looted and destroyed.

The Holy Sepulchre drew al-Hakim's attention. Massive pilgrimages went to the shrine and wealth was bestowed on it. Might such wealth go better to Muslims? Melkites, Arabic-speaking churchmen, had developed the miracle of the holy fire, lit by their patriarch at Easter. It was believed there was trickery here and that a filament was smeared with oil so that all lamps would magically be lit up simultaneously in the ritual. If Jerusalem, as a sacred place for Muslims, was to be purified then might the removal of the greatest of Christian shrines be an efficacious means to this end? Al-Hakim acted. He was nothing if not thorough. In September 1009 Constantine's basilica of the Sepulchre was utterly destroyed, stone by stone. Only the massive pillars of the rotunda, or at least the lower portions of them, remained because they were resistant to the workers' tools. And yet in the last six months of 1020 there were signs that he was weakening in his obduracy towards the Christians: the chronicler Yahya of Antioch records how casual personal contact with a Melkite led to some reconstruction of Christian buildings. The Copts had a similar story of restoration on a whim and personal contact.

Eccentricities grew. Early in his reign al-Hakim had taken to riding, inspecting streets and alleys or passing into the desert, often with very limited personal security. When he rode on a donkey, mostly simply clad, he was, however oddly, echoing the simplicity of Ali. This night riding grew more frequent. In 1021, after riding into the desert at night with a young groom, he disappeared. All that was found was a hamstrung donkey and bloodstained clothing, with tears made by a knife. The likeliest account of what happened is that seven Bedouin accosted him and demanded money. In his usual generous style he promised them 5,000 dirhams. Four Bedouin went off to the Treasury with a groom as a guarantor of good faith. The remaining three murdered him and buried him in an unmarked grave which was never found, leading to the legend, still believed by the Druze, that al-Hakim was divine, had left his temporary body and would one day return. Al-Hakim's formidable elder half-sister promptly took charge and saw to it that his son reigned as the next caliph. The continued vitality of commerce in Egypt sustained the regime.

Cunning in the removal of leading personalities, al-Hakim kept some of his supporters to the end. Cancellation of non-Quranic taxes, flashes of humour, good sense in foreign affairs all saved him from deposition. Talents, political as well as intellectual, fine taste in poetry, scientific knowledge and interest, and the outline of an extreme but coherent Ismaili programme were all lost to a cruel and arbitrary temperament.

The Silence of the West

Muslims had destroyed the Holy Sepulchre, one of the greatest of Christian shrines, and in response Pope Sergius IV (1002–14) issued an encyclical addressed to all Christians calling on them to restore it and kill 'the impious pagans' who had demolished it. The encyclical aroused so little response and was issued so long before the First Crusade that it has generally been regarded as a forgery. Not so. The finest expert of his day on medieval manuscripts has demonstrated that it is authentic and that the pope was proposing to lead an Italian expedition to go to the Sepulchre and was appealing for donations.* 'For all of us Italians,' Sergius wrote, ' – whether you are Venetians or Genoese – with your financial help, wish to prepare a fleet of a thousand ships to travel across the sea to Syria to claim back the Redeemer's tomb.' Those who responded were enjoined neither 'to fear the sea's turbulence nor dread the fury of war', because if they died they would receive the reward of eternal life.

And yet nothing happened. No dog barked after the Sepulchre was broken into pieces. No expedition set out. There were no ships dispatched. No military effort was made. Sergius's encyclical had outlined in essence all the features of later crusading – armed force to recover the Sepulchre, papal leadership, heavenly reward for those who died – but without moving those who read or heard it. There ought, on the face of it, to have been a response. Jerusalem, known to all Christians through Scripture and liturgy, was becoming increasingly a place of pilgrimage. Rome, and the tombs of Peter and Paul, the prime objective in earlier centuries, was now giving way to Jerusalem. Monasteries speculated about the role of a Last World Emperor who at Jerusalem would inaugurate the end of the world. Pilgrimage to Jerusalem increased; hosts went on the occasion

---

* H. M. Schaller, 'Zur Kreuzzugsenzyklika Papst Sergius IV', *Papsttum Kirche und Recht im Mittelalter*, ed. H. Mordek (Tübingen, 1991), pp. 135–53.

of the millennium of Christ's Passion in 1033. New shrine chapels to accommodate pilgrims were built in about 1037 when a Byzantine emperor, collaborating with a Fatimid caliph who valued pilgrim traffic, built a smaller Church of the Holy Sepulchre on the site of the destroyed Constantinian basilica in the aftermath of an earthquake.

There is a startling contrast between the response in 1009 and that in 1095. In 1095–6 the First Crusade set off to make the arduous journey to Jerusalem, but in 1009 nothing happened. The cause must lie in events and changes in attitudes in the West rather than the East.

Localism in the West

The historian of the First Crusade, John France, puzzled by the 'curious incident' of the lack of response of Western Christendom to the destruction of the Sepulchre by al-Hakim, set himself in 1996 to work out just why nothing stirred after 1009, and systematically worked through the chronicles of the time for clues.* He concluded that at the heart of the matter lay the intense localism of the sources. Authors, sponsored by local aristocrats, wrote about local saints and were themselves devoted to particular limited objectives – the history of one monastic house, the story of its founders or the career of one bishop who interested them or of one notable, probably a local benefactor – and saw no farther. However, two chroniclers, Adémar of Chabannes and Raoul Glaber, monks from south-central France, report the destruction with dismay. Glaber says the Sepulchre was destroyed by the ruler of Babylon, a common term for Islamic Egypt, but, like Adémar, he attributes the motive for the destruction to Western Jews. It was they, both chroniclers assert, who egged on Muslims. It was an extraordinarily unhistorical piece of anti-Semitism and was accompanied by pogroms. Despite their limited historical sense, both chroniclers cared greatly about Jerusalem and Adémar himself died on pilgrimage there in 1043. There is no reason to doubt the reality of the

* J. France, 'The Destruction of Jerusalem and the First Crusade', *Journal of Ecclesiastical History*, 47 (1996), pp. 1–17.

attacks on Jews reported by both chroniclers but, beyond that, the al-Hakim destruction had no further impact. Historical understanding was very limited. A number of other chroniclers never mention the destruction by al-Hakim at all and it is striking that Fleury on the Loire, a reforming monastery and a leading intellectual centre, has no word on it. Further to the east, German authors developed a genre of world history based on compiling biblical and classical sources to illustrate the working of God's providence in history but had no awareness of a wider Christian world. The Annals of Hildesheim record the death of Gunther, bishop of Bamberg, in 1065 but do not say that he was on pilgrimage to Jerusalem. Western Europe had turned in on itself: intensely local, it had very little awareness of events in the East, even so vivid an atrocity as the destruction of the Sepulchre.

Pope Sergius had an exclusively Italian emphasis and this dampened his appeal. Italian cities were participants in far-flung trade: Venice had established privileges in the Byzantine Empire and although the leading municipalities – Venice, Pisa and Genoa – later developed a true crusading zeal themselves, they were at this time preoccupied and involved in peaceful trading ventures. Sergius does not seem to have touched the aristocracy of northern Italy who also had their own preoccupations. Popes of Sergius's day moreover mattered little and tended to be victims of faction politics in Rome and its locality. Passive guardians of the shrines of St Peter and St Paul, they had scant means of publicising their views.

Compostela and Cluny

How did this change? One part of the story is the rise in popularity of an old pilgrimage route over the Pyrenees to the shrine of the Apostle James (Sant'Iago) in Galicia in remote north-western Spain, fruit of the mysterious discovery of his bones on this site by a ninth-century bishop. It could be an arduous journey over the mountain range, comparable to the austerities of the ascent of the Alps to reach Rome, and its austerity could have been an attraction. By the second half of the eleventh century there had come to be three important pilgrimages: Jerusalem outstripping the rest,

Rome still there for traditionalists and then Compostela itself. The new route was taking pilgrims into or close to Muslim-dominated lands in Spain and the hostels and refuges on the journey were outlets for anti-Muslim sentiments and seed-ground for the indignation at the Muslim hold on Jerusalem, which issued finally in the 'stirring of hearts' of the West and the First Crusade.

The abbey of Cluny, in Burgundy, gave the lead to the growing pilgrimage and was itself an outstanding example of the new Romanesque architecture of the eleventh century, roofing over great spans, providing for a flow of pilgrims up to a dominant high altar and giving room for massive choirs. Cluny in its glory days had 200 choir-monks and the beauty of its liturgy, its chanting of masses and its skilled management moved military men, who felt that this was the liturgy performed as it should be. Aristocrats were drawn to join the monastic life and to seek the prayers of Cluny and its priories for their dead relatives. It was a focus for a new and peaceful piety. Cluny had been generously endowed by a duke of Aquitaine, William the Pious, and given freedom from secular ties. It was exempt from the power of bishops, at this time only too often secular in their interests in sees which they had bought. It acquired a great congregation of reformed monastic houses, some 2,000 by 1109, all of which accepted its leadership. It was a forerunner of the fully fledged monastic orders of later times. Other leading abbeys, such as Hirsau in the Black Forest or Jumièges in Normandy, followed similar courses with dependent monasteries. Cluny and its fellows exercised spiritual influence over the fighting elite and imposed on them penances often of a very demanding kind. When the call came to go to Jerusalem and fight for it, it appeared to many of the elite a means of doing penance all in one go and saving their souls.

The sculpture of the time produced dramatic images of the suffering of those condemned to hell. Sculpture in Romanesque churches of the pilgrim route also showed cavalrymen riding against enemies – a stimulus to the great cavalry-led expedition of 1095. The great churches of the Compostela route had their own saints whose monuments stand to this day in obscure country places in south-western France as a reminder of the piety of the pre-crusade age.

Anti-Muslim Conventions

Anti-Muslim sentiment was static in the early Middle Ages; the Compostela route did not increase it but did keep it alive. The Church of the day was preoccupied with the task of converting barbarians in the aftermath of the collapse of Rome and consequently had little to say about Muslims. It was aware that death was the penalty for attempting to draw Muslims into Christianity, just as death was the penalty for apostasy by Muslims; sometimes Christians deliberately sought martyrdom by publicly abusing Muhammad and Islam and there were executions. Intellectual life was dominated by monks who were preoccupied with recovery of the legacy of Greece and Rome and had no eyes for anything else; consequently conciliatory and understanding writing which came from Byzantium or other Eastern Christians was disregarded and a crude polemic prevailed on the cruelty, idolatry and sexual misbehaviour of Muslims. Hagiography treated Islam in unsympathetic terms. A convention that Saracens were evil was established and nothing dislodged it. When Urban II, launching the crusade, spoke of Muslim atrocities against Christians, he was echoing a well-established genre of stories.

The Reform Papacy

Cluny and its affiliated priories, their exemptions and their influence in public life, mattered in another way as they buttressed the developing reform papacy emerging in the course of the eleventh century and provided reformers. The story began as the Holy Roman Emperor Henry III, seeking in the traditional way coronation by the pope and concerned that the existence of three rival candidates for the papacy might invalidate his crowning, descended on Rome in 1046, dismissed the candidates and appointed a German bishop of his own, who reigned as Clement II. Henry's action launched a sequence of German or north Italian reforming popes, who declared war on simony, the regular practice of payment to kings in return for appointment to high ecclesiastical office, especially bishoprics. They also opened a campaign against nicolaitism, the marriage of clergy – again a regular practice involving the continuance of a hereditary priesthood in which no issue of merit or vocation arose and fathers instructed sons on their ceremonial duties in a form of apprenticeship. Initiatives of this kind from an emperor were not controversial, for he was solemnly anointed as he took office, conferring on him a special status with authority over clergy and the right to deliver to bishops their symbols of office, the ring and the shepherd's staff.

Of these new-style popes the most notable was Leo IX (1048–54), a Lorrainer, for many years bishop of Toul and a relative of the emperor. He was distinguished in his tireless journeying out of Rome in the cause of reform through Florence, Pavia and Cologne and then to the diocese of Rheims. There he was to consecrate a new church for the translation of the relics of St Remigius, the most important saint for all the Franks as he was the missionary who had baptised their king, Clovis. In an unusual move, Leo exposed the saint's relics on the high altar and then confronted the bishops and abbots whom he had summoned to a great council there and asked them one by one if they had paid money for their respective offices. In dramatic scenes bishops were confounded; one bishop was even struck dumb. Some bishops were deposed and all who had failed to heed Leo's summons to the council were automatically dismissed from office. The moral authority of the papacy was established at a stroke. The pope also sought a concomitant reform for the laity by the institution in the Rheims diocese of the Peace of God, restricting fighting and requiring protection for the vulnerable, women, monks and merchants.

The pope led his own forces against marauders attempting to conquer papal lands, and was defeated by Norman rulers of south Italy at Civitate in 1053. He died in the year following this catastrophe, but not before he had established that force could be used on behalf of the see of Peter. One error lay in his use of the Cluniac monk Humbert of Silva Candida, who in an irritable and careless fashion issued a declaration of excommunication with far-reaching consequences for the patriarch of the Byzantine Church over a trivial issue, leaving it on the altar of the great church Hagia Sophia in Constantinople.

Pope Gregory VII (1073–84) was inspired by Leo, to whom he habitually referred in conversation. Passionate, devoted to St Peter in a long career dedicated to Rome, a monk and a man of relatively humble origin in contrast to the run of aristocratic holders of the papal office, Gregory had titanic energy and turned the world upside down. Force, he believed, was necessary to achieve his great objective, that 'holy Church, the bride of Christ, Our Lady and mother should return in her true glory and stand free, chaste and catholic'. In his opposition to simoniac, unchaste clergy and their backers, he turned to all kinds of allies: he welcomed Erlembald, a street fighter in Milan, distributed banners to warriors, used barbaric Normans to fight for him and developed the notion of militias of St Peter as a fighting force for the papacy. He broke wholly with the tradition under which Leo IX and his predecessors had worked as reformers under a beneficent and reforming emperor. The Church and its ordained clergy, abbots and bishops should stand in independence of all secular power. It was a vital moment in western European and Christian history, for the division between Church and State adumbrated by Gregory lasted and it differentiated the situation in the West profoundly from the Muslim East, where the caliphate in the tradition of Muhammad exercised authority in matters both religious and secular.

The death of Emperor Henry III and a long regency for his son Henry IV, who succeeded at the age of six, opened the way for advances in papal power and independence to the advantage of Gregory when he embarked on his extraordinary challenge to the Church and society. 'Cursed is he who keeps back his sword from bloodshed' was his favourite text, taken from the prophet Jeremiah, and the use of every weapon against the enemies of his reform led to dramatic clashes and a war of pamphlets. No longer would statements from the papacy be left in obscurity, as in Sergius's day. Step by step his natural supporters deserted him, even those sympathetic to reform. He humiliated Henry IV, but then had to witness the emperor's ravaging of his beloved Rome while he took refuge in the fortress of the Castel Sant'Angelo. He was forced into exile and died under the protection of the Normans.

He left behind a multitude of initiatives, letters and schemes. Among them was a letter he sent to the young Henry IV in December 1074, before they quarrelled. This sketched out to the emperor a plan for Gregory himself to lead an army to aid Christians overseas, 'who are being daily butchered like herds of cattle'. 'I have been touched with great grief', he went on, 'and I have taken steps to stir up certain Christians who long to lay down their lives for their brethren. Already more than fifty thousand men have prepared themselves, so that, if they can have me as their Pontiff and leader they may go all the way to the Lord's Sepulchre.' He had been influenced, he concluded, by the desire of the Byzantines to heal quarrels, which included the major issue of the Procession of the Holy Spirit in the doctrine of the Trinity, which continues to disturb and damage the relationship between the Latin and the Greek Churches in modern times. Here Gregory, the great radical and the dynamic defender of the rights of the papacy, was surprisingly ready to seek reconciliation.

It was all fantasy; there never were 50,000 men in readiness and the scheme got nowhere. But the man was revealed. His 'great grief' was typical of a man of compassion, and his scheme sketched out all the themes of the First Crusade – Saracen atrocities, relief of Eastern Christians, the journey to the Sepulchre, the will to assist Byzantium. The plan, which remained in his head, cohered with his vision of the Church as he believed it had once been, free of greedy and oppressive lay powers, its leaders openly chosen on merit and in peace with all fellow Christians. A desire for peace might seem an odd outcome of Gregory's stormy actions, yet there was a logic and a vision to it, widening out Leo's decree for Peace in the diocese of Rheims. Gregory was seeking the Peace of God over the whole Christian world and the action to aid Eastern Christians, healing the split with the Byzantine Church, was designed to make universal Peace a reality.

Gregory's tempestuous reign left an important legacy for the beginning of crusading, both positively and negatively. On the one hand, his actions alienated all crowned heads: consequently no kings responded to the summons to Jerusalem and armies had to be commanded by princes. On the other hand, he implanted in papal circles a notion of the rightfulness of war for a holy cause and of the injustices done to Eastern Christians. The sketch of a crusade lay, so to speak, on the table to be picked up later.

Behind the localism and limited horizons of the chronicles investigated by John France lay the misery of anarchic, perennial warfare, dominant in the eleventh century as a result of the progressive disintegration of public authority after the breakdown of Charlemagne's empire. There remained some residual awareness of the idea of the power and duty of the ruler to maintain order which had been inherited from the Roman Empire; but in practice, over the years, power had devolved only too often down to the level of the castellan. In the lands of the western Franks there was indeed a monarchy, which reached back to the insignificant figure of Hugh Capet, chosen in 987, but his power and that of his descendants for many years had remained minimal. Philip I, for example, who reigned with frailty from 1060 to 1108, towards the end of his life remarked that his vain attempts to capture the insignifcant castle of Montlhéry, to which he held a claim, had made him old before his time. The king was a landlord among many others and the real unit of power was the *mouvance*, a circle of influence based on landholding. Struggles to maintain or expand these circles form the stuff of history in the most anarchic regions. Raiding and plundering were central.

A vernacular poem composed between the late twelfth and early thirteenth centuries describes a scene which had been typical of the eleventh century as well. As an army moved forward, preceded by scouts, fire-raisers and foragers, who were to collect the spoil and carry it away in the baggage train, villages were set on fire. Terrified inhabitants were led off to be held for ransom: 'Everywhere', the poem continues, 'bells ring the alarm; a surge of fear sweeps over the countryside, wherever you look you can see helmets ... pennons ... the whole plain covered with horsemen. Money, cattle, mules and sheep are all seized. The smoke billows, flames crackle. Peasants and shepherds scatter in all directions.'

Churchmen denounced these practices as the work of mercenaries but were aware that this was only a formula, for they knew only too well that ravaging was part of general warfare and carried out by arms-bearers who were, of course, their relatives. It fell grievously on peasants, the surplus of whose labour sustained the way of life of landholders. They were over and over again the victims in battles over *mouvances* as a besieging force stripped a locality of its stores of grain, seized crops to feed its horses and took away livestock. The object was to intimidate and humiliate the land-holder under attack and to shake the loyalty of vassals, who viewed their lord as an effective protector. The peasant, in any case, lived precariously: the barrier between living and starving was a thin one and could be broken by climatic conditions, epidemics, murrain of cattle, poor harvests and ravaging.

Landholders for their part were subject to the pressures of their kindred: they had to struggle in order to provide for their sons and daughters, to gain plunder to satisfy their troops, maintain their weapons and support cavalrymen who were the best-trained and best-equipped warriors of the day and remained expensive. Multiple homage was usual, so that one lord had obligations to a series of other lords; conflict settled which homage was going to be the most important. Horizons were dominated by the struggles to retain lands, peasants and castles in this fluid and uncertain world in which the distinction between public and private war had virtu-ally disappeared. Emperors also could be frustrated by recalcitrant land-holders and by the problem of castle-breaking. The great duchies of the eastern Franks, where the Empire was reborn, had a tradition of independ-ence and included leading families with allods, tracts of land which owed no homage to the ruler at all and which were virtually independent. Eve-rywhere lords, both spiritual and temporal, were concerned to protect their lands and rights.

Little wonder that there was much talk of peace. There is evidence of great men, such as the dukes of Aquitaine, using their resources to enforce a measure of order. Adémar of Chabannes wrote of crowds crying out for peace. The Emperor Henry III (1046–56) spoke of creating peace when he defeated the Hungarians. There is some evidence of influence emanating from St Martial in Limoges to popularise the use of an appeal for peace in the tropes of the Agnus Dei; 'Lamb of God have mercy on us' twice repeated, was followed by a verse appealing for peace: ' Dona nobis pacem', 'Grant us peace'. As the century wore on, it was clear the attempts to bring peace to a warring world had not succeeded.

It is against this background that we should examine the startling summary of a leading modern British historian, confessing with moving honesty to the problems he encountered in trying to understand the minds of those who went on the First Crusade and subsequent expeditions. 'I have recognised', he wrote,

> that the task I have set myself is in many ways an impossible one. We are too distant from the personalities concerned to understand them fully, and anyway we have to reconcile their bleak, obsessed, savage and religious world with ours and describe it in our own terms before we can comprehend them at all ... Their priorities often seem alien to us, and the movement in which they were engaged madness, because the basic religious elements common to Christians in any age were transformed in their case by adaptation to a society in which lordship, honour, family solidarity expressing itself at all times in vendettas, reputations and commitment to extravagant social generosity played powerful parts.

'I do not suppose', he concludes, 'that I am alone in finding it very hard to stretch my mind to encompass the amalgam of piety and violence, of love and hate which was characteristic of their response to the call to arms.'* This grim assessment of the nature of the lives of arms-bearers and their men who formed the core of the immense numbers going on the journey to Jerusalem is borne out by the events of the crusade, which reveal a most daunting blend of internecine conflicts, needless vain display, savagery to opponents and distortion of Scripture both in the preparations for the crusade and on the great march to Jerusalem. Mixed in with this was much raw courage and endurance, plus an only fitful awareness of its religious aim. Inevitably, the crusaders carried with them the grievous characteristics of their turbulent world.

---

* J. Riley-Smith, *The First Crusaders, 1095–1131* (Cambridge, 1997), p. 6.

4

THE FIRST CRUSADE

Urban II

The pope who succeeded in 1088 and reigned for ten years, took office at a nadir of papal power after the short pontificate following Gregory VII's death. Effectively Urban II was Gregory's successor and heir and thought just as he did. He wrote to the German bishops who still supported Gregory's cause, 'Believe me just as about the most blessed Gregory. I want to follow in his footsteps: everything he abhorred, I abhor; what he condemned, I condemn; what he loved, I warmly embrace.' He was as radical as Gregory in his acceptance of profound change in Church and society as a sacred duty and favoured armed action just as Gregory had done; but he was pragmatic and realistic where Gregory had not been.

Writing in 1945 Carl Erdmann, the pioneer of modern crusading history, said, 'Gregory did not reckon with men as they actually are.' But Urban did. He understood the political world and the making of alliances. In 1089 he arranged the marriage of the indomitable supporter of Gregory VII in Italy, the Countess Matilda of Tuscany, and Welf, son of Welf IV of Bavaria, leader of the opposition to the Emperor Henry IV in Germany. The alliance worked and eventually defeated the emperor, leading to the blocking of Alpine passes against him and the loss of prestige of his antipope, leaving Urban free to re-enter Rome in 1093 and restore the papacy's authority. By calling the crusade to Jerusalem in 1095 Urban created a foreign policy for the popes giving them a prestige and spiritual power which lasted until the great clash between the king of France and Pope Boniface VIII at the turn of the fourteenth century.

His realism sprang, in part, from his experience. Born Odo of Lagery in the arms-bearing class of north-eastern France at Châtillon-sur-Marne in Champagne, he took orders, studied in the cathedral school at Rheims and served as its archdeacon, thus coming into contact with the reforming zeal of Leo IX and with the Peace of God mechanism for restricting warfare and protecting clergy and the vulnerable from the effects of war. Then he was professed as a monk of Cluny and was influenced by its tradition, the discipline of its liturgy and its intimate links to Gregorian reform. He showed his administrative powers as he rose to become prior, second in command to the abbot. Released from the monastery to become cardinal bishop of Ostia in about 1080, he entered into intimate service to Gregory in his last, fraught years. It was an unusually wide experience. His greatest asset was nonetheless his origins in the aristocratic society of France, which gave him understanding of this noble world, the majority force behind the crusade.

The Councils of Piacenza and Clermont

The Council of Piacenza in March 1095 was the first great council of Urban's pontificate, demonstrating the progress which he had already made in moving forward from the disaster of Gregory VII's expulsion from Rome in 1084. Here he assembled higher clergy to debate Gregorianism, to denounce the sins of the simoniacs, the breaches of celibacy and the lay powers who abetted them. The enemies of reform were rejected; both Henry IV and Philip I of France remained excommunicate.

The Byzantine emperor Alexius Comnenus, aware of not only the need he had to recover much of Anatolia from the Seljuqs but also the weaknesses of his own forces, sought outside help and accordingly sent emissaries to the Council. Alexius knew the quality of professional soldiers in the West and may well have looked for a mercenary force to help him recover Anatolia. Emperors practised sophisticated diplomacy, and

Alexius may have thought that it was wise to plead the sufferings of Eastern Christians through his representatives to move pope and clergy, rather than plainly acknowledge his prime purpose – to recover ancient Byzantine lands.

The patriarch of Constantinople, Symeon II, seems to have wished to end the split with the Western Church and may himself have given information on atrocities wreaked by the Saracens. It is a paradox that the two popes, Gregory VII and Urban II, who believed in the use of violence to force reform on the recalcitrant, nonetheless had as their overall aim a general peace, not only quelling the violence of warriors but also making a final end to the schism with Constantinople.

Four months after Piacenza, Urban was in Provence at the start of a long tour within France, preaching, promoting peace, saying Mass, consecrating churches and altars, giving his blessing to the great wave of ecclesiastical building that had taken place there. No doubt a moment especially dear to the pope was when he consecrated the high altar at Cluny in October 1095. For quiet country towns the appearance of this elderly man wearing the papal insignia of the time – a conical white cap with a circlet of gold and gems accompanied by the supreme relic of the True Cross – was a moving occasion and great crowds came to see him. This was the essential background to the Council of Clermont.

At Clermont in November 1095 there was a massive international attendance of higher clergy to engage in discussion of the great themes of Gregorian reform: ecclesiastical discipline, simony, clerical marriage, lay investiture and appointment. There was a call for a general Peace. These matters so occupied the churchmen that they kept record of them and not of the appeal for a crusade to Jerusalem which was made at the end of the long deliberations. The exception was the bishop of Arras who recorded one sentence. 'Whoever,' the text ran, 'for devotion alone, not to gain honour or money, goes to Jerusalem to liberate the Church of God can substitute this journey for all penance.' This vital sentence offered hearers a means of expiating all their sins in one great act, fulfilling either all the imposed penances that they had been unable to complete or the penances that their consciences led them to think they ought to perform because of their sin and enabled them to do so by fighting. It has to be remembered that the machinery of confession and penance was very ill-developed at this time and heavy, cumbersome penances were demanded from penitents. There is an illuminating passage in a chronicle from the abbey of Monte Cassino after Clermont, describing the pope urging some arms-bearers to go on crusade. They explained to him that the penances they had to fulfil required them to be unarmed and in their locality that left them quite unprotected, liable in this violent society to be murdered. In going to Jerusalem, the pope urged, they were going to fulfil a penitential task in personal safety, using their arms against the enemy.

It has been argued that we cannot know what Urban said at Clermont. Chroniclers, who described the scene and wrote well after the event in the light of the astonishing success of taking Jerusalem, were concerned to interpret the workings of providence that had enabled this to happen, or to give honour to their heroes in this great odyssey. Yet the bishop of Arras's solitary report can be put beside other contemporary evidence to form a whole. The pope wrote to the reformed monastery at Vallombrosa, ordering the monks not to go on crusade; the fighting men who were going to Jerusalem, he said, were going to 'liberate Christianity' and restrain 'the savagery of the Saracens'. In a letter to Bologna in 1096 he wrote similarly of the 'liberation of the Church' and of 'total penance' being remitted; in an appeal to Flanders one month after Clermont he denounced the Muslims saying, 'the barbarians in their frenzy have invaded and ravaged the churches of God. Worse still they have seized the Holy City of Christ.'

These letters show the pope was summoning men to fight in substitution for all penance, recruiting only arms-bearers and denouncing the mal-treatment of Christians in the East and the alien occupation of Jerusalem. In support of the call he repeated stories of Muslim cruelties to Christians that had been commonplace in Christian sources well before the eleventh century.

There is evidence that a call to liberate Jerusalem had been in the pope's mind before he went into a meadow outside the cathedral at Clermont, that it had been broached with great men on some earlier occasions and that he had chosen certainly a spiritual and probably a lay leader before Clermont was called. Adémar, bishop of Le Puy, who had great resources and a reputation for skill with horses, was present at Clermont; he filled the role of leader on the spiritual side. Raymond, count of Toulouse, although not present, had clearly been informed and recruited beforehand and was the natural choice as lay leader because of his experience in fighting Muslims in Spain.

The Call of the Cross

On 27 November 1095, at the end of the Council, the pope went into the meadow outside the cathedral and launched the journey to Jerusalem with an extraordinarily potent set of actions. In a largely illiterate society gestures were of immense importance. He built on the existing symbolisms of pilgrimage – the napkin, satchel and staff – and added one more: the 'taking of the cross' as a symbol of an armed pilgrimage to Jerusalem. The sculpture in the cloister of the priory at Belval in Lorraine gives us a rare glimpse of a crusader standing in pilgrim clothes with the cross on his chest, as his wife clings passionately to him. We see here that the cross was made up of strips of cloth measuring in all 6 inches by 6 inches (15cm by 15cm). The pope's actions in the meadow were those of the organiser of a revivalist meeting in our own times, who puts together a team of supporters to set the ball rolling and encourage others to participate. We know that Baldwin, archbishop of Canterbury, did just this in his campaign in Wales in 1188 to preach the cross for the Third Crusade. At Radnor the archbishop preached and an interpreter translated into Welsh, whereupon, as earlier arranged, Gerald of Wales, chronicler and archdeacon, came forward to take the cross and so move others to do likewise. Thus, after Urban exhorted his hearers, pleading atrocities against Christians in the East and the wrongful occupation of Jerusalem, Adémar of Le Puy came forward to take the cross and sew it on his clothing, as arranged. He had thoughtfully provided a basket of textile crosses for others to do the same – and they did.

It was Urban's master stroke. He had built on the increasing vogue of pilgrimage in previous years, with its established symbols and rights, and added to that a special armed pilgrimage to the East and to Jerusalem, with the symbol of the cross backing it. By this time the cross had become the symbol of Christianity, part of the potent world of relics. Urban skilfully associated three things: firstly the magic name of Jerusalem, known to all through sermon and liturgy and acknowledged to be the greatest target of pilgrimages; secondly, the act of sewing on a cross; and thirdly, linking that 'taking' of the cross with a vow and with the appeal of the wrongful taking of Jerusalem by alien people, the 'pagans', as he called them. To arms-bearers used to disputes over the rights and wrongs of occupation of land, the plea that Jerusalem had been occupied against all justice automatically had a resonance. They were also used to vows – to the promise of fidelity a vassal made to a lord and to the vow that a monk made on his profession in a monastery. Urban linked all three: Jerusalem, the sewing on of the cross and the vow, and created an act which went on moving the minds of medieval humanity for centuries to come. The revivalist atmosphere was completed by a pre-arranged chant by supporters with the cry 'Deus lo volt': 'God wills it.' That the providence of God was behind it all was the assumption to be conveyed to the laity by the pope's backers.

It turned out to be a revivalist meeting that fell flat. It all worked, but there were not enough arms-bearers present in the meadow to make up the number of warriors clearly desired by Urban to go to Jerusalem. The preaching of the cross had to go on, and not only by the pope but also by other preachers acting for him. It was a long-drawn-out affair, albeit a mightily successful one in the end, accounting for 'the great stirring of hearts' which moved the chroniclers and contemporaries. We can trace the pope preaching the cross again, for example, at Limoges at Christmas 1095, when he dedicated the basilica of St Martial; in 1096, just before Lent, he preached the cross at Angers and in mid-Lent at Tours.

Charters issued by arms-bearers who went on crusade give us vital clues on the reasons why they went on this hazardous journey. In 1096 a certain Ingebald, for example, wrote about his sins as a reason for going. 'Considering', his charter ran, 'that God has spared me, steeped in many and great sins, and has given me the time for penance …'. The words will have come from the hand of monks, since the weak level of education of parish priests and their social class ruled them out as mediators between arms-bearers and the demands of the Church. The eleventh century was a great age of monastic vitality and of a new asceticism. In theory monks were not supposed to be in close touch with the secular world, but in practice they were and monks, reformed canons and, of course, truly Gregorian bishops all had influence to move men to go to take Jerusalem and did so. An established way to salvation was to enter the monastic life as death approached, accept celibacy, be buried in the monastery and receive the prayers of the monks. But death could not be accurately forecast. Little pilgrimages were one way of assuaging guilt and one that took the arms-bearer generally to relics. But the march to the Holy City came as a special outlet, a kind of monasticism for the moment, an assuaging of guilt in one act.

Charters may show us acts of repentance by crusaders before setting off and one can surmise how this came about, as the would-be participant discussed the decision to go and an abbot would draw his attention to outstanding injustices to be done away with before the journey. Some of the most clear-cut examples come from families who went to Jerusalem to fight after the First Crusade, but they give clues as to what happened after Clermont and before the host set off. Monasteries had a vital role to play in securing the welfare of the crusader and his dependants by their prayers, and because they were landholders they could provide loans and mortgages to meet the extraordinary costs participants faced. With helpful financial arrangements could come hints and suggestions about acts of reparation. So Stephen of Blois, married to William the Conqueror's daughter Adela, gave a wood to the abbey of Marmontier 'so that God at the intercession of St Martin and his monks might pardon me for whatever I have done wrong and lead me on the journey ... and bring me back healthy and safe'.

The hosts which assembled in consequence of the preaching of the cross must have been far greater than the small body of professionals anticipated by the Byzantine Emperor Alexius. It astonished contemporaries; the word used was 'inaudita', 'unheard of'. A good estimate would be that the total of the separate contingents who set off on the land route to

Jerusalem amounted to 60,000. Nothing like this had ever happened. To provide a comparison: 14,000 would be a fair figure for the army of adventurers and vassals assembled by William, Duke of Normandy, to conquer England in 1066 and even that may be too high.

In one point the influence of Gregory VII lived on. The crowned heads, the Emperor Henry IV and King Philip I of France, remained excommunicate and did not come – though the extraordinary appeal of crusading led Philip to have his brother Hugh of Vermandois join the expedition. The crucial figures were princes, men of high rank and resources, who could pay the immense cost of the journey: only they with their entourages and their contacts could do it. The cost of supporting and equipping just one arms-bearer for the great journey from northern France to Jerusalem, 2,700 miles along a difficult land route, has been calculated at five times the normal annual income of such a man. The leader had to provide for arms, armour, transport, horses, mules. He also had to make arrangements, provision and assist vital auxiliaries such as farmers and grooms, squires and armourers, and allow for the care and feeding of large numbers of men on a long journey in a hostile environment. Idealism was in the forefront: the notion, beloved of an earlier generation of historians that younger sons starved of inheritance went for the sake of land, is knocked out by these calculations. A younger son could get land elsewhere much more easily.

Of those who went on crusade, a substantial number can be related to the pope's journey in France. Others came from farther afield, moved by 'the great stirring of hearts'. Two deserving special mention are the Count of Flanders from the Empire, who brought great resources, and Godfrey of Bouillon, Duke of Lower Lorraine, who departed with the permission of the Emperor Henry IV, taking with him officials including his seneschal and his chamberlain. He was no Gregorian and had fought on Henry IV's side. Aware of his faults before leaving for Jerusalem, he restored the priory of St Dagobert de Stenay which his men had wrecked.

Albert of Aachen, a chronicler who, though he did not himself go on crusade, received reminiscences from Lorrainers who did, gives us a description of the activities of an ascetic evangelist from Picardy called

Peter the Hermit, who in old age retired to a monastery he had founded at Huy on the Meuse. This is not far from Aachen and there is a reasonable supposition that Albert had special information based on the old man's memories. He describes Peter going on pilgrimage to Jerusalem lamenting 'unlawful and wicked things' and 'calling on God himself as avenger of the wrongs he had seen'. He asked the patriarch of Jerusalem why he 'allowed gentiles and wicked men to defile the holy places, and let the offerings of the faithful be carried off, churches to be used as stables, Christians beaten up, holy pilgrims robbed by excessive fees and distressed by the many violent acts of the infidels', and received the reply that he had no power to prevent these acts. Peter then had a vision at the Church of the Holy Sepulchre calling on him to cleanse the Holy Places himself. He resolved to inform 'the pope and the leaders of Christian peoples'. It looks as if Peter was an entirely independent preacher, acting with the authority of his vision. He flourished a celestial letter, calling for aid to Jerusalem. His themes were harsh and apocalyptic, stressing atrocities committed against Christians. He drew the poor in great numbers. For his hearers, Jerusalem really was a land flowing with milk and honey, as in Scripture, and would deliver them from a harsh, confined world in which they were so often close to starvation or made sick by ergotism caused by mould or rotting grain. Their lot had worsened in the course of the eleventh century, binding them more closely and harshly to lords. So they responded massively to Peter and to other preachers like him, and the People's Crusade was launched.

However, modern research has shown that Peter's followers were not exclusively poor. Clearly there must have been trained fighting men providing a cadre of leaders. For example, the lord of Boissy Sans Avoir, an arms-bearer with his own lands, has had his name mistranslated as Walter the Penniless. There were a number of foot soldiers and cavalry: undisciplined as they were, they still had elements of a fighting force. Another straw in the wind suggesting factors at work creating the conditions for crusading quite independently of Urban II comes from the Muslim world. The chronicler al-Azimi from Aleppo recorded harassment of Frankish and Byzantine pilgrims at Syrian ports resulting in some loss of life as they attempted to make their pilgrimage to Jerusalem in 1093–4.

The People's Crusade soon showed the dark side of society as anti-Semitism, which had emerged earlier in the days of Adémar of Chabannes, again reared its head. Jews were vulnerable. They had liquid cash and they were in the dangerous position of moneylenders. Godfrey of Bouillon blackmailed the Jews of Cologne and Mainz so that each of the two communities provided him with 500 silver pieces. A Swabian Count Emich and his followers, presumably recruited by Peter the Hermit, killed Jews at Speyer after attempting to force baptism on them, massacred others at Worms and looted and killed at Mainz, where the archbishop failed to keep his promise to protect them. No doubt local tensions aided the looters. When Emich and his gangs came up against a capable army led by the king of Hungary, they gave up. Emich escaped, never did go on crusade and went back to Swabia.

Another sub-leader, Volkmar, persecuted Jews in Bohemia, while a group passing over the landward route imposed forced baptism in the Danube at Regensburg. Vengeance and vendetta were a part of society, and there is Jewish evidence not only of the looting of Jews for money for the great expenses of the journey but also of persecution born of twisted logic – if crusaders were taking great risks to expel the unjust occupiers of Jerusalem, should they not avenge Christ's suffering by also repressing and killing Jews who had been responsible for His death? Inexperienced leadership and the sheer size of the People's Crusade led to quarrelling and tension over provisioning in the localities through which they travelled. There was great wastage of personnel: a sub-leader, Gottschalk, and his group, creating trouble in Hungary, were killed off by King Coloman.

Alexius, confronted with an ill-equipped army far larger than he wished, wisely provisioned these unwelcome arrivals at Constantinople so as to prevent damage to the empire through foraging, then ensured that they were taken on to occupy and garrison Kibotos, on the Gulf of Nicomedia, but control was lost once they were there and elements, looting and foraging round about, were caught by the Turks of Nicaea and massacred. Remnants had to be rescued by the Byzantines. Alexius had expected mercenaries, who would have been under his control. Instead, he received a great and miscellaneous host and was consequently determined to bind them to him as closely as he could. In return for oaths, the leaders would receive aid and guides through difficult terrain. Determined to rebuild Byzantine power after Manzikert in 1071, the emperor's prime targets were strongpoints in Anatolia and the city of Antioch, lost in 1086. Jerusalem, lost in 638, was merely a distant objective.

Bohemond of Taranto was odd man out. He had fought a war against Alexius in pursuit of his own brigand-like claim to Byzantium, the legacy to him of his father, Robert Guiscard, Norman ruler of the multi-ethnic and multicultural kingdom of Sicily. He took the cross, then moved very slowly and cautiously to Constantinople, no doubt with the aim of allowing time for the emperor to accustom himself to the extraordinary notion that he should accept his skilled and dedicated enemy as a member of the crusade army sent to aid Christians in the East (that is, first and foremost, Byzantium) as well as conquer Jerusalem. Alexius had little real choice. He had never intended to lead the army in person – he was not a talented general and he had a need to continue to manage the difficult politics of the Empire, constantly confronted as he was by recalcitrant, manoeuvring aristocrats. He moved the great armies on. Bohemond approached Godfrey of Bouillon and suggested that, together, they could take over Constantinople and supplant Alexius; Godfrey refused.

In the end the emperor secured from the leaders of the great contingents an oath of vassalage, requiring them to hand over conquered lands and cities in return for vital logistical and personal help. Mistrust ruffled relations; Godfrey used ravaging in imperial lands to emphasise his dissatisfaction, while Alexius played one leader off against another and calmed the situation by supplies of provisions. Tancred, the Norman nephew of Bohemond and a tearaway, attempted to avoid taking an oath altogether, but was finally compelled to do so.

The crusaders were unaware of changes in the Islamic world which eased their passage to Jerusalem – while still leaving them a very difficult pathway to their objective. Alp Arslan, the victor at Manzikert, died in 1072 and was succeeded by his formidable son Malik Shah, a man of high culture, deeply knowledgeable about Persian literature, the sponsor of beautiful mosques in Isfahan and the poetry of Omar Khayyam and also a ruthless organiser of military power. He kept control of the fluid situation created by the coming of the Seljuqs using traditional slave soldiers, Mamluks, of the type used by the Abbasid caliphs in the ninth century. He was aided by a long-serving vizier, Nizam al-Mulk, the author of a standard work on the conduct of a Muslim ruler and an administrator of high calibre. But they had both been removed on the eve of the Council of Piacenza and the intervention of the Emperor Alexius, as in 1092 Nizam al-Mulk was stabbed to death by an emissary of the Assassins, extremist Shiites who were offended by Nizam al-Mulk's part in the revival of Sunnism and resented the corruption of the Fatimid caliphate in Cairo. The Assassins were ensconced in an almost impregnable site at Alamut, in the Elburz mountains. A team of inspired devotees under a talented Grand Master, Hasan i-Sabah, they needed no hashish to deaden their pain, only the inspiration of the rewards of paradise, dealing out death to Sunni leaders and Franks at the Grand Master's will.

By pure coincidence Malik Shah died of natural causes a week later. Conspiracy theories sprang up. Seljuq leaders were succeeded by opportunist *atabegs*, ostensibly looking after youthful princes and in practice taking over power from them. The Seljuq sultanate, created by Tughril Beg's journey to Baghdad, was fragmented so that instead of Malik Shah mobilising Sunni Islam against the crusaders, they had to grapple with individual *atabegs*. One such was their first antagonist, Kilij Arslan, who had been imprisoned by Malik Shah. He escaped after Malik Shah's death and set about creating a mini-empire for himself in Anatolia, with Nicaea as his capital, just as the crusaders began their journey from Constantinople.

Battles with the Atabegs

While the crusader armies moved on towards their first major objective, Nicaea, an ancient Roman and Byzantine city with substantial walls and towers, Kilij Arslan, confident in his soldiers, left the city to take Melitene, a key point on the route to Mesopotamia and Iran. Frustrated there, he came back to harass the crusaders as they encamped around Nicaea. The city was defended on its western side by the Ascanian Lake – thus diminishing the area of wall to be manned. Kilij Arslan had intended the city to be a key point in his developing leadership and he had put in a garrison that was more stable and better disciplined than garrisons elsewhere. As part of his plan of Byzantine revival, Alexius was determined to recover a city with so long and distinguished a history and he saw the crusader contingents as a unique instrument put in his hands for this purpose.

Crusader contingents, arriving piecemeal under their leaders and with no effective overall command, occupied different sides of the city, with Bohemond and the Normans along the north wall, Godfrey of Bouillon and Robert of Flanders on the east. Raymond of Toulouse, who came up later, occupied a position by the south gate and was setting up camp when Kilij Arslan arrived with his archers. Seljuq mounted archers were expert in discharging showers of arrows in order to disconcert opponents and break up their formations, finally to encircle and destroy them. Raymond's forces stood firm, outfaced the shower of arrows and then drew the attackers into close-quarter fighting: hard, slogging work with heavy losses on both sides. Meanwhile Godfrey rallied speedily, came round from the other side of the city as Raymond held his ground and took Kilij Arslan in his right flank, forcing him to retreat. The terrain had been decisive, the hills and woods enclosing Nicaea leaving scant room for manoeuvre by archers, and the crusaders had shown courage. It all raised morale and readied them for the siege proper.

Siege engines and mangonels came into play but were not at first effective. Missiles made insufficient impact on stout walls and siege engines of the *testudo* type, wooden penthouses pushed against walls, with armoured roofs to protect miners working below, failed under attacks from the garrison. One such penthouse from Godfrey's force collapsed, killing those within. Raymond of Toulouse used mangonels to protect his men as they bridged the ditch and pushed forward another penthouse-type engine, which the garrison burned. Finally a massive sum was paid from the common fund of the armies to a Lombard engineer who designed an engine which was pushed across the ditch. Under its protection miners worked on the stone, made holes and in classic fashion put in wood supports, then fired them. As the defence began to crumble, the garrison surrendered on terms and went free, to the displeasure of some crusaders.

The city went to Alexius, not the crusaders, who were nonetheless compensated with loot. The emperor had given vital help, supplying wood and nails for the siege engines and food for the besiegers – enough to prevent dispersal for foraging but not enough to succour all the poor, some of whom starved. He had forced the garrison to spread manpower across their defences by blockading the Ascanian Lake with his boats. After Nicaea fell, some crusaders abandoned the march onwards to Jerusalem and enlisted under the emperor. Alexius had kept the confidence of the leaders and it is reasonable to suppose that it was under his influence that they sent envoys to the Fatimids in Egypt, who believed this Western force might aid them in recovering lost territory in Syria and Palestine. Neither Alexius nor the Fatimid caliphate had understood the overwhelming passion to recover Jerusalem which animated the crusader army.

They marched on heading south towards Antioch, aided by the imperial representative Taticius leading a contingent of Byzantine troops guiding the crusader army through the terrain and, where possible, receiving cities and strongpoints for the emperor. Ahead lay Dorylaeum, an old Roman way-station in a key position at the gateway to the plateau of Anatolia. Kilij Arslan came back from Melitene aided by a force of Danishmends, another Turkish group normally his rivals, whom he had persuaded to join him in order to destroy the western army in open country where nomad cavalry could be most effectively deployed. His intelligence was better than that of the westerners and he caught the vanguard of the forces led by Bohemond, Robert of Normandy, Stephen of Blois and Robert of Flanders as they had just crossed a bridge near modern Bozüyük and were entering on a wide valley north of Dorylaeum separated by about three miles of stragglers from the rearguard of Godfrey of Bouillon and Raymond of Toulouse. Bohemond showed his high calibre as a commander, placing infantry, priests and non-combatants in a camp with a marsh behind where they stayed overnight, terrified by the howling war-cries of the nomads. Cavalry were placed in a forward position to block the enemy's advance, but not all held. Some of Bohemond's force panicked and had to be rallied by an intervention of Robert of Normandy. The blocking force of cavalry retreated to form a carapace with infantry round the camp, which was attacked from three sides. A morale-raising phrase passed round the hard-pressed crusader force to maintain morale: 'Stand fast together, trusting in Christ and the victory of the Holy Cross. Today may we all gain much booty.' Booty was the gift of God.

For five critical hours in daylight infantry and cavalry together stood against mauling attacks, heavy losses being inflicted on both sides, till the rearguard came up in response to the desperate demand of the vanguard. Stragglers on the road between the vanguard and the peasants generally were massacred. The vanguard broke Kilij Arslan's army, forcing them away from the camp. Arslan's men turned to try to meet attacks on their left and rear from Godfrey and Raymond, then lost cohesion and fled pell-mell, leaving a trail of corpses and every sort of loot, precious jewels, horses, pack animals, cows and sheep. Kilij Arslan's attempt at empire-building was finished. The crusaders felt the hand of God upon them, and they met no more serious resistance being welcomed at Iconium and brushing aside a Turkish ambush as they approached Heraclea which then fell to them.

Though the Turks had been overawed, the army faced grievous conditions on the high plateau of Anatolia after the fight near Dorylaeum, waterless, subject to extremes of temperature. There were many deaths, horses and mules were lost, cavalrymen sometimes were mounted on oxen; thirsty men, taking advantage of a pause on fertile land in Pisidia, drank too much and died. Godfrey of Bouillon out hunting was injured by a bear.

At Heraclea armies diverged. Baldwin of Boulogne, the brother of Godfrey of Bouillon, and Tancred turned away south and east into Cilicia to exploit contacts with Armenians, restive at the oppressive rule of the Seljuqs, and win over cities where they had a strong presence. There is little doubt that the diversion had the approval of the crusade leaders and was the fruit of collaboration with Taticius acting in Alexius's interests, who had put the crusaders in contact with the Armenians at the time of the Nicaea siege. Baldwin and Tancred mopped up the cities of Tarsus and

Adana, then clashed over Mamistra. There was open fighting between them and men were killed.

Meanwhile the main army decided against the shorter coastal route to Antioch and took a longer route through the Taurus Mountains for just the same reason as drew Baldwin and Tancred into Cilicia, to forge alliances with the Armenians. They took Comana and Coxon, then turned south through the Amouk valley to seize Artah, east of Antioch, and a vital strategic post for the defence and supply of the city. Armenians rose against the Turkish garrison and opened the gates to the crusaders. The Turks counterattacked but were beaten off.

The links established in Cilicia, between Baldwin and the Armenians turned out to be of major importance as Baldwin, probably a failed priest who had abandoned orders for a military career, came in contact with a more distant Armenian leader, Thoros, ruler of Edessa, 45 miles east of the Euphrates. Thoros was uneasy in his power over the city because he had deserted Armenian allegiance and ruled as one of the Orthodox Byzantine faith. Thoros asked Baldwin to join him and be his son and heir and in a ceremony celebrating their agreement the childless Thoros embraced his newfound ally; both stripped to the waist and Thoros wrapped a shirt round them both. He was unwise to trust Baldwin, the most ruthless of all the crusaders. Not long after, in March 1098, a rising took place in the city in which Baldwin had complicity. Thoros was lynched and Baldwin took over one of the great cities of Mesopotamia. It was the first of the Crusader States of Outremer, a tripwire against Muslim attack and a nursery of kings. Baldwin gave vital aid to the crusaders who besieged Antioch, but he was unwilling to do anything to endanger his new possession and he had no part in the climax of the crusade, the siege and capture of Jerusalem.

The Siege of Antioch

Some time after Baldwin's triumph, the main body of the crusaders passed on to Antioch. They decided they could not afford to bypass it on the journey to Jerusalem; moreover, they were still working in collaboration with

Alexius. For all its troubles, plague and earthquake, the city remained a great fortress girdled by the Orontes river with a perimeter of some 7 ½ miles, its wall studded with defensive towers, ascending to the heights of 19,500 feet (500 metres). A citadel near the summit gave observation of all movements on the plain below and a garrison of about 4,000 under the ferocious leadership of Yaghisyan, a Mamluk appointed by Malik Shah, who forced Armenians and eastern Christians to serve as defenders by holding their wives hostage.

The princes had learned lessons from the episodes of crass individualism in the arduous journey from Constantinople and exercised a collective leadership. On 21 October 1097, in front of the gates on the north-east, they debated. The choice was between a policy of either waiting and resting their army, relying on the Armenians' supplies and their own officers scattered at strongpoints across much territory, or one of open siege, enveloping the city as best they could and exerting pressure on the garrison. Raymond of Toulouse urged the importance of holding together and focusing on the overriding objective of Jerusalem. He won the debate and in the autumn the crusaders moved step by step to limit the free movement of the garrison and its reception of fresh troops and supplies, gradually inhibiting the garrison's use of the multitude of gates of the city.

The crusader force dared not try a close siege for the perimeter was far too great and the danger of their troops being overwhelmed by an unexpected sally from the garrison too strong. Mr Micawber would have recognised their policy: they were aware that they, unaided, could not achieve a decisive result but hoped something would turn up – perhaps a major mistake by Yaghisyan or reinforcements from Byzantium. The rival sides were like evenly matched wrestlers neither of whom could achieve a decisive throw. The road to St Symeon was bitterly fought over: men and materials could win their way from the port, but at heavy cost in fighting en route. The crusaders were still making progress before Christmas, putting a squeeze on the garrison as Genoese reinforcements enabled Bohemond to build a siege-fort, Malregard, to inhibit Turkish attacks from Harem on his side of the perimeter by St Paul's Gate; besiegers assembled a Bridge of Boats across the Orontes and Tancred established a presence near St

George's Gate. But at Christmas 1098, in the struggle for supplies that was a central factor in the siege, the balance of advantage tilted towards Yaghisyan's garrison and away from the besiegers, as cold, hunger and disease began to have their effect and Yaghisyan sought a counterweight from Muslim allies outside Antioch. His first choice was Duqaq, *atabeg* of Damascus, who surprised Robert of Flanders and Bohemond as they led a mixed force of infantry and cavalry on a distant expedition to secure forage. In the battle against Duqaq on 31 December 1097 the cavalry kept their nerve and avoided encirclement but had to beat a retreat to the besiegers' camp, abandoning both the forage collected and their infantry, who were massacred. Thereafter besiegers were reluctant to set out on foraging expeditions with manpower of less than 200–300 for fear of garrison counter-attack. Men began to leave. The poor tried to stay alive 'eating dogs and rats, the skins of beasts and seeds of grain found in manure'. Bohemond, distressed at seeing the suffering of his Christian supporters and their mounts, thought of leaving and his half-brother Guy did abandon the siege. Peter the Hermit tried to slip away but was intercepted by Tancred. Taticius left in February with the reasonable objective of calling up supplies and Byzantine troops; his move was later interpreted as cowardice.

As morale fell away, Adémar sought to recall the crusaders to their mission with prayers, processions, psalm-singing and Masses and a search for divine help through repentance and discipline, as he dismissed women from the camp and in a vivid demonstration had two adulterers, stripped naked and flogged through the camp. It checked desertions.

Then Yaghisyan called to his aid Ridwan of Aleppo with a substantial army which approached the city via the Iron Bridge, a control point for the crossing of the Orontes to the north of Antioch. The leadership gave command of the crusaders' counter-attack to Bohemond, who led out from the crusader camp all the cavalry they had, 700 in all, on every kind of mount, including pack animals and even oxen. From these 700 he kept in reserve his best men and horses. Two advance squadrons of Ridwan were reconnoitring. In tight formation the miscellaneous force on the crusader side ambushed them, catching them in their flank. They fell back and in the ensuing mêlée were enmeshed in Ridwan's main force. As Ridwan's mass of cavalry by sheer force of numbers began to push the crusaders back, Bohemond saw the crisis of the battle had come; he led his reserve in a charge with couched spears, checking Ridwan's archers, whose bows were wet after a shower, and achieved total surprise. They all fled. It was a high-risk tactic against overwhelming hostile forces, and it worked.

The prestige of victory was well demonstrated by an array of severed heads of the crusaders' enemies and impressed emissaries from al-Afdal, vizier of the Shiite Fatimid caliph in Cairo, discussing a possible arrangement for the crusader army to be given privileges in Jerusalem or even the city itself in return for their help in checking inroads of Sunni Seljuqs and recovering lost Fatimid territory. For a year the crusaders had their emissaries in Cairo. It all proved inconclusive. Al-Afdal cut the Gordian knot in August 1098, took Jerusalem and expelled the Artuqids (alias Ortoqids), heirs to Artuk I, Seljuq governor of the city. In the event, the crusader passion for taking Jerusalem for themselves exclusively took over in 1099, and any thoughts of a deal vanished.

Recovered from illness, Raymond of Toulouse took a hand after Christmas and used his resources to establish a counterfort, Mahommeries, on a hill opposite the Bridge Gate. A common fund established by the princes helped to meet expenses. Tancred received payment and established a tower on the base of a monastery to act as counterfort to St George's Gate. So military successes and the relighting of the beacon of sacred mission fought against gnawing hunger, disease and despair.

At this moment Yaghisyan threw the dice for the last time and invited to his aid Kerbogah of Mosul, with an army that dwarfed anything yet brought against the crusaders. While Kerbogah, instead of going straight to Antioch, spent three weeks trying in vain to capture Edessa, Bohemond used the general alarm created by news of Kerbogah's approach to make his move, suborning with rich promises Firuz of the non-Muslim defenders, probably an Armenian, to betray his towers and promised entry to Antioch to his fellow princes in return for his own dominion over the city; they agreed, subject to the rights of the Emperor Alexius, should he wish to exercise them, and in a night movement on 2–3 June Bohemond and others broke in, opened a postern gate and let in the besiegers while also seeking to take the citadel. In darkness and confusion many were massacred, Muslims, Armenians and Eastern Christians alike. Yaghisyan was killed but his son held the citadel despite Bohemond. The besiegers had got in at last after over eight months but Kerbogah's great menace still loomed and the citadel was still in Muslim hands. Desertions multiplied. Stephen of Blois became convinced that all was lost and said so when he met the Emperor Alexius, coming up with his army. Crusaders assumed that he was coming to relieve them in Antioch. When the news reached them that Alexius was not coming to help them in their desperate straits, the link between Byzantium and the West was broken; nothing healed it, and the capture of Constantinople by the Fourth Crusade in 1204 merely confirmed the 'fait accompli' of June 1098.

On 8 June, Kerbogah launched an assault among the heights at the north-west seeking to link up to the citadel and there were fierce encounters at other points on the perimeter as Kerbogah made diversionary moves. In the last phase of the battle for Antioch there was a familiar blend of emotions: the warrior's delight in heroic battle, overwhelming fear and moments of crusading fervour as visionaries brought new assurance of God's favour in dire need. On 11 June a priest, Stephen of Valence, while in a state of terror, had a vision of Christ with the cross, Mary and Peter promising aid if the crusaders prayed, did penance and recognised their sinfulness. Shortly afterwards another visionary, Peter Bartholomew, was given assurance from St Andrew that the Holy Lance which pierced Christ's side at the Crucifixion would be found if he excavated in the floor of the cathedral; urged on by Raymond of Toulouse, a party assembled and dug. On 14 June, when all seemed lost, Peter Bartholomew found a piece of metal. One of the holiest of all relics had been vouchsafed to the surviving Christians as a sign of divine support which aided morale. In the end the desperate need for survival led to final action and on 28 June the leaders committed all their forces under Bohemond's command. 'It would be better', they thought, in the words of Albert of Aachen, 'to die fighting than to succumb to the cruel famine and watch the miserable Christian people perish day by day.'

In daylight they broke out of the Bridge Gate, each prince's group having been allocated a function in a skilfully devised sequence of movements: Hugh of Vermandois at the outset with his bowmen demolishing a Muslim attempt to block the crusaders as they emerged from the Bridge Gate; Godfrey of Bouillon and other northern leaders marching up the plain into the path of a series of Kerbogah's units, keeping the Orontes on their flank. Renaud of Toil safeguarded their rear and Raymond in the mountains blockaded the Muslim forces in the citadel while Adémar with southern French troops in a great sweeping movement sought to outflank the Turks, bringing strong forces to bear where they least expected it.

Kerbogah had been careless with his great host, deploying it widely round the Antioch perimeter and leaving a nucleus of his force up in the north, probably hoping to destroy the crusading army as a whole as it debouched. Dismayed, his men began to flee. Bohemond had kept one squadron in reserve with every single surviving mount, 200 in all, and charged at a critical point. That settled it. Kerbogah up in his camp simply broke off the engagement. The citadel surrendered to Bohemond, and the army fell on Kerbogah's camp, absorbing loot and killing wholesale. Although he was, technically speaking, going to war on behalf of the Abbasid caliph, Kerbogah was no *jihadi* himself, even if he had *jihadis* in his host. He had bargained and delivered a hostage to Yaghisyan; at heart an opportunist, he belonged in the 'fractured borderlands of Islam', the world of self-seeking *atabegs* that proliferated after the breakdown of Seljuq unity and he gave in fairly easily. The crusaders, by contrast, and for all their flaws, were driven on by a combination of the will to survive and the recurrent crusading sense that they must conquer or die. It was a great achievement by Bohemond and all his troops.

No sooner was Antioch won and loot and forage absorbed than the leadership fell back to its default position of quarrelling, individualist self-seeking and casual marauding. The fierce Syrian heat caused disease and many died. On 1 July the leaders decided to delay the advance on Jerusalem; a month later, on 1 August, Adémar died, probably of typhoid. He had been an irreplaceable spiritual leader. Raymond of Toulouse refused to accept Bohemond's possession of Antioch and used his troops to hold on to the Palace and the Bridge Gate while even the Genoese, contracted to keep supplying Bohemond, were uneasy about Alexius exercising a claim to the city because of the princes' oaths to him and disconcerted by the rivalry between Bohemond and Raymond for Antioch. Raymond set about making more territorial conquests so as to disrupt Bohemond's supply line. The poor grew cynical about the princely leaders, called for an advance to Jerusalem and were frustrated about the lack of forage and foodstuffs for them: some in desperation went to attach themselves for the sake of food to Baldwin's garrison at Edessa.

Eventually, still in pursuit of his claim to Antioch, Raymond set about besieging the Muslim town of Maarat-an-Numan and was joined temporarily by Bohemond, hoping to exercise a part-claim to Maarat by right of conquest and so frustrate Raymond. There was a devastating massacre of inhabitants, made worse by heavy looting and a night-time assault by the desperate poor. Their frustrations led at one stage to a group called the Tafurs practising cannibalism by openly feasting on the haunches of dead Muslims, an episode which shocked contemporaries. On 13 January Raymond, in effect abandoning his claim to Antioch, seized the chance to assert leadership, ordered the ruined Maarat to be fired behind him, called praying clergy to accompany him and walked out in front of them in bare feet, clad as a pilgrim, symbolically asserting his claim to lead troops on to Jerusalem.

However, some character trait damaged Raymond's claim to leadership: for all his wealth and achievements his fellow princes never accepted him and, in the sequence of events after his departure from Maarat, schemes for territorial aggrandisement tripped him up. With strange obstinacy he insisted on besieging the insignificant town of Arqa. He was still accompanied by Peter Bartholomew, the visionary and discoverer of the Holy Lance, who in the dead months of 1098 had gone on insisting on the need to advance to Jerusalem. But he became wild and bloodthirsty in his revelations and in April 1099 was subjected to the ordeal to prove the authenticity of his visions. After fasting, he committed himself to the judgement of God, running the barefoot gauntlet of burning fires; he did not survive, either being crushed by excited onlookers or succumbing to the effects of his injuries. With the end of Peter Bartholomew and a rebellion by the poor came the finish of Raymond's solitary leadership. The princes swept him aside, abandoned the Arqa siege, reasserted collective leadership and all together moved to Tripoli, thereafter marching at speed along the coastal road to the south and to Jerusalem. Compromise with al-Afdal and the Fatimid caliphate or collaboration with Byzantium was abandoned: they would conquer. They turned aside from the coast at Jaffa and came in sight of the Holy City on 7 June. They were a much diminished force.

Jerusalem

John France estimates that the total surviving crusader force consisted of 12–13,000 cavalry and 12,000 foot – too few for a conventional siege. They had to storm the city and to do this it was essential to have siege towers or ladders, rams and mangonels and sufficiently flat ground in proximity to the walls. Both sides were conscious of the economic and military power of Fatimid Egypt and the prospect of a relief army aiding the garrison and catching the besiegers in the classic, devastating position of being caught in the open by a fresh, equipped army, spurred the besiegers to a rapid sequence of action and the besieged to comparative passivity as they waited for help. Before the arrival of the crusade, the Fatimids had given the garrison 400 mounted men with the brief of galloping to any critical point, then dismounting to reinforce troops hard pressed. The city had strongpoints at the Quadrangular Tower and the Citadel to deter attack; the Seljuqs had dug moats and there were double walls, plus the deterrent for attackers of a grave lack of water on the arid plateau and an absence of timber to construct siege towers or ramps. Improvisation and the help of the Genoese and skilled men got over the problem of constructing siege towers but lack of water remained a grievous handicap, especially for the poor, and made defence against *naphtha* harder.

A hermit from the Mount of Olives addressed the leaders on 12 June and assured them that it was time to attack. Wood was too scarce to provide more than one ladder. On 13 June Reybold of Chartres, from Tancred's contingent, was first to put his hand on the top of the city wall and had it chopped off. After this the leaders conferred and two siege towers were constructed. On the southern side one built by Raymond of Toulouse made an additional point of pressure but his position on the high land made him vulnerable to missiles from the garrison, which in the end burnt his siege-tower. The second, a ramshackle construction the height of a four-storey house, created out of frail materials by Godfrey of Bouillon and a coalition of French princes, was taller than the wall in places but nevertheless was light and manoeuvrable.

Adémar in death was still potent. When he appeared in a vision to another prophetic figure, Peter Desiderius, calling for the host to process round the city as Joshua did before the walls of Jericho fell, everyone responded, marching barefoot with relics and music round part of the walls up to the site of the Ascension of Christ on the Mount of Olives. Princes' quarrels were stilled and all were called back to their purpose. The procession took place on 8 July; decisive action followed on the night of 13–14 July, when Godfrey's siege tower was taken down and conveyed under cover of darkness to a new site on flat land on the north, probably near to Herod's Gate. With it went a carefully prepared battering ram and the besiegers' mangonels. The garrison was taken by surprise: their ropes, padding, projectiles and mangonels had been readied for assault near the original assembly point of the siege tower and had to be shifted to the new site. Signallers using reflectors on the Mount of Olives co-ordinated attacks on the northern and southern fronts. But everything now hung on the assault mounted on the northern side on 14 and 15 July, as the besiegers in great numbers pushed forward a massive ram while the garrison protected the wall, lowering straw and ropes, swinging beams against the tower and assailing the attackers with arrows. Godfrey of Bouillon, a master of the crossbow, used his skill to fire the padding protecting the wall. The ram was attacked with *naphtha* by the garrison, forcing besiegers to use precious water to prevent the fire taking hold. Then the ram stuck in the hole made in the outer wall, leaving the inner wall unbroken, and the position was reversed as the besiegers tried to destroy their ram with fire and the garrison poured on water to keep it in position in order to block the approach by the siege towers. At last the decision was taken to abandon the ram and bring the siege-tower, well prepared against fire with wet hides, directly up to the wall in an attempt to scramble up and over. The garrison's mangonels' arc of fire carried some projectiles beyond the tower, relieving pressure on its defences. A battle followed, with the garrison's *naphtha* being countered by vinegar to douse the flames, till at last an improvised bridge carried besiegers across the wall; in one account a critical part was again played by Godfrey of Bouillon in the crossing. Once the besiegers had reached the rampart, the defence collapsed and was overwhelmed by the incoming host.

It can be seen that success in achieving the object of the whole expedition hung by a thread. If the garrison never launched sallies to unsettle the besiegers – as they easily could have done – they were still subjecting them to heavy fire from missiles, arrows, *naphtha* and stones from mangonels if they came within range of the walls. They had the interior lines, their own supplies of water and the 400 mounted men. The ladder attack on 13 June subjected the attackers to heavy losses and the movement of the ram and the siege tower up to the final assault point on 13–14 July was brought about by very large numbers, exposed to sustained, heavy attack by projectiles, pushing the ram and tower by muscle power. John France suggests that one quarter of the attacking army was lost in the course of the siege, leaving a frail force for an inevitable battle with the Fatimids from Egypt after the city had fallen. There was one ingenious improvisation in the overnight movement of the northerners' siege tower and ram, disconcerting their opponents and much courage, tenacity and further improvisation in the use of the siege tower in the last stages to fire arrows to drive away defenders. But there was nothing inevitable about this victory. Lethal damage to the tower, following on from the contretemps over the jammed ram, could have led to stalemate and despair.

A religious passion periodically held the army together. Some on the approach stopped short at Montjoie, the point in the Judaean hills where the city can first be seen, put off their shoes and walked barefoot for the last miles – a scene splendidly captured by Gustave Doré in Michaud's classic popular history of the Crusades.

Princes quarrelled, as they always did. Raymond of Toulouse was angry with Tancred because of his diversion from Jerusalem to capture

Bethlehem. The princes disputed among themselves about the rule in Jerusalem once the city was captured. Who was to hold power? Raymond remained in tension with Godfrey and the northern group. But the vision of Adémar led to the Jericho-style procession, which gave the opportunity, in the emotion of the moment, for Tancred to be reconciled with Raymond and for the princely quarrels to stop. When the last, dangerous assaults were being made on 14–15 July there were priests on hand singing hymns and exhorting soldiers. As on the march, some acute generalship, improvisation and military techniques made up in part for the adventurism, pride and ambition of fighting princes and their disputes, with religious zeal, discreetly guided, holding the army together at critical points.

Massacre in Jerusalem

The city fell. The massacre which followed was overwhelming. The 400 mounted men made for David's Tower at top speed, where they joined the Fatimid garrison in refuge. Gates were opened. The Josaphat Gate on the east side brought in yet more besiegers. Raymond of Toulouse's force, seeing the enemy abandon their positions, climbed the walls with ladders and joined in the attack from the southern side. Attack from a series of angles left no easy position where defenders could rally. Raymond's chaplain, Raymond of Aguilers, who was an eyewitness, described grievous scenes of beheading, wounding with arrows, torturing, burning, and victims forced to jump to their deaths from towers. Raymond himself went to the Citadel and joined the Fatimid governor with his garrison. The abandoned horses of the 400 were seized gladly by the crusaders who saved them for battle with the Fatimids from Egypt which they knew would come. Raymond took charge, extracted ransoms from the garrison, who were joined by a small number of Jews and with a high probability some Muslims; the garrison was subsequently given safe conduct with some who had joined them, albeit in small numbers.

Some have seen in the descriptions of babies smashed against walls by clerical chroniclers an echo of Psalm 137, with its bitter conclusion from the Israelites in Babylonian captivity, 'Happy shall he be that ... dashes your little ones against the stones'. Kedar, himself a Jew, poignantly reminds us that exactly the same actions were undertaken by SS troops in the murder of Jews in the Holocaust and believes that in 1099 we are encountering an actual, literal event. He is surely right. In the terrifying excitement of forced entry, some crusader horsemen were crushed to death with their mounts. Poorer soldiers forced their way into houses, killing inhabitants and extracting loot, making some richer than they had ever been. Tancred showed a keen eye for plunder and took precious items from the Dome of the Rock which he believed to be the Temple; to Muslim refugees who had managed to save themselves and were on the roof of the al-Aqsa mosque he offered banners of identification so that he could gain ransoms for them; he was angered when his promise was dishonoured later on by other crusaders, who killed them all. Ransoming saved some Jews, as is shown by correspondence deriving from the Cairo Jewish community who paid to save co-religionists and preserve rolls of the Torah. But there were Jews who had taken refuge in a synagogue and were burned to death.

Albert of Aachen describes Godfrey of Bouillon avoiding the slaughter and going out of the city, circling around with three of his men and then re-entering via the eastern gate to pray and give thanks at the Holy Sepulchre. This is in some contrast to the author of *Gesta Francorum*, who in a famous phrase describes the end of the slaughter and goes on to record the crusaders picking their way to the Sepulchre with the words 'all our men came rejoicing and weeping for joy to worship at the church of the Holy Sepulchre'.

Conventions of warfare in the crusaders' homeland put the defenders of a town or castle at mercy if they declined terms put by besiegers and their strongpoint was stormed. Often in practice there were last-minute bargains to be made, with variable treatment of those who were at mercy: they might, for example, be forced to leave without any possessions but still with their lives. It is apparent from the sources that the effects of the victory after this siege had a quite unusual ferocity and, further, that examples of the results of storming in the West in this age, sometimes cited by historians in mitigation and explanation, do not in fact compare with what happened in Jerusalem.

The besiegers had suffered grievously on their long journey from the West, had been bombarded with projectiles during the siege and subjected to insults and ostentatious desecration of crosses. A great release of tension as the city at last fell was not surprising. And yet the massacre extended to sacred buildings and included women and children and involved many atrocities. Moreover, there were in fact no fewer than three massacres in Jerusalem: the opening onslaught, the subsequent killing of Tancred's victims on the roof of the al-Aqsa mosque and, on the third day after the victorious entry, a decision by the princes to kill in cold blood Muslims who remained, whether captive or subject to what were in effect ransom contracts, consequently in breach of agreement. In effect, despite minor survivals, both Jewish and Muslim communities in Jerusalem after the siege ceased to exist. Fulcher of Chartres, chaplain and chronicler to Baldwin, the conqueror of Edessa, who arrived with his master one month after the fall of Jerusalem, observed the masses of bodies lying in the city, the great stench of the corpses and the measures taken to remove them, with some Muslims being forced and some poor Christians being paid to take bodies out of the city and heap them up in great mountains outside the walls. It has been argued that descriptions of the killings in Jerusalem have been influenced by Scriptural rhetoric from the Book of Revelation and the massacres artificially heightened in the chroniclers' accounts by the text in Chapter 14, verse 20, about blood rising to the level of horse bridles – a clear impossibility and an excitatory phrase in clerical eyes, as bloodshed could be seen as fulfilling the divine words. Chroniclers do speak about bloodshed, especially at the Dome of the Rock and its portico, and of the blood rising to the ankles of men and horses or to the knees of horses. This echoes the words of Revelation which contrast the rewards of the blessed and the torments of the damned, who 'drink of the wine of the wrath of God', and then describe the grim actions of an angel with a sharp sickle who gathers the clusters of the vine of the earth, now ripe, and casts them into 'the great wine press of the wrath of God'. Then the text goes on: 'and the wine press was trodden outside the city and blood came out of the winepress even unto the horse bridles'. The crusaders who came into the city were led to believe they were the agents of the wrath of God, and so acted.

After the city fell, the question arose: who was to rule? It was no idle query, for there was an honourable view that the city of Christ's Passion and Resurrection should be under the rule not of laymen but of a spiritual authority. However, on 22 July the leadership rejected the claims of a patriarch and offered the crown to Raymond, who refused it; the offer then passed to Godfrey, who accepted a position as Advocate. A primacy of honour, it was felt, should go to a patriarch, while the practicalities of gathering resources, making grants and sustaining an army should be in the hands of a layman. Raymond was at first reluctant to surrender the citadel but finally gave way and Arnulf of Choques, chaplain of Robert of Normandy, was made patriarch.

Ascalon and the Aftermath of the Crusade

There remained the menace of Fatimid Egypt. Over twenty years Badr al-Jamali, an Armenian mercenary, had restored the defences of Cairo and acted as financier to the caliph. It was just this military dominance which offended the founder of the Assassins but Badr al-Jamali was a leader to be feared, as part of the surviving defences of the citadel of Cairo – built by specialist Armenian stonemasons imported by Badr al-Jamali and made of the highest quality of masonry from Badr's native Cilicia – witness to this day.

Al-Afdal, who succeeded him in 1094, was not as secure or as experienced as his father but he was conscious of the high traditions he had inherited and was determined to fight. Godfrey took the lead by taking his forces from the city and moving forward to challenge the Fatimids and their army outside the port of Ascalon, a crucial link between Egypt and former Fatimid lands in Palestine. Reluctantly, Raymond and Robert of Normandy followed Godfrey and accepted his plan of action, assembling the Christian army in squadrons, enabling them to meet attack from any quarter and moving with speed through the countryside towards the gates of Ascalon. As they came out of their night camp on 12 August to the north of the port they met herds of animals assembled to provide for the Egyptian army. The soldiers showed a discipline gained over years of campaigning and at first declined to disperse and forage; instead they moved through the herd, giving the impression of being a much larger army than was the case.

All the princes were now in action, assembled with their contingents. Godfrey and the princes, despite being a much smaller force, had seized the initiative and surprised the enemy encamped outside Ascalon. A crucial part was played by Robert of Normandy's cavalry, which captured the enemy's standard and broke their morale. Many were crushed as they tried to swarm through the gate to take refuge in Ascalon. Al-Afdal escaped and promised to destroy the Christian settlers with the power of the Fatimid army. Godfrey and Raymond quarrelled over possession of Ascalon: the garrison, at first ready to surrender, got wind of the dispute and decided to stand firm. It was a fateful decision, for Ascalon was a menace to the Crusader States for half a century thereafter.

An armed conflict between Godfrey and Raymond was narrowly averted; at length the princes, including Raymond, left for home, and Godfrey faced the chronic problems of creating a land base for Jerusalem, pulling in new manpower and somehow acquiring the seaports that were essential for trade, pilgrims and reinforcements. The continued dangers of the land route to the Holy Land were dramatically revealed in the crusade of 1101, an ill-fated and ill-thought-out affair in which a blend of enthusiasts attracted by the triumph of 1099 and erring would-be crusaders, who had not yet fulfilled their vows and were rounded up by reproaches of bishops and of Pope Paschal II, came to grief through neglect of all the lessons of the First Crusade, failing to co-ordinate armies' movements and make use of close-quarter fighting skills to neutralise the mounted archers of the Seljuqs. Most perished, including Stephen of Blois, dispatched to the East once again by his formidable wife. One survivor was Raymond of Toulouse, crusading yet again, who after some vicissitudes found a lasting home in the County of Tripoli which he founded and handed on to heirs.

This collapse threw into focus the achievements of the First Crusade and gave a new and even greater status to those who had served in it. Kingship and lordship, which all too often sullied the crusading ideal and halted armies, also kept crusading in being over decades. Investigations of charters reveal the degree to which the decisions of lords and their followers to go on crusade and the traditions of extended families over time established crusading families. They link to the preaching of Urban II and to the very different preaching tour of Peter the Hermit. Names of families recur right down to the Second Crusade, in 1147–8. Why some families and not others with similar backgrounds and monastic connections took up crusading remains a mystery. Women bore the brunt of their husbands' long absences, but Jonathan Riley-Smith suspects they were often key personalities in maintaining crusader kin groups.

As the 1101 Crusade floundered to its end, Godfrey was already dead. On 18 July 1100 he had succumbed to fierce heat and, maybe, typhoid. He was being entertained by a Muslim emir at Caesarea; rumours of poisoning spread, but are an unlikely explanation. The first man to rule in Jerusalem and a leader both in the siege and the battle of Ascalon, he was buried in a position of great honour within the entrance to the church of the Holy Sepulchre. He was succeeded, not as Advocate but as King, by his younger brother, Baldwin of Edessa, backed by the Lorrainers among the settlers. He seized power after travelling down with his small army and beating off a Muslim attack at the Dog river. Daibert of Pisa, former papal legate, who had displaced Arnulf as patriarch, wisely forbore to push his claim to rule Jerusalem and anointed and crowned Baldwin in the church at Bethlehem on Christmas Day 1100, leaving behind in Edessa as successor an obscure crusader, supposedly a cousin, Baldwin of Bourcq.

In power Baldwin at once showed his extraordinary energy and capacity, taking oaths of fidelity from his new vassals, heading his army in a brief attack on Ascalon and reconnoitring desert territory south of the Dead Sea even before his coronation, and thereafter working hard in liaison with the Italians to take ports, build up a demesne and establish money fiefs to attract recruits to the kingdom. Al-Afdal was as good as his word and tried repeatedly to use his army to expel the Christian settlers, fighting a battle in September 1101 in which there were heavy losses on both sides and trying again in May 1102, when Baldwin came close to disaster through his own arrogance. He ignored advice to wait for reinforcements, attacked al-Afdal and was forced to flee and hide in the mountains, then escape via Arsuf and Jaffa before re-assembling his troops and, in a new encounter, forcing the enemy to give way at the end of May. Opinion thought that he had lost in the first battle because he had not got the relic of the True Cross with him. Unconquered, Ascalon remained a threat because it enabled the Fatimids to ship in troops more or less at will to attack Baldwin's lands and, when al-Afdal mounted his last offensive in 1105, he seized the opportunity to combine his own Shiite forces from Egypt with an army from Sunni Damascus under a Turkish leader. But Baldwin was ready for him, having assembled men in the presence of the patriarch of the day with the True Cross, and now had a much bigger army with more mercenaries and local Christians in his service. Al-Afdal was forced back to Ascalon with losses.

It was the end of his interventions but not of other opportunist attacks on the Ascalon garrison. Baldwin remained a risk-taker and, though there were still dangerous Muslim jabs at him, he believed in pressing them hard, interrupting their caravan trade and seeking opportunities to take land from them. He left to posterity a coastal state with an all-weather port at Acre, strong maritime power and a closely integrated relationship with his bishops and fighting men. A line of Crusader States along the coast formed: the County of Edessa, the Principality of Antioch, the County of Tripoli, the Kingdom of Jerusalem.

Cairo, the seat of the Fatimids, was only 264 miles from Jerusalem and Baldwin took the view that it was vital for the future of his kingdom and allied states to destabilise Egypt and seize land within it to provide money fiefs for arms-bearers in the future. He died in pursuit of that objective. On an expedition deep in Egypt, he felt death approaching. Hating the prospect of being buried there and his grave becoming an object of ridicule, he urged his army to carry him back in a litter as fast as they could. When he died in 1118, at el-Arish, still in Egypt, his cook, following his wishes, eviscerated his body and the army carried his remains forward to be taken through the Golden Gate on Palm Sunday and buried with great honour next to his brother Godfrey in the Church of the Holy Sepulchre. He deserved his place; he, more than anyone else, was the true creator of the states of Outremer.

Massacres of Muslims by Muslims were part of Near Eastern history, yet there was a specially baleful quality about the crusaders' killing of Muslims which followed the capture of Jerusalem. The Abbasid caliph's court in Baghdad was moved to tears by a description of what happened. Poets wrote lines meant to be declaimed, fiercely criticising the inaction of Muslim leaders in the face of massacres. In 1094 an unusual sequence of deaths of seasoned leaders, not only among the Seljuqs but also soon afterwards in Fatimid Egypt, bewildered the Islamic world and created a vacuum. No heir of Malik Shah took the field against crusaders: there were too many other problems of plague and internal disorder for the sufferings of their co-religionists in Syria and Jerusalem to stand out and there was a lack of understanding of the determination of these strange interlopers to capture Jerusalem. As an objective for Muslim pilgrimage Jerusalem had fallen back in importance, well behind Mecca and Medina: it was the First Crusade which gave it a renewed importance and created a link between crusade and *jihad*. But this took time to happen.

The preacher and scholar al-Sulami wrote a far-sighted treatise, the *Kitab al-jihad*, on the implications of the crusade and attempted to rouse contemporaries to action, preaching early in the twelfth century in Damascus, recalling the massacres, linking the assault on Jerusalem with the Norman takeover in Sicily and proposing the total expulsion of the Franks and a restoration of the status of Jerusalem as a holy city for Muslims. It fell flat: military and political leaders did not respond and were preoccupied with their own survival. A popular delegation from Aleppo journeyed across the desert to Baghdad in 1117 to protest against the depredations of the Franks. It broke into the Friday prayers and destroyed the *minbar*, trying to put pressure on the sultan who had succeeded Malik Shah; a little later there was a similar assault in the mosque of the caliph in Baghdad, again disrupting prayers and breaking a *minbar*. There was clearly a concerted drive against the *de facto* Seljuq power and the authority of the caliph. The latter was displeased at the disruption to the occasion of his formal welcome to a new bride from Isfahan. Merely formal, meaningless expeditions were launched to satisfy agitation. So long as military leaders did not respond to the scholars and preachers and the popular agitations against the Franks, the Crusader States remained broadly secure, profiting by the disturbed and confusing world of the *atabegs*.

Actions by the Franks continued to irritate Muslim opinion. The firing of Maarat by Raymond of Toulouse was not forgotten and there was indignation at the loss of Qurans in the destruction of a library in Tripoli in 1109. A *qadi* in Aleppo distinguished himself by riding up with a spear to troops assembling for battle in 1119 and calling for *jihad*, but nothing came of it. However, a concerted drive for expulsion of the Franks, bringing together the theory of *jihad* and the moral rearmament believed essential by al-Sulami at Damascus for a successful *jihad* under effective military leadership, was a long time coming. All this was to the benefit of the crusader settlers in Syria and Palestine.

They were the heirs to a unique enterprise, an expedition of astonishing size, led by princes and not by kings, brought into being by Urban II's inspired linking of the symbols of pilgrimage with the vow, the taking of the cross and the promise of remission of penance. Its great size as an army helped it to weather the extraordinary hazards, with concomitant losses of personnel, on its long, dangerous journey. It succeeded against all the odds of terrain, distance and hostile forces equipped with unfamiliar military techniques, narrowly surmounting the virtually endless quarrels of their leaders by a passionate wish to recover Jerusalem and by the repeated, sometimes almost despairing, appeals of the poor to the consciences of nobles. Self-preservation, the slow growth of a sense of common purpose and some collective funding checked individualism and, coupled with the emergence of capable and valorous commanders, carried them by the narrowest of margins to their victory. At critical moments the spiritual leader Adémar (in life and death), visions of saints and martyred crusaders, an opportune discovering of a relic and echoes of scripture stiffened morale and recalled the fearful and the quarrelsome to their central purpose. The memory of the First Crusade, 'the odyssey of the barons', stirred the imagination of the West for centuries to come.

5

THE GREAT
MIGHT-HAVE-BEEN

The Crusader States have sometimes been thought culturally barren, ruled by military men with limited horizons. This does them an injustice. They included both men of true piety, anxious to adorn sacred sites captured in early years at great sacrifice, and the secular-minded, aware of the value of pageantry and display for attracting pilgrims and impressing both allies and enemies. The states lay at a crossroads between the Byzantine Empire and Eastern Churches, long divided but brought into contact and sometimes reconciliation through the needs of settlers and the interests of queens. Queens had great patronage and the marriage policies of kings of Jerusalem and the Byzantine emperor Manuel Comnenus (1143–1180), intent on developing friendship with the settlers to establish ancient Byzantine claims, issued in the arrival in the kingdom of an Armenian as queen and a Byzantine princess, who attracted craftsmen from far and wide, ready to exercise their skills on sites of international renown. Their work reflected a pot-pourri of interests and traditions. Sculpture, mosaics, working of copper and illustrated manuscripts all flourished and a significant number of fine buildings were erected and embellished, especially in and near Jerusalem.

Jerusalem had pride of place as the object of pilgrimage, overflowing in the season and quiet in the winter. Pilgrims brought income to the burgesses and to the ports. At times of political and economic crisis, during famines and outbreaks of plague, refugees sought help, and not in vain. Kings and patriarchs had a well-deserved reputation for feeding and succouring them. In the 1070s, when Jerusalem was still in Muslim hands, men from Amalfi obtained permission to open a hospital, a place of refuge where pilgrims could recover from the hardships of their journey and those expecting to die in the Holy City could be looked after and given the sacraments. After the crusaders' conquest it began to expand on a site south of the church of the Holy Sepulchre. Capable of holding a thousand patients, it tended Christians and Muslims alike: pregnant women, for example were cared for and temporary arrangements made for looking after their children. Only lepers were denied entry. There were individual beds, coverlets and slippers. The diet was of a standard normally available only to the rich, with meat three times a week, pork and mutton for the stronger, chicken for the weaker and white bread.

The most important centre of all was the Sepulchre, transformed into a pilgrimage church designed to carry visitors through ambulatories and chapels to the Sepulchre itself under a Byzantine rotunda; a splendid Byzantine representation of the 'Harrowing of Hell' was moved, then reassembled on the ceiling of the choir. This rescued and refurbished church was re-consecrated by the patriarch at dawn on the morning of 15 July 1149, the fiftieth anniversary of the capture of the city. In the entrance to the Dome of the Rock, thought to be Solomon's Temple, an iron grille was set up by the crusaders; a beautiful creation of an original delicate fleur-de-lys design, it would have captivated the eye when the rows of candles lit up the interior of the building.

Inside the city Queen Melisende built a beautiful Gothic church dedicated to St Anne; outside, she created an abbey at Bethany for her sister Iveta to be abbess, reworking an ancient building and adding a church over Lazarus's tomb. Around the city, shrines were created or repaired to provide a full experience of visits, prayers and memories. At Hebron a happy discovery of the remains of the Old Testament patriarchs Abraham, Isaac and Jacob made possible the conversion of a mosque into a basilica visited by Jews and Muslims as well as Christians.

The scriptorium of the Church of the Sepulchre had a distinguished history. According to tradition, the Melisende Psalter was the fruit of reconciliation between Fulk and his queen after a serious political and matrimonial conflict, taking the form of a presentation to the queen for her private devotional use. Ivory covers of Byzantine workmanship illustrated two aspects of kingship: David, warrior and psalmist, on the front with medallions of virtues and vices in conflict; and on the back a Byzantine-costumed figure performing the classic works of mercy, also shown on medallions. The warrior defends his city; the ruler on the back uses his power to look after the weak and helpless. The inclusion of English saints in a calendar within suggests the influence of the English prior of the Sepulchre, William, and its colouring reveals Armenian influence. There were other beautiful manuscripts: a sacramentary for use at Mass and illustrated gospel books.

Bethlehem had a Byzantine church where Baldwin I was crowned on Christmas Day 1100. Here a tomb was created for Joseph of Arimathea and a series of mosaics initiated to commemorate the marriage of King Amalric with the Byzantine princess Maria of Antioch, carrying forward Manuel's project of drawing together Christian churches against the Muslim menace while disregarding points of difference and, in the case of the Western Church, not standing pat on the vexed question of the Procession of the Holy Spirit. Manuel and Amalric were recorded together as sponsors and the work was carried out by both a Byzantine churchman and a Melkite. At Nazareth there was a church of the Annunciation and a grotto dedicated to the visitation of the Archangel Gabriel. Sculptured capitals were prepared to adorn its walls. The Mamluk Sultan Baybars destroyed the building but capitals were buried, presumably in hopes of better times and, discovered in 1908, were revealed as attractive and graceful work in the style of the French Romanesque.

One scholar of note gave his life to the kingdom. William of Tyre was born in Jerusalem about 1130, most probably a son of one of the city's burgesses. He studied at the school attached to the Sepulchre, then went for some twenty years to immerse himself in the best schools of the day, following liberal arts and theology at Paris and Orléans and civil and canon law at Bologna. Unlike others of non-aristocratic origins who broke the glass ceiling of the time and went on to make careers in the West, William chose to come home to the Holy Land to serve king and Church until his death, probably in 1184. He wrote his *History of Jerusalem* to stimulate Western churchmen of his own stamp to much greater efforts to exhort the faithful to preserve Jerusalem. He started with eight books on the First Crusade, then others, turn by turn, on the kings. No reader can fail to be gripped by the memorable passages on, for example, his discovery that King Amalric did not believe in the resurrection of the body or the moment when, as tutor to Baldwin the Leper, he realised that his pupil had a fatal disease. He also shows an awareness of just acts carried out by Muslims – not a common feature of Western writing. It is one of the finest chronicles of the twelfth century. Not only that, but William also wrote an account, tragically lost, of the Muslim princes from the time of Muhammad. What is most significant is his patriotism. The kingdom he served had its fair share of adventurers and opportunists and squalid disputes. It was loosely multicultural, a very imperfect unity. And yet it could make this very able man into a true patriot. Given more time, William might have had more successors with the same emotions, providing a vital glue for this fighting society.

The multicultural aspect worked tolerably. In his utilitarian fashion Baldwin I invited into Jerusalem Arabic-speaking Orthodox Christians from beyond the Jordan to make up for those lost in the massacre of 1099. A Latin episcopate ruled, but it did not matter much for relations with other Churches, since the Orthodox episcopate was accustomed to the position of *dhimmis* under the Muslims. They kept their own courts, albeit always subordinate to the Franks, and were free to worship in Jerusalem at their own churches. Monasteries were undisturbed and Armenians and Jacobites (Nestorians), condemned by the Byzantine Church, had greater freedom under the Franks. Trade helped. In market courts at Acre witnesses swore on their own sacred books: the Quran for Muslims, the Torah for Jews, the Gospel for Christians. There were always Bedouin, ever unmanageable, and there were resentful Muslims and Muslim slaves. But by and large the divisions, ethical and ecclesiastical, of a crossroads kingdom did not work against kings' interests; some actually helped them.

Defence

Superiority in naval power was crucial for the Crusader States. It was the one point where the Muslims of Egypt were at a disadvantage because of their lack of timber for shipbuilding. They could and did win naval battles at times, but could never commit their ships without inhibition. The climate made it imperative to have the opportunity for crews to obtain fresh water at frequent intervals, and in consequence they were perennially in an awkward, even dangerous, situation because of their lack of secure sources for water supply.

The obtaining of ports, ships and watering-sources along the littoral had been seen as an imperative need by the kings of Jerusalem and it is in this light that one should look at the treaties which they made with Italian cities. The Genoese made a critical contribution via the timber supplies they made available in 1099. They, and their rivals from Italy, were vital for securing the littoral of the Holy Land and its ports.

The treaties Baldwin I made with the cities to secure Arsuf, Caesarea and Acre in his early years were rents in the unity of jurisdiction of the kingdom but the concessions thus made cemented its security, giving a general maritime domination to the Crusader States and ensuring the passage of warriors and pilgrims from the West as the land route was given up. In the 1170s during the sailing season there might be as many as seventy pilgrim vessels at anchor in the harbour at Acre — and pilgrims were a source of reward to kings as well as to the Italians, because of the profits from royal markets and the taxes which kings could levy at the ports. Baldwin I bequeathed to his successors demesne in Judaea and Samaria and drew rewards from his domination of the great caravan route from Egypt to Damascus. He built at speed a castle by the route at Shawbak on a ridge near the plateau of Edom, acting as a focus for Christian settlement with its productive hinterland and water cisterns. In the following year he built two more fortresses, creating a line stretching down to Aqaba; only Shawbak remained for his successors. In 1142 Pagan the Butler, who had become lord of Transjordan, refortified Kerak in Moab, farther north of Shawbak and 10 miles to the east of the end of the Dead Sea, continuing the menace to Muslim caravans.

The military orders were of great importance to the kings with their perennial shortage of money. The West's passion for sustaining Jerusalem issued in the foundation of these orders, combining, not without some controversy, the role of monk and warrior. Pilgrims travelling along the vulnerable road from Jaffa needed protection from banditry; the Hospitallers seem to have started hiring fighters to escort them. The notion of the monk-knight evolved from this and was so valuable and so popular that it came to be more important than the care of the sick – still not neglected, but given second place. In chivalric style, patients were referred to as 'our lords, the sick', but the Knights took the spotlight. They took vows, as monks did, and sustained a modified Benedictine liturgy while devoting their lives to fighting, castle guard and castle-building, giving kings the immense value of a standing army, a dedicated, highly trained body, fine horsemen with a musculature and control of weapons to match anything the Muslims could offer. In the West they received many donations, legacies and endowments, providing the resources to sustain the Knights and sergeants indefinitely, and they took on the distinctive uniform for the Knights in action: a white cross on a red surcoat and the Maltese cross on capes. Their takeover in 1142 of an Arab castle in Syria, which became Krak des Chevaliers, was crucial as it protected the north-east flank of the County of Tripoli and blocked access of Muslim forces to the coast.

The Templars grew out of an initiative of a knight who was a vassal of the count of Champagne; like the Hospitallers, they were charged to protect pilgrims and developed from what was a very small initiative to a substantial enterprise through the eloquence of St Bernard of Clairvaux, his personal contacts and the encouragement of Baldwin II. To the patriarch's anger, both orders were exempt from his jurisdiction. On the Second Crusade the Templars helped save the day in an ill-conceived land expedition, showing their calibre in war, in knowledge of the terrain and in the ready availability of their treasure. The elite Knights and the sergeants who served them were never numerous: they worked with auxiliaries and mercenaries. In medieval style, Templars and Hospitallers were great rivals. Yet this drawback was far outweighed by the professional quality they brought to castle and battlefield.

At an early stage kings established an unusual degree of control. A dispute over succession to the County of Tripoli after the death of Raymond of Toulouse in 1109 was used by Baldwin I to establish the king's authority in a territory where he was not, strictly, overlord. He had become the arbiter of Outremer. Temperamentally out of kilter with the Gregorian reformers, the bishops who served in the Crusader States were of a kind well adapted to serve kings and barons and looked back to an earlier style of episcopal action, working closely with secular authority. Baldwin II had his residence at the southern end of the Haram. He was impressed by the activities of the Templars, saw a vital need for more trained manpower and so gave them space. The al-Aqsa mosque became their headquarters and they constructed great stables in vaults below. The belief that they were on the Temple site gave the Templars their title. The earliest bishops were chaplains of the crusaders; subsequently, recruitment generally came from clergy who had originally come from the West and might well have family connections with the settlers, rather than from the younger sons of aristocrats in the Holy Land, who were needed for military service. William of Tyre himself, although he became archbishop of Tyre in 1175, served as chancellor from 1174 to 1183. It was the proper business of the episcopate, it was felt, to aid leaders with their charters and their records. Frederick, William's predecessor as archbishop, came from Liège, was an Augustinian canon at the Temple of the Lord who became bishop of Acre and had a career as a secular administrator, a peacemaker and a diplomat, representing in Rome both the patriarch and the king of Jerusalem. William described him as 'a nobleman from Lorraine. He was extremely tall and although he was not very well educated, he took great pleasure in warfare.'

Another duty of the episcopate was to carry the True Cross to battlefields. This was above all the duty of the patriarch of Jerusalem but it could be carried by bishops. The kingdom also attracted men with a strong sense of liturgy, seeing a prime duty in ensuring that rites were performed to a high standard in the multitude of shrines welcoming pilgrims, and those who had a practical, outgoing piety, looking after the sick and poor and organising their care.

The assembly of Nablus, summoned in 1120 by Baldwin II, an avaricious but devout king known for the hard skin on his knees created by hours of prayer, was designed to avert the wrath of God on his kingdom by a series of decrees repressing immoral behaviour and to ensure that tithes were not sequestrated by barons but paid to the Church. It included a blunt clause permitting clergy to engage in warfare – a decision that went beyond anything officially permitted hitherto in the Western Church but characteristic of the general role of clergy in the kingdom.

Settlement

Between 1115 and the mid-1160s the armies of the Christians, not the Muslims, were the aggressors. Once Baldwin I had secured the position of the Crusader States, the armies of the settlers, sometimes reinforced by crusaders from the west, sometimes not, generally ruled battlefields and maintained military superiority with their cavalry charges and their insistence on seizing the initiative. Of course, there were set-backs. Antioch soon became a worry. It lay as far away from Jerusalem as Edinburgh lies from London, and it was subject to pressures both from Byzantium and from Muslims. Normans ruled in Antioch but in one catastrophic episode in 1119, known as the Field of Blood, in an act of impetuous folly Roger of Salerno, regent for Bohemond's young son, did not wait for settler reinforcements from Tripoli and Jerusalem, and, with his own limited resources, took on a Muslim attacker, Il-Ghazi the Artuqid, once co-governor of Jerusalem. Roger and all his knights were lost. Baldwin II rose to the occasion, used all the powers of decision which the kings had acquired, distributed the widows and saw that Antioch stayed a Christian bulwark. But he had to spend time in the north and so did his successor, Fulk, causing resentment among Jerusalem barons.

In the south the initiative remained with the Christians until the rise of a counter-force on the Muslim side based on Mosul and Aleppo later in the century. The Israeli historian Ronnie Ellenblum argues that Frankish rule achieved a level of security in its key lands which the Levant had not had for generations and permitted a hitherto unsuspected peaceful agricultural settlement on certain sites. This attracted fresh craftsmen who enjoyed friendly working arrangements with local Christians, probably underpinned by intermarriage between Franks and Eastern Christians, echoing at a lower level the marital arrangements of kings.*

It is clear that historians have underestimated the peaceful survival in parts of the Holy Land of Christians who lived on as *dhimmis*, did not succumb to the long-term pressure to convert to Islam and thus avoid the tax imposed on them. The work of Ellenblum has fleshed out this hypothesis. He has looked more closely at the nature of fortification in these areas and concludes that the so-called 'castles' were often simply fortified manor houses, widespread in western Europe as the vogue grew for these structures, designed to assert a lord's power and give focus to a settlement, rather than guarding against some armed threat. Records of boundary disputes imply that Franks in these settlements took a close personal interest and were not distant absentees dependent on a dragoman, in the manner of the absentee lairds in the Highlands of Scotland or the Protestant Ascendancy in southern Ireland with their harsh local representatives.

Where records allow, they reveal another surprising fact – that the economic migrants who made the long journey from the West to work in these small settlements came not from northern France but from central and southern France, Catalonia and Italy. The truly enterprising in the Middle Ages, as Marc Bloch long ago taught us, were willing to travel great distances to earn well and improve status. Magna Mahumeria, north of Jerusalem, gives us a picture of the pattern of skills within that settlement. Here were construction workers, carpenters, gardeners, vineyard workers, metalworkers, butchers and bakers, clearly freemen with skills, willing to travel and make new lives where local shortages had forced better pay for their talents.

Significantly, the settlements had adapted to the conditions of Near Eastern agriculture, such as thinner soils, locusts and much greater aridity. They had developed the technology needed to cope with problems of

---

*Ronnie Ellenblum, *Frankish Rural Settlement in the Latin Kingdom of Jerusalem* (Cambridge, 1998).

climate and pests and were practising terracing, making irrigation canals and using oil presses. This is likely to have involved co-operation with Muslims and small farmers. Ibn Jubayr, who travelled through the Holy Land in 1184 as Saladin threatened the Crusader States, noted Christians and Muslims working the land in co-operation and he concluded that some Muslims, badly treated by their co-religionists elsewhere, had come to prefer Christian-occupied territory. On Ellenblum's map various indicators – the *burgus*, the manor house, the church or the monastery – guide the reader towards the sites of these settlements while a set of numerals act as keys to the detailed information on which Ellenblum's reconstruction is based. At a glance one can see a conglomeration of settlements clustering north of Jerusalem, another cluster farther north round Neapolis (Nablus) and a line of others by the coast and near Acre. There are a few west of Galilee,* and Ellenblum reminds us that Christians there were at peace and not exposed to Muslim attack until as late as 1169.

In and around Jerusalem churchmen carried on the quiet work of consolidation and improvement of rents and holdings, characteristic of many a monastic house in western Europe. So, for example, the canons of the Holy Sepulchre contracted in 1132 with a widow in Jerusalem to provide her with an annuity and food from their kitchen for life, specified as a loaf of bread per day, half a litre of wine and a cooked meal, a meat meal or whatever the canons ate on Sundays and great feast days. They also made immediate repairs to her property and in return gained possession of her orchard and the reversion of her house on her death. The cartulary of the Sepulchre is a full one in good preservation; no doubt similar quiet economic advances, less well recorded, took place elsewhere.

The Fatal Flaw

The Crusader States were not weak and artificial entities, fragments of western Europe in an alien world doomed to a short life, as has been commonly believed. Step by step, building a case within his narrative of events,

---

*Also known as the Lake of Tiberias.

Malcolm Barber in 2012 destroyed this view.* The Crusader States were viable and their weaknesses surmountable. They could have lasted a lot longer, Jerusalem remaining Christian, but for one major flaw: the lack, generation after generation, of a male heir of full, fighting age. 'Woe to the kingdom when the king is a child!' In the medieval world that could easily be disastrous.

The genealogy of the kings shows their misfortune. Baldwin I left no child at all. His cousin Baldwin II was happily married to the Armenian Morphia but had only four daughters. A suitable husband was found for Melisende in Fulk V Count of Anjou, a warrior and a pilgrim who knew the kingdom well. They were married in 1129 and had two sons, Baldwin and Amalric. After Fulk's early death Melisende was crowned together with her thirteen-year-old son Baldwin III. They ruled together until Baldwin, after some struggle with his mother, insisted on ruling alone. He married Theodora, niece of the Emperor Manuel, who gave a handsome dowry. But she was only twelve years old and after over four years of marriage there were no children. She and Baldwin died young and the crown descended to Melisende's second son, Amalric, albeit not without controversy. Amalric's first marriage to Agnes of Courtenay was annulled. With Agnes he had a son, Baldwin, and a daughter, Sibylla; by his second marriage to Maria Comnena, great-niece of the Emperor Manuel, he had a daughter, Isabella. Amalric, in the tradition of both Baldwin I the Conqueror and Baldwin III, aimed at extracting tribute or land from Egypt or even achieving outright conquest with the aid of Byzantium. He worked hard at the project but failed to break through and in 1174 died of dysentery.

There followed a succession disaster. Baldwin IV, the eldest son, was a leper who led in battle and in council as best he could, winning one important victory, but he was doomed to an early death and could never sire a son. Which of the daughters would succeed? Sibylla or Isabella? It turned out to be Sibylla. In a bad case of romantic love triumphing over duty, she insisted on marrying as her second husband Guy of Lusignan, an

---

*M. Barber, *The Crusader States* (New Haven, CT, and London, 2012).

aggressive, insecure adventurer, outwitting opposition in the kingdom. Unhappily aware that hereditary right could bring in as heir the leading baron Raymond of Tripoli, a descendant of Baldwin II's daughter Hodierna, Guy succumbed to the slanderous suggestion that Raymond was seeking to discredit him, made a fatal decision to fight and in three days lost the kingdom's field army. The kingdom never recovered. Its promise of future prosperity and vitality was snuffed out.

6

FROM WARLORD TO *JIHADI*: NUR AL-DIN AND SALADIN

Two events were crucial for the rise of the emir Nur al-Din to be the master of the Islam of his day, its most effective propagandist and thinker — a world changer. One was the capture of the city of Edessa at Christmas 1146, the other the collapse of the Second Crusade in June 1148.

Zangi's Legacy to Nur al-Din

Nur al-Din's father Zangi, *atabeg* of Mosul then master of Aleppo, was a ferocious disciplinarian, governing a mixed army of Turcomen, Kurds and slaves by the terror of crucifixion for the least infraction of his will. His first-class intelligence service warned him that Joscelin II, an indolent count of Edessa who had quarrelled with his neighbour settler Raymond of Poitiers, prince of Antioch, had vacated the city altogether and had left inside a garrison of mercenaries. Using all his resources, Zangi took Edessa in one month, capturing it at Christmas 1146 and leaving no time for the Christians to relieve it, massacring the Franks but sparing Eastern Christians and their churches. It gave him undeserved fame as a *jihadi*, rewarded with praise, titles and robes by the caliph of Baghdad. He paid panegyrists to praise him in their poetry for preparing to cleanse the *sahil*, the coastal lands of the caliphate, from the Franks. But they were not wholly committed and one even developed a liking for Christian Antioch and wrote amorous verse to Frankish ladies. In reality, Zangi was a warrior against fellow Muslims rather than Christians, a collector of cities, passionately devoted to adding Damascus to his existing bag of Mosul, Aleppo and Edessa.

Damascene leaders lived in terror of what might happen to them in the light of the fate of their dependency Baalbek, where the garrison had been promised their freedom if they surrendered but were promptly massacred when they did, their place being taken by Zangi's men under the command of a Kurdish mercenary Najm al-Din Ayyub. Consequently they sought defence against Zangi by having the Franks as their allies.

Zangi's life ended dramatically. He was knifed to death in his tent, by a slave, allegedly while in a drunken state, on 11 September 1146 during his siege of a Muslim fortress on the Euphrates. The chronicler Ibn al-Athir, however, had a different story. An attendant found him seriously wounded. 'Master,' he asked, 'who has done this to you?' He was about to reply when death took him. Not a casual killing, then, but a planned assassination by someone who had got past the guards – so, much more likely to be a Damascus emissary.

Zangi had ruled by fear alone. As soon as he died, his corpse was hurried into the ground without ceremony, his followers looted his treasure and there was anarchy. His eldest son, Saif al-Din, seized Mosul while Nur al-Din, his second son, moved with speed to Aleppo where he knew the governor and was also viewed with favour by Shirkuh, Ayyub's brother. The gates were opened to him, delivering the citadel, a natural feature which towered 200 feet over the city and gave him a vital security in these uneasy early years. Meanwhile the careless Joscelin, invited back to Edessa by the surviving Christians, slipped into the city without preparing any siege engines. As the Christians welcomed him, the Muslim garrison barricaded themselves in the citadel and could not be overcome. Nur al-Din moved up from Aleppo with maximum speed, catching Joscelin, his troops and the luckless Christians between his army and the garrison. All the Christian men were killed, all the women and children were enslaved and smoke rose from Edessa. It never recovered. Joscelin, although he escaped, was captured in 1150 and died in Nur al-Din's prison nine years later. Nur al-Din had established his credentials as warrior and true *jihadi*.

The first loss of a crusader state, the tripwire against Muslim attack from the north, was bound to stir a major reaction in the West and its fruit was the expedition known to historians as the Second Crusade. It had the potential to crush Nur al-Din.

The Second Crusade

This crusade had as its leaders Louis VII, king of France, and the emperor elect Conrad, king of the Romans, a man who had twice served in the Middle East. It included his nephew Frederick of Swabia, the future Emperor Frederick I Barbarossa, an extraordinary number of high-ranking aristocrats and a plethora of top-ranking churchmen. Behind its summoning lay the golden voice of the Cistercian monk Bernard of Clairvaux, who had worked with the first pope of the order, Eugenius III, the summoner of the crusade. In a major ceremony in the presence of St Bernard at Speyer Cathedral, Conrad had taken the cross and in an atmosphere of exaltation, a multitude had done the same. Bernard was indeed the voice of the epoch. In preaching tours he had the adulation of a modern pop star, with enthusiasts pulling off pieces of his clothing. The cadences of his preaching in French as he travelled in German-speaking lands still moved many who did not understand his language. They wept and took the cross.

Louis was moved by the French tradition of crusading, and, working on that tradition, Abbot Suger presented to him the standard of Charlemagne at the royal shrine in the abbey of Saint-Denis and exposed for his veneration the relic of St Denis, the converter of France. There were strong links to the past. Detailed examination of charter evidence shows a continuity of noble families who in the years after the First Crusade sent their sons to serve in the Holy Land. Broadly associated with the preaching tours of Urban II or Peter the Hermit, all looked back to the achievements of the First Crusade. Louis's expedition was viewed with alarm by the Emperor Manuel of Byzantium, who feared an attack on Constantinople and as a precaution made a pact with the sultan of Anatolia — a truce to ensure

Muslims and crusaders did not combine against him. This contributed to the mistrust of Byzantium which dated back to Alexius's supposed abandonment of the First Crusade at Antioch.

The approach to the Holy Land was botched. There was insufficient shipping to carry so large an army by the preferred seaward route, so it had to go by land. Louis, a devout man repenting of an atrocity in his past, was no skilled general. He coped inadequately with the perils of the landward route through Anatolia and, in a fight for survival against the Turks, was forced to leave his infantry to be massacred and take ship to Antioch with his aristocrats. He was affronted by subsequent events in Antioch. His queen, Eleanor of Aquitaine, was an attractive woman and a child of the south, an heiress bringing Aquitaine to the French crown, and was in contact at Antioch with Raymond of Poitiers, the prince, a scion of the house of Raymond of Toulouse. They spoke Occitan to each other, which Louis did not understand and made him feel excluded. Supposedly there was an amorous entanglement and so Louis was unwilling to co-operate in any way with Raymond and left Antioch with Eleanor and his leading men to travel to Jerusalem.

Failing to co-ordinate with Louis's army, Conrad suffered heavy defeat near Dorylaeum and lost many of his German infantry when he moved back to Nicaea. In poor health, he went to Constantinople and the medical care of Manuel, causing some Germans to abandon the expedition altogether. Finally Conrad and survivors took ship to Acre. Conrad, as emperor elect, may well have felt he was the man of highest rank and the rightful leader of this crusade; originally a supporter of an attack on Edessa, he seems to have become convinced that it was no longer feasible. The decision to abandon the north and instead capture Damascus was probably taken at a small assembly in Jerusalem in April 1148, where Conrad stayed with the Templars: it was later ratified in a massive assembly of leading aristocrats and churchmen.

The galaxy of high rank assembled for the crusade may have been a source of over-confidence. Newcomers would have believed that what was still a substantial army with great men leading was bound to win through but settlers knew more about the wiliness of the enemy and the hazards of Near Eastern climate and geography. The primary position of honour in any assembly was that of the king of Jerusalem and it was his natural function with his barons to provide the newcomers with counsel based on experience. The misfortune of the crusaders at this juncture was that Baldwin III was inexperienced, lacked full independence and also the prestige to be won by successful warfare.

The strategy of the Second Crusade was defensible. Louis had received a daunting report on Edessa, wrecked by Nur al-Din and lacking any Christian population. It was reasonable to strike it off the list and defensible to look towards Damascus, the greatest city in Syria, a trading centre and key point on the Silk Road from China to the west, with special expertise in producing silk and steel blades for swords. Control of its commerce and the fertile lands near it would be an advantage. Restoration of the military reputation of the Christian crusaders and settlers was essential and to take this city was to remove a vital building block of power from the Muslims.

News of the coming of a great army reached Unur, the *atabeg* of the Burid dynasty in Damascus. In the emergency he sent for help to Saif al-Din in Mosul and Nur al-Din in Aleppo, who readied their armies. In the city crowds came together in the Great Mosque, an immense structure dating from the eighth century with a *mihrab* whose ornament was one of the masterpieces of Muslim art of its day. Damascus had been the seat of the Umayyad caliphate and contained an object of great emotional significance, the blood-spattered Quran of the third caliph, Uthman. It was exposed to rouse the populace to resistance against the Frankish enemy. There were prayers for the safety of the city and repentance for sin, ashes thrown over their heads by supplicants for divine help. Two passionate elderly scholars chose the way of the martyr, *shahid*, deliberately riding out to be crushed under the hoofs of Christian cavalry. Their names have come down to us, one being given a tomb revered by pious inhabitants and visitors, with an inscription recording his martyrdom.

By this time, the Kurdish mercenary Najm al-Din Ayyub had become garrison commander under Unur. It is difficult not to believe that the spectacle of an aroused populace then began to change his attitudes and develop sympathy for *jihad* against the Franks.

It is clear that no one mind had analysed the tactics for the great incoming army and the hazards it might have to face once it had moved forward from the settlers' strongpoint at Banyas to reach Damascus on 24 July. The army's leaders seem to have staked all on a coup that would deliver the city into their hands in short order and not to have thought through the possible consequences should this not happen. They brought with them neither timber nor siege engines: Damascus had no massive fortifications comparable to Antioch but it still had walls to surmount.

The defence was determined. The army attacked the west of the city, where a mass of smallholdings divided the fertile orchards irrigated by a system of canals fed from the Barada river, and pushed through to the riverbank. Here was water aplenty for men and animals. The defence used the mud walls dividing the smallholdings to poke through lances held by soldiers invisible to the invaders and shot arrows on the advancing troops from watchtowers. Then, mysteriously, having fought so hard and broken through to the river, the crusading army apparently followed advice to switch the attack to the eastern side of the city, a waterless area with no orchards, on the plea that there was a low wall, easy to surmount. As they considered returning to the western side and its water supplies, the crusaders found their way blocked by defenders assembling palisades manned by archers. They felt unable to face them and the retreat was sounded at dawn on 28 July. It was extraordinary. After four days they had given up the siege and trailed back south, harassed by the Muslims and suffering heavy losses.

Once back at Jerusalem, morale understandably destroyed, the crusaders were unwilling to follow Conrad's suggestion to win back prestige by attacking Ascalon, another strongpoint and port still in Muslim hands. He despaired and went home. Louis's army went but he himself stayed on for another year as a resident pilgrim in Jerusalem before returning to his kingdom.

Why the advice to the crusade to switch their attack to the eastern side of Damascus was given remains mysterious. Had Unur, as *atabeg* of Damascus, promised hefty tribute to the Kingdom of Jerusalem if the attack held off? Did Jerusalem barons discreetly wreck the crusade by

shifting the attack to an impossible location? The settlers lived in a different world from incoming crusaders – had so to live – a world of attack and
counter-attack, of tribute-taking and Muslim alliances. They could see the
attempt at a swift coup was doubtful and getting tribute instead was an
attraction. An Islamic chronicler believed that the army's leaders grew
fearful of Saif al-Din and Nur al-Din with their armies ready to move on
to the attack; the army had not scaled the walls and, left outside the city as
in Edessa, would be caught in the classic nutcracker position between an
undefeated garrison and an outside relieving force. Local commanders had
come to believe in the vital importance of conserving military manpower.
Incoming crusaders did not think in this way. The mass of troops, who had
suffered much on the journey and lost so many friends and supporters,
would play no games. They had come to fight a decisive action and would
settle for nothing else and so went home.

Whatever the truth of the Second Crusade's collapse, there was no
doubt about its effects. It was generally believed that innocent crusaders
coming from the West had been bamboozled and betrayed by settlers in
the Crusader States and that belief inhibited action to come and help them
in Outremer for decades after 1148. Clergy might appeal and talk about the
vow to crusade and its celestial reward and St Bernard might reflect on the
consequences of the sins of the West. It all had no effect.

Nur al-Din after the Failed Crusade

The battle over Damascus played into Nur al-Din's hands. It discredited
the Burids and Unur the *atabeg* as allies of King Fulk of Jerusalem. The
climate of opinion began to change – *jihad* came back into fashion.

In 1108 the legist al-Sulami had thoughtfully argued the necessity for
jihad to be revived and directed against the Franks, who should be expelled,
and had pleaded for a return to Jerusalem as a Muslim holy city. Beginning
his appeal in his suburban mosque in Damascus, he then transferred to the
Great Mosque – but his entreaties fell on deaf ears. As the number of
victims of Frankish aggression grew, there would be more audiences
willing to hear sermons on *jihad* and to act on them. Forty years after

al-Sulami, crowds in the Great Mosque cried out for *jihad*. Nur al-Din continued to have propagandists working for him and was the more inclined to encourage them to do so because, whereas Mosul had at its back rich agricultural land, Aleppo did not and it was prudent to make up for this by establishing volunteer supports. But he was not always consistent.

Nur al-Din the Man

Contrary to a widely accepted view, Nur al-Din did not take advantage of the problems of the Crusader States and drive on with *jihad* against the Franks in the aftermath of the Second Crusade but instead played a subtle game, cutting away at Antioch's security by seizing two strongpoints at Harim and Apamea and killing Raymond of Poitiers in battle at Inab in 1149, a success hailed in verse by the poet Ibn al-Qayrasani as a *jihadi* triumph.

In fact, this was part of a set of moves designed not even to attempt to take Antioch but to emasculate the Christian city and fortress so as to prevent it giving help to Damascus when the time came for Nur al-Din to overrun the city and to establish a stranglehold on supply routes from the north for grain to feed its massive population. Damascus was his true objective all along. He proclaimed his will not to enter into conflict with Muslims but patrolled in the Hauran, the fertile lands which also fed Damascus, ostensibly to give protection against marauders to the Muslim peasants working in the fields. He imposed such discipline on his troops that they never succumbed to the temptation to forage at the peasants' expense. At the same time he engaged in manoeuvres against Abaq of the Burid dynasty in Damascus, ruler after the illness and death of Unur, warning him of subversion against his authority within the city. Meanwhile he knew full well that *jihadis* on his side were at work influencing the population and arguing for Nur al-Din's superior claims as a true Muslim campaigner and that Ayyub, in Abaq's employment as a military leader, had a complicity with this.

In the winter of 1153–4 it all came to fruition as he began to stem the supply of grain from the north, leading to food shortages, and then sent

Shirkuh from Aleppo to intimidate the city before arriving outside Damascus himself in April 1154. There was only token resistance: the city surrendered. Abaq was treated mercifully and compensated for his loss of power with land elsewhere. Ayyub, member of an ethnic group looked down on by both Turks and Arabs, had been a mercenary and had served a bewildering variety of employers as a soldier, but within Damascus he found a cause and became Nur al-Din's loyal adherent. He was the one man whom Nur al-Din allowed to sit in his presence and it is easy to understand why – he had helped to bring the greatest city in Syria to his master's camp.

Nur al-Din had fulfilled his father's long-held ambition to take Damascus and had done so peacefully, without shedding Muslim blood. But it was not *jihad*. The mainline policy was that of a warlord like Zangi, and to Damascus he added other acquisitions at the expense of Muslims. There were great benefits to his capture of Damascus: he brought stability to the city, aided its economic life, engaged in building and was happy to witness a valuable increase in population under his rule. Nor was he immune to appeals for Muslim reform – provided they did not intrude on his central drive to extend his own power within the Islamic world. He would have liked to seize Mosul when his brother died and a child succeeded, but had to draw off. How far the extending of his own personal power was still the priority is demonstrated by the truces he established with Jerusalem in 1155 and 1156, the latter with the stipulation that tribute to the king of Jerusalem would be paid from Damascene revenues.

But later in the 1150s fortune turned against Nur al-Din. Byzantium threatened. Manuel Comnenus, who had succeeded his brother as emperor in 1143, turned his attention to the Crusader States and began to develop a policy of marriage alliances designed to create a common line of action against the menace of the Muslims and to recover ancient Byzantine territory. In 1159 the Emperor's solemn entry into Antioch was a portent, as he rode in majesty, followed at a distance by Baldwin III without symbols of office, a clear sign of his subordination to the wealth and ancient authority of Byzantium. When Manuel prepared to use his army to assault Aleppo, Nur al-Din thought disaster had come. In the end he made a settlement with Manuel, who dropped his plans for attack in return for the freeing of crusader prisoners taken during the Second Crusade and a promise of support against the Seljuqs in Anatolia. Thus pragmatism and diplomacy prevailed over military action.

Failure to pursue *jihad* and become a genuine *mujahidin* nonetheless worked on Nur al-Din's mind. He fell so seriously ill in October 1157 that he made a will. That illness recurred in 1158 and he felt God's hand upon him in reproach for failure to pursue *jihad* and expel the Franks. While he was thus preoccupied, Baldwin had captured Ascalon, stopping the repeated pinprick attacks from the garrison and opening the means to fulfil Baldwin the Conqueror's dream of pushing into Egypt and tapping her wealth. In 1157 Nur al-Din's territory was afflicted by a massive earthquake and aftershocks, which damaged Muslim fortresses, walls and living quarters and forced him to expend wealth and energy in repairs. The Antiochenes revived their strength and recaptured Harim in 1158. Only a characteristic princely quarrel between Thierry of Flanders and the marauding Reynald of Châtillon (second husband of Constance, heiress to Antioch) saved Shaizar, the fortress of the ibn Munqidh, a Muslim clan on the Upper Orontes, from recapture by the Byzantines. Nur al-Din had never before undertaken the *hajj*; it was part of his growing spirituality and sorrow for past inactivity on *jihad* that he took time from pressing responsibilities in 1161 to do so.

A catastrophic defeat in the Bouqia valley in the north of the County of Tripoli, when he was surprised by a mass of Antiochene troops, forced Nur al-Din to reassess his aims and principles. He had narrowly escaped with his life on a donkey released by a Kurd, who had sacrificed his own life to cut the beast's tether. The episode led him to undo the effects of this disaster, to compensate relatives of his troops who had been killed, to replace personally all the lost horses and equipment and to abandon compromise with the Franks in favour of total commitment to *jihad*.

He was encouraged by a major victory over a force of Christians near Artah in 1164, outmanoeuvring them, recapturing Harim and taking a rich haul of high-level captives to his prison at Aleppo. It was a prestige victory because of the surrenders and Nur al-Din chose not to release his victims, with the exception of a young prince of Antioch, ransomed because he wanted nothing to disturb Manuel Comnenus – better a weak Antioch, he calculated, than Manuel as neighbour. In Reynald of Châtillon he recognised a particularly dangerous antagonist and imprisoned him for sixteen years. He similarly confined Raymond, count of Tripoli, and Joscelin of Courtenay, of the disgraced line of Joscelin II of Edessa. In the following years he continued to drive on towards the south, next capturing Banyas and putting pressure on King Amalric, who was forced to defend on two fronts while still continuing to attempt to gain land or tribute from Egypt in the fashion set by Baldwin the Conqueror.

The drive down towards Egypt has often been misunderstood: Nur al-Din was not simply racing his opponent, the king of Jerusalem, to the supposedly rich pickings of Cairo but he was, above all, fulfilling the duty he had undertaken at the instigation of the Baghdad caliphate to destroy the Fatimid heresy. The importance to him of ensuring that orthodoxy utterly defeated the Ismaili heretics has been brought out by recent research. In fact, two targets for *jihad* had emerged – one against the Franks and the other against Islamic heresy. The first was precisely what had been sketched out by al-Sulami in Damascus: the total elimination of the Franks, destroying their churches and crosses, casting out their pollutions and restoring Jerusalem to its rightful place as a Muslim holy city. Late in his life he commissioned a beautiful symbol of his intention to recapture the city for Islam – a *minbar* carved by four local wood-carvers, erected in the great mosque at Aleppo and prepared to be re-erected in the al-Aqsa mosque when Jerusalem had returned to Islamic hands. It had on it a humble prayer of Nur al-Din, dated 1168, asking God to allow him to put it into the mosque.

Ecumenical Sunnism and the Battle against Heresy

In 1154 centuries of disunity between the two great cities of Aleppo and Damascus came to an end when Damascus opened its gates to Nur al-Din. It was clear that a single major power had come into being in the central Islamic lands and the Abbasid caliph al-Muqtafi responded to the new opportunity to carry forward the long battle of the Baghdad caliphate against the rival caliphate of Cairo and its Ismaili heresy. Here was a new instrument for the cause and the caliph accordingly required his vizier ibn Hubayra, a jurist and theologian, to write to Nur al-Din acquainting him with the need for action. Caliphs had the authority to grant land and so in the same year he issued a charter for Nur al-Din to have the rights to the Fatimid lands in Egypt and Palestine if he conquered them and returned them to the rightful allegiance and doctrine of the Abbasid caliph. Nur al-Din, a military man making his way in the fractured world of the *atabegs*, was developing a network of propagandists and literary support-ers and, listening to his scholars, over time incorporated the struggle against the Fatimids into his *jihad* against the Franks.

In the 1160s the battle against the Fatimids and its heartland in Egypt became a major preoccupation, accompanying his growing commitment to Islamic prayer and ritual. Scholars who had assented to his *jihad* against the Franks gave a more enthusiastic response to the struggle against the dangerous errors of the Fatimids. Nur al-Din's network of supporters in the Islamic world became formidable and aided his campaigning. Pleas of *jihad* could be used to disarm his opponents. It was difficult to oppose a leader who claimed that he was carrying out a *jihad* in accordance with the will of the Prophet and that opposition to him was tantamount to obstruc-tion of the *jihad* itself. At the same time, as Nur al-Din assumed the gar-ments of a Sufi, practised prayer and fasting and banished alcohol, music and dancing, to the dismay of his troops, he took on the role of the ideal Muslim ruler, rebuilding the walls of Medina, issuing coins with his name and the title the 'just prince', building hospitals, mosques, orphanages, Sufi cloisters and a House of *Hadith* Scholarship in Damascus which he attended in person.

Orthodoxy based on the doctrine of an uncreated Quran and an empha-sis on the inscrutable will of an all-powerful God in the world He had created had become the basic tenets of the Baghdad caliphate. Beliefs were accepted *bila kaif*, without speculation, and accompanied by full adher-ence to the rites of Islam. This followed from the rejection of Mutazilism and was Baghdad's weapon against the rival caliphate of Cairo, seen as heretical with its teaching about the infallibility of a correctly designated Fatimid caliph and his right to decree doctrine. The ultimate vision was of a Muslim world both temporal and spiritual, united under the leadership of the Baghdad caliphate, securing Sunnism for Islam everywhere and putting down the Ismaili heresy for ever.

Part of the preparation for that ultimate victory was *jama-ı* Sunnism, an ecumenical movement uniting in harmony the four main schools of Sunnis and even moderate Shiites untainted by doctrines of infallibility. Once the initially impoverished Fatimids had secured power in Egypt, they became formidable opponents and a special effort to overcome past dissensions of Sunni scholars was felt to be the right means of destroying the heresy. Thus the staffing of the *madrasas* – training places for judges, public officials and Islamic holy men – was key and so to a lesser degree were the *khanqahs*, which had grown up as convents for the instruction of Sufi mystics. Here were the centres of literacy and education in the Quran and law.

Looking back on the history of the *jihad* from his standpoint in the thirteenth century, Abu Shama recalled Nur al-Din intervening in a dispute between jurists over the choice of a new professor. Calling them in and addressing them via his spokesman in the citadel at Aleppo, he decreed that both rival candidates should be appointed and each should preside in his own *madrasa*. It was not quite the full ecumenism envisaged by the caliphs and viziers but it was a step in the right direction. In his early years, as he confirmed his power in Aleppo and suppressed the Shiites, Nur al-Din had done away with the deliberate sign of Shiite presence, the sectarian addition to the words of obligatory daily prayer 'Come to the best of works: Muhammad and Ali are the best of men'. But later in his career he found reconciling formulae for inscriptions he commissioned in the Great Mosque at Damascus, mentioning with the Prophet both Ali and the Emigrant caliphs of the early years and even, in one case, including the murdered victims of the anti-Alid reaction.

Sustaining traditionalism and deterring heresy, Nur al-Din stands out as a patron and innovator seeking to banish obscurity from copies of the Quran. Copying was a highly specialised activity demanding great skill, fine material – that is, papyrus – and wealthy patrons. Classic Kufic Qurans show plainly that their makers, both patrons and calligraphers, were more interested in creating high works of art to honour God than in providing easily readable texts.

Abbasid reformers were impatient with the obscurities of Kufic, however beautiful, and sought a script whose meaning was plain and which could be read simply by any literate. They wished to eliminate the Ismaili distinction between the surface meaning of the Quran (*ẓahir*) and its deeper meaning (*batin*). Texts, which required a specialist interpreter to explain the true meaning to the uninitiated, lent themselves to exposition of alleged hidden secrets within the Quran to be unveiled to their initiates by specialists in the Shiite movement. Nur al-Din checked obscurities by using a plain, legible cursive script for the Quran derived originally from the Maghrib and used widely for administrative documents. The process was aided by the Abbasid caliphate's practice of making cheaper paper from rags. By using the cursive in public inscriptions, Nur al-Din was also putting down a marker – it was a visible change from the style of earlier inscriptions and designed to inform the public that, where it prevailed, power had shifted and the religious reforms of the Abbasid caliphate had taken over.

Nur al-Din sustained the long Islamic tradition of generosity in founding public buildings and making provision for the sick. A hospital in Aleppo founded in 1150 offers an example of high-calibre woodwork marquetry in its double doors with geometric patterns in some contrast to the beautiful but mysterious floriated Kufic. Here again a more austere, clearcut style largely supplanted the efflorescence of the older tradition. Kufic, however, was not completely eliminated – it was there in the most beautiful of all works issuing from Nur al-Din's patronage, the now lost *mihrab* in his mosque in the Aleppo citadel. The *minbar* for the al-Aqsa mosque, destroyed in 1968, is well recorded and has been remade: it was one of the greatest masterpieces of Islamic woodwork, with a richness and variety of geometric patterns and vegetal ornament.

Muqarnas had a part to play in conveying to the observer the atomistic nature of the universe of the Abbasid orthodoxy. *Muqarnas* vaulting, sometimes referred to as honeycomb or cubic vaulting, is purely decorative; it floats, as it were, reflecting the fragmented and perishable nature of the universe, held up by the will of the creator, without whom everything would collapse. A multitude of cubes inside a dome have a visual effect of impermanence; if associated with windows, they may also suggest the radiance of a mass of stars in the heavens. The eye flickers from one cube to another. There is nothing fortuitous here: the technique conveys what is commonly referred to as an occasionalist theology, mirroring in stone, brick and stucco a continuous process of 'annihilation and re-creation' by God of the atoms making up the universe, modifying the hemispherical dome of early Islamic architecture so as to conceal the squinches and ribs and all visible supports in the interest of the impression of impermanence, as understood by the theologians of the Sunni revival of the eleventh and twelfth centuries. God's will dictates immediately and directly everything in His universe. The architecture, the cursive script and, to a lesser extent, the trend in geometric patterns of decoration reflect the doctrinal position of the Baghdad caliphate, its belief in God's relation to His universe and its opposition to the Ismaili heresy. Nur al-Din stands squarely in this tradition and it is no surprise to find excellent examples of *muqarnas* vaulting early and late in his career, in a portal of the hospital he built in 1154 at Damascus and in the mausoleum he designed for himself in the same city in 1168.

The Drive for Egypt

The Fatimid caliphate was in decadence. In 1160 powerbrokers in Egypt had lighted on the expedient of choosing the eleven-year-old al-Adid as caliph, with all the associated Fatimid powers and attributes. Surrounded by the magnificence of the caliphal palace in Cairo, his foot kissed, his decisions having God's approval, al-Adid was in practice the plaything of any contender with sufficient military power. In his gift was the office of vizier, with its high claims to authority under the caliph, including military power and the duty to protect judges and scholars, conveyed in such phrases as 'sultan of the armies, friend of the community and glory of the dynasty, protector of the *qadis* of Islam and chief protagonist of believers'.

The outcome of this power vacuum at the centre was a highly personalised struggle among, in the first place, local contenders for power and their followers, secondly, the Franks under a strong military leader, King Amalric of Jerusalem, and thirdly, Nur al-Din, operating under his best general, Asad al-Din Shirkuh. The vizierate could be competed for only by Muslims, which meant either one of the local contenders or Shirkuh; Franks, however, remained in the wings, available to be drawn in as allies while they pursued their own interests in obtaining tribute or land. The situation was still more complicated by the gulf between the Abbasid and the Fatimid caliphates: Nur al-Din and his generals in the long run sought the destruction of the heretical caliphate but they could not afford to show their hand as they fought and manoeuvred. Caution decreed that they had to proceed slowly in view of the interests which still clustered round the Fatimid caliphate. Shirkuh, for example, could only contend for the vizierate in the guise of a supporter of Shiite principles, a 'protector of the *qadis* of Islam', rather than as the agent of a leader determined to bring down the caliphate which energised and defended these *qadis*. Ethnic tensions and other divisions of belief complicated the scene still further: Sunnis within Egypt were potential supporters of a doctrinally sound intervening power, but Egyptians were often hostile to uncivilised Turks; Kurds were despised; under Fatimid rule Jews and Christians still occupied administrative posts of importance.

The Kurd Shirkuh, elderly, short, fat and disfigured by a cataract in one eye, was an improbable inspirer of men. His virtues were shown in action and, as with any successful general who won victories and looked after his troops, gained him a willing following among his Mamluks despite his oddities. He was a brave man with an understanding of terrain and tactical possibilities, well able to shift his forces rapidly to deceive the multitude of spies deployed by opponents. Nur al-Din backed him cautiously, aware of geographical difficulties for invaders of Egypt and the dangers of sandstorms and of fatigue for men and horses crossing desert territory. The Franks had benefited from Baldwin III's capture of Ascalon in 1153 and had grown familiar with the routes and the terrain, making them more tricky opponents for the Muslims but they had to fear a squeeze on the Crusader States from two angles – Syria and Egypt.

Against Nur al-Din and Shirkuh stood one of the finest fighting kings Jerusalem had ever had, Amalric the son of Fulk and Melisende. The actions of Zangi and Nur al-Din had created a reservoir of need. Jerusalem had worked hard to feed poorer Christians in flight from their ancient city in the first crisis and harboured needy aristocrats who had lost their lands. Amalric was encouraged in his advances by the dissatisfaction of Edessan exiles and the possible danger they represented to his authority if not provided with substitute territories; and he was moved by the need of the elite in over-crowded lands to strike out and win new areas for expansion. He launched no fewer than five expeditions into Egypt. Open-minded about alliances if they served the central need of providing adequate forces to stand up to the Muslims, he was, for example, willing to accept a subordinate position to the Emperor Manuel Comnenus, if it brought Byzantine fighting strength, above all sea power, to his aid. William of Tyre knew him well, was uneasy about his theology but aware of his regular attendance at Mass and his devotion to his kingdom. A weakness lay in his liking for affairs with married women. In a vision St Bernard upbraided Amalric for his lechery but ended by blessing the fragment of the True Cross he wore round his neck. Amalric believed the relic saved his life in battle the next day.

He made great progress in Egypt at various times but was unable to sustain his alliance with Byzantium, suffering from weaknesses in supply arrangements, and made a grave error on his fourth expedition in 1168 in burning Bilbais and massacring its inhabitants, turning Egyptians against him. He breached a truce and was forced to withdraw from Egypt in the face of a substantial army led by Shirkuh. It was a turning point for, although he made an attempt with Byzantine aid on Damietta in 1169, the balance of forces had moved against him. Overall, he won a great deal of tribute in various encounters but never made the conquest of land within Egypt for which he worked so hard.

Uncertainty concerning the vizierate within Egypt opened the way to Frankish interventions and also facilitated the drive of Nur al-Din and his men to take the caliphate. Shawar, the governor of Upper Egypt, had attained the vizierate in 1163, only to find himself displaced by his Arab chamberlain, Dirgham. Shawar appealed to Nur al-Din in Damascus, with a promise of great Egyptian grain revenues, and Nur al-Din, at first a little reluctantly, agreed to back him and send in Shirkuh. Shawar was an opportunist and not to be trusted, but in the tripartite battle over Egypt each participant feared giving an advantage to another. If Shirkuh did not intervene, would the Franks gain a dangerous advantage? Dirgham was killed in battle and Shawar, again vizier, promptly set about betraying Shirkuh and inviting in Amalric. In a unique episode Shawar, as vizier in 1167, had conducted two Frankish emissaries to the presence of the caliph to ratify a treaty. One of them, Hugh of Caesarea, had no idea of the majestic seclusion in which the caliph resided. Al-Adid sat on a golden throne behind curtains, only withdrawn after Shawar had prostrated himself three times. To ratify the treaty Hugh, ungloved, strode forward to shake hands in sturdy western style; unwillingly the caliph abandoned protocol and exposed his hand too. Two worlds collided.

The Rise of Saladin

Within this confused arena of war, tribute-taking and diplomacy, one new force was quietly beginning its rise as Shirkuh noted talent in his nephew Yousuf ibn Ayyub. The young man became known to history as Saladin, by virtue of one of the titles of honour he was given, Salah al-Din, 'uprightness of religion' – latinised by his Frankish opponents as Saladinus. Instead of appointing one of his sons as aide-de-camp in the usual way, Shirkuh decided to take him on instead. Saladin had begun his career as police chief in Damascus, where his enemies said he raised revenues by taking a rake-off from prostitutes' earnings, then showed courage and battle sense in an encounter between Amalric and Shirkuh at al-Babayn in 1167 and proved himself as a garrison commander in Alexandria, where Shirkuh left him commanding troops numbering no more than a thousand but in charge of a much larger population which had mixed feelings about Turks and was by no means to be relied on. Outside, cutting down orchards, setting up a watchtower to observe everything and pressing very hard, was a much larger besieging Frankish force. Blockade created hunger, but somehow, by a blend of diplomacy with the inhabitants and tight discipline over troops, Saladin lasted three months till Shirkuh came to relieve him. The experience left him with a lasting distaste for Egypt but nonetheless made his name as a resourceful general and manager of men. He never looked back.

Early in 1169, still believing he could negotiate with Shirkuh, Shawar was attacked and killed by Saladin and a Syrian. Shirkuh was accepted as vizier but in March succumbed to his overeating, following Juvenal's recipe for a sudden end, by taking a hot bath after a heavy meal. There was again a vacancy for a vizier. Saladin played a cautious game, allowing rivals to counter each other's claims, dropping hints, using a 'silver-voiced' Kurdish spokesman to promote his candidature, giving the impression that he would be manageable. He won. The caliph accepted him and Saladin soon showed his decisive power. He dealt with a eunuch's plot to spearhead an Egyptian reaction against Syrians. In the story, which has a flavour of the *Arabian Nights*, the scheming eunuch aimed to call in the Franks, then stab Saladin in the back as he pulled troops out of Cairo to fight. So a beggar was sent out with a message to the Jerusalem Franks, but he was not a beggar. An apostate Jew, converted to Islam, spotted his fine new sandals and uncovered the trickery. The message never got through and it was the end of the beggar and of the eunuch. Saladin then turned on the uncontrollable black Sudanese troops, given to rioting and mugging travellers. They were numerous, but Saladin secured an immediate tactical advantage over them in Cairo by setting fire to the quarter where their women and children lived. They ran to their defence and were killed.

Supposed treasure in Egypt, the fertile (albeit variable) lands fed by the Nile, the commerce of the Delta and the weakness of the caliphate all drew military leaders into a game of winner-takes-all. Shawar had tried and failed. Shirkuh gave every sign he would go beyond his role as Nur al-Din's general and stake out a major territory for himself. Nur al-Din did not overtly oppose him but began to hedge and consider placing Turks with him who could check his ambitions. Finally, the gifted and ambitious Saladin aroused his disquiet as well. Nur al-Din urged him to complete the task for which Shirkuh had originally been sent and abolish the Fatimid caliphate altogether.

Fortune favoured Saladin. He had a gift of friendship, not all of it simply an element in his skilfully crafted diplomacy, and he came to be in intimate and trusted contact with al-Adid. In 1171 the caliph, just short of twenty-one, died. It was said that he called for Saladin in his illness and he did not come. It may be so: presence in the caliphate palace at such a juncture could have been dangerous and Saladin still had his enemies. The end of the Fatimids passed off smoothly and in September 1171 the name of the Abbasid caliph was substituted for that of the last of the Fatimid caliphs, first in Fustat, to test the water, and then in Cairo. There was no uprising and no disturbance and so after 202 years the rival Shiite-orientated caliphate, that had once looked as if it was going to rule the world, passed into oblivion. The family of the last Fatimid caliph was sequestrated and the sexes kept apart, all under the eye of a eunuch faithful to Saladin. The women were soon freed but the men were kept in an honourable isolation until they died – on no account was the risk to be taken of the Alid line being continued.

The caliphal palace now stood vacant. It was of extraordinary richness, reached through passages guarded by Ethiopians, with pavilions, fish pools, gardens, exotic birds and animals. But for all its magnificence, there was no money to be found, only horses and weapons. In 1174 an Ismaili was crucified by Saladin in the hope of getting to this missing treasure but he revealed nothing. Nothing was ever discovered, although the story was that many years later, in the days of the Mamluks, a store of money was found under a house at a gate of the eastern palace.

Meanwhile Saladin revealed how close he still stood to the barbaric, militaristic world of the professional mercenary, as he let his soldiers sell off loot and manuscripts from the magnificent caliphal library under the presidency of his eunuch. Bindings were torn off, quires scattered, then reassembled. Later he grew in stature, listened to scholars and treated with care a library that came into his hands in 1183, but he always lacked the intellectual breadth of Nur al-Din. He had something of the Bedouin in his nature and spent heavily, gaining recruits and rewarding family.

As Saladin's superior, Nur al-Din could reasonably expect to cash in on the economic vitality of Egypt and receive tribute. He sent an accountant to investigate but still did not get what he wanted and grew suspicious. Nur al-Din had distractions. In 1170 another great earthquake damaged Muslim cities and castles compelling him to make a truce with the Franks and occupy himself with repairs. As Nur al-Din came down to attack Kerak and Shawbak, key fortresses of the Franks in desert terrain, Saladin came up from Cairo but, warned by his entourage of the danger that Nur al-Din could take advantage of the situation to destroy him, drew off. Ayyub in Cairo gave counsel to his son and urged caution against hotheads in Saladin's council. Profess loyalty, he said. Tensions remained and Nur al-Din still questioned Saladin's finances. Both Nur al-Din and Saladin mustered troops, perhaps as much to prepare for bargaining as outright war. However the threat of civil war passed when Nur al-Din died after a polo match in 1174, leaving a young son, al-Salih.

Saladin was fortunate. Amalric succumbed to dysentery in the same year. It looked as though he had reached the top of the world and problems which had beset him for years were being dissipated by two fortunate deaths. Nur al-Din's empire broke up and Saladin aimed to reunite it under his leadership. Damascus surrendered to him early on, yielding to persuasion rather than military force. Then he made a fatal mistake by assuming the role of regent in Aleppo and trying to take advantage of the youth of Nur al-Din's eleven-year-old heir, but in a moving speech in the hippodrome in Aleppo the young al-Salih denounced him as a 'wicked man, who repudiates my father's goodness to him'. Saladin took all the Muslim territory and cities he could and extended his power to Yemen and even fought a battle in 1175 against a Zangid contingent. In pursuit of his objective, he married Nur al-Din's widow (not the mother of al-Salih) in 1176 – with a surprising result. He fell in love with her and they remained a happy romantic couple.

Still, for years he acted as nothing other than a raw, self-seeking warlord. Only in 1183, after complicated manoeuvring and diplomacy and the death of al-Salih, could Saladin take Aleppo. By then he had grown in under-standing and stature but still faced residual problems of recognition as a leader of Islam, stemming from both his Kurdish background and the obdurate resistance of Mosul and Aleppo to his regency. These were com-pounded after 1180 by the arrival of a new Abbasid caliph, the twenty-two-year-old al-Nasir, more decisive than his predecessor and highly sensitive to the possible proximity of Saladin-ruled lands to his own caliphal territories in Mesopotamia. At first the outward signs of recogni-tion were available and Saladin received from the caliph a black satin robe with gold-embroidered sleeves, a black and gold turban and a jewelled necklace, and rode in these symbolic accoutrements through Damascus but the relationship went wrong two years later and never recovered. He was twice attacked by Assassins and had to redouble his security arrange-ments, a decision which reinforced his existing custom of carefully staging every move and gesture.

Saladin's continued success depended on a flow of propaganda, sus-tained faithfully by his secretary, Imad-al-Din, once in the service of Nur al-Din, and the claim he continued to make of being God's instrument in the unification of Islam and ultimate *jihad* against the Franks, which drew support for him over a wide area. His followers and admirers recognised that he was not a gifted general – his strength lay in diplomacy, the applica-tion of finely tuned and occasional force and a skilled propaganda and information service. He had a weakness for employing his family members, some of whom, such as his brother Turanshah, were disreputable and incompetent. He could not afford defeats, for his claim to rule in Islam could never rest secure relying solely on his own paid troops and Mamluks – the distances were too great and the enemies he still had too varied.

In his dealings with the Franks the shock had come in 1177 when Amal-ric's successor, Baldwin the Leper, took charge in person, even though he had to be carried in a litter, and caught Saladin unawares. The bulk of Frankish forces had been active to the north besieging Harim and Saladin then saw an opportunity to attack. Baldwin came out to challenge him but was forced to retreat to Ascalon. Relaxed, as he saw an early opportunity and aware of the weakness of Baldwin's forces ensconced in Ascalon,

Saladin dissipated his forces foraging and ravaging and was caught by Baldwin at Montgisard, between Ramla and Ibelin, and suffered a nasty reverse. He only just escaped, leaving behind a piece of his mail stained with his blood.

The battle at Montgisard damaged Saladin, however much he argued, and justly, that the Franks had suffered heavily too. There were his own losses, his precipitate flight and the capture of his friend Isa, subsequently ransomed at a heavy price. Baldwin took advice from Reynald of Châtillon, who had emerged from his long imprisonment and had become lord of the key desert fortress and town of Kerak through marriage. Influenced by Reynald, Baldwin took a bold step by placing a new fortress only one day's march from Damascus as an obstacle to Muslim forces passing from that Syrian redoubt to attack the Crusader States. It covered a vital crossing of the Jordan river, known as Jacob's Ford, and was also – a clear insult to Islam – the site of a Muslim shrine. Baldwin interested the Templars in the site and spent heavily on the construction of what was to become a great castle in the latest fashion, with two concentric rings of fortification. Saladin used all the force of diplomacy and finance to try to stop the building of the castle and offered massive sums – first 60,000, then 100,000 dinars – if the Franks would give up the project. Baldwin refused. The inner ring of the castle was completed when Saladin moved to a major assault in August 1179; Baldwin accepted the challenge, assembling his army at Tiberias, but Saladin was too fast for him, using specialist miners to make a passage under the walls. The wood supports, fired in classical fashion, failed to bring down the wall but he retunnelled at speed and forced an entrance on 24 August, just before Baldwin came up. On seeing the smoke rising from the destroyed castle, Baldwin withdrew. Templars and others had fought gallantly but were overwhelmed. There was a wholesale execution of the defenders: Saladin felt the need to react ruthlessly to this major challenge to his power and the castle was never rebuilt.

Jacob's Ford did something to efface the damage done by the debacle at Montgisard but still left Saladin facing the long-term problems of military expenses and the drain of manpower in a series of raids which he mounted in the years after 1179. He did not have a united Islam behind him. The settlers abandoned the tradition of aggression which had so often sustained them and followed a defensive policy, relying on the security of their castles and towns, while Saladin ravaged and raided in the hopes of tempting his opponents to battle. An encounter at Forbelet in 1182 was inconclusive and in the same year he failed to take Beirut; movements in 1183 and 1184 were also ineffectual. He could take comfort as Aleppo finally yielded to him in 1183, but Mosul remained recalcitrant. A dramatic episode in the same year saw Reynald of Châtillon constructing ships that could be dismantled, moved and then reassembled to menace Red Sea commerce, one squadron passing down to blockade Aqaba, the other moving to the western bank of the Red Sea and harassing Muslim pilgrims and traders. Reynald's move struck at Saladin's reputation. Was he worthy of his position as the leading force within Islam when its holiest sites were threatened and the leader was preoccupied with manoeuvres against Muslim rivals? As the potential was there to threaten Mecca and Medina, Saladin reacted with fury and counter-attacked, capturing Reynald's men, parading them throughout his realm and finally executing them in public; two were slaughtered like sacrificial animals before a baying public outside Mecca.

Well aware of the faction-fighting and problems of succession in the Crusader States, he made a treaty with Raymond of Tripoli, who had been so alarmed by a possible attack from Guy of Lusignan in Galilee that he allowed free access to Saladin's troops across crusader land in return for a Muslim reinforcement of his garrison at Tiberias – which could fairly be called treasonable. Kerak continued to defy him and under Reynald remained a pressure point on troop and caravan movement between Damascus and Cairo. In 1187 Reynald broke a truce and looted a caravan. The years following 1179 had the effect of leading both the Crusader States and Saladin himself to desire the decisive battle – the settlers to end the drain of men in the varied encounters of the 1180s, Saladin in order to establish himself unequivocally as a true *mujahidin* who would deliver Jerusalem. Events moved fast. When Sibylla's young son Baldwin V died and she mounted her coup, crowning herself and Guy in 1186, Raymond of Tripoli and his party, lying in wait at Nablus, tried one last desperate throw to secure their succession and called on Humphrey of Toron, the husband of Isabella, Sibylla's half-sister, to support them. With a gallant sense of the needs of the kingdom, Humphrey refused to help and promptly paid homage to Sibylla. Guy reigned and held command against Saladin. Mosul accepted the overlordship of Saladin in 1186 and so the scene was set for a final encounter.

In the meantime Saladin had a problem of another kind, concealed from his troops. He had fallen ill in the winter of 1186, so seriously that his death was expected, and he made his will. Imad al-Din believed that the illness was divinely sent to wake him 'from the sleep of forgetfulness'. Despite proclaiming his fidelity to the Quran and his commitment to the *jihad*, in practice Saladin had spent years subduing other Muslim rulers and conquering their cities and strongpoints. Proximity to death changed him. Still weak, in 1187 he emerged from his experience with a more profound commitment in his heart to what he had professed with his lips. He was so much more dangerous.

The Battle of Hattin

Both sides felt the time had come for an encounter. Guy may have been a controversial figure but he was the king and the forces of the kingdom rallied to his summons, giving him one of the most formidable armies the kingdom had ever had: part settlers, infantry and cavalry, and part mercenaries hired with money granted to the Templars by Henry II of England. Castle garrisons were drained to create the host.

In preparation for the showdown Guy led a delegation, including Templars and Hospitallers, to seek reconciliation with Raymond of Tripoli. When Saladin's son al-Afdal raided into Galilee and approached Nazareth, local inhabitants appealed for protection to these military orders, who felt honour-bound to leave the delegation and go to their aid. Outnumbered by a Muslim force some 7,000 strong, they were massacred; only Gerard of Ridefort, Grand Master of the Templars, and three others escaped. In accordance with the previously mentioned treaty, Muslims rode over Raymond's lands carrying their victims' heads on spears. Raymond was horrified at this, did homage to Guy, repudiated the deal with Saladin and expelled the Muslim reinforcements from his garrison at Tiberias. It was thus a united force which faced Saladin.

As he prepared for battle, Saladin cast aside the hesitancies of his earlier career and prepared a plan for luring the Christians to their destruction. In a sudden coup he struck at Raymond of Tripoli's base in Tiberias, capturing the town and leaving Eschiva, Raymond's wife, in the citadel. Eschiva sent to the Frankish army to seek relief. Safe at the massive springs of Sephoria, the greatest in the whole area of Lower Galilee, with a discharge of water adequate for all the needs of men and horses, Guy held councils to decide what to do. The aggressive party, Gerard of Ridefort and Reynald of Châtillon, spoke for advance to confront Saladin and destroy him. A cautious view was put by Raymond of Tripoli and prevailed. A veteran, as Raymond was, understood that, if Saladin did take the citadel, his wife, Eschiva, would be ransomed in the usual way. Advance without adequate water supplies in the July heat stacked the odds against any army. In effect, Raymond pleaded for delay, waiting for Saladin to make a mistake, then pounce; at Sephoria the army could be cut off from the coast, so a possible move could be made to Acre with secure water and supplies and still await an error by Saladin. Guy accepted the decision.

Then in the night Gerard of Ridefort called on Guy to change his mind. Gerard had a long-standing grudge against Raymond of Tripoli, who had wrecked his chance of a rich marriage before he joined the Templars, and he was well aware of Guy's insecurity. As *bailli* to Baldwin the Leper, Guy had been accused of cowardice for standing on the defensive; now he was doing the same, and, Gerard suggested, it was all a plot by Raymond to destroy him. Moreover, as depository for massive sums bequeathed to the Temple by Henry II, he needed to justify the bequest with a decisive attack, and so Guy gave the command and the army moved off before dawn. It was 3 July 1187.*

Saladin prepared for a battle in which water supplies and archery would

---

* Based on B. Z. Kedar 'The Battle of Hattin Revisited', in *The Horns of Hattin* (London, 1992), pp. 190–207, which shows there are too many conflicting sources to allow certainty to any narrative.

be crucial. He laid down massive stocks of arrows, used camels to bring up water in skins, kept access to springs for his army at the Wadi Fididjas and at Hattin and waited with reinforcements based at Kafr Sabt and Lubiya as well. There is little doubt that Guy had intended to bring about a battle in which the enemy could be pinned against higher ground and exposed to the attack of his cavalry, but Guy underestimated the size of his opponent's army, which was so huge that it allowed Saladin to keep substantial forces to block all possible routes Guy might choose to take his army to Tiberias and to leave enough military force to block his line of retreat. Guy moved to Mount Turan, which only had a small spring, and then on to the plateau of Maskana where he and perhaps Raymond of Tripoli as well made a crucial mistake in deciding to camp overnight on 3–4 July, with the aim of resting his army. There was some pooled water by the site, suitable for animals, but still quite insufficient, and any attempt to rest was destroyed as Saladin's men set fire to the scrub which proliferated on this bare terrain. Saladin sent two wings of his army towards Mount Turan to fan out behind Guy and block his retreat. Saladin had also positioned his troops on a line somewhere west of the watershed stretching from Nimrin to Lubiya. On the morning of 4 July Guy's army moved forward again. Saladin, who had blocked the way to the springs of Hattin, gave time for the sun to rise high and increase his enemy's discomfort, then succeeded by relentless archery in breaking the formation of the army. Arrow showers tormented the infantry and induced them to flee to the volcanic promontory of the Horns of Hattin where they took refuge within the walls of the two prehistoric fortresses within the Horns. From the protection of the walls they could fire back at Saladin's men, but no entreaties persuaded them to return to protect the cavalry, still the most devastating force Guy had, and whose charge Saladin feared. In heavy armour they suffered dreadfully from thirst and some horses were killed by arrows. Raymond of Tripoli, Balian of Ibelin and supporting cavalrymen broke through Saladin's lines and made their way to Lake Tiberias. Fighting under Guy, however, still went on into the afternoon of 4 July when the surviving cavalry prepared final desperate charges. Were they aiming to force their way through to Lake Tiberias and water or the Hattin springs, or did they take advice from a cavalryman who had served with the Muslims and charge down to capture Saladin's tent? The latter is likelier. The cavalry at this last stage assembled in the crater between the two horns and made last pushes. Al-Afdal, in his first battle with his father, remembered well his father's fear of these last charges. The battle, Saladin told his son, was not won till they stopped. Only at the final failure did he dismount from his horse, fall on his knees and thank God for victory. Surrender came when the True Cross was taken, a fatal blow to morale. Carried off to Damascus, it was never seen again.

Leading captives were brought before the sultan and Guy, treated with consideration, was given iced julep to drink. When he handed it on to Reynald of Châtillon, Saladin intervened to point out that he had not given him the drink and therefore had not established the duty of hospitality and care towards him, the tradition founded on desert life. Saladin personally beheaded Reynald and sent his head to be paraded in Damascus. Subsequently members of the military orders in their hundreds were offered a choice between conversion to Islam or execution. Most stood firm and were executed by inexperienced Sufis or volunteers: there followed grim, botched beheadings. Turcopoles, Muslims enlisted for pay and viewed as traitors, suffered the same fate. Distinguished captives were assured of their lives. Grand Master Gerard, in return for his freedom and that of ten others, was persuaded to use the Templar vow of obedience and so order his knights to surrender key strongpoints. Guy was used as a bargaining tool to induce Ascalon to surrender. The inhabitants demurred, but as Saladin began his siege and no help came, they surrendered on terms. Thus Ascalon, vital for the uninterrupted channelling of troops and supplies from Egypt, fell to Saladin and the scene was set for an attack on Jerusalem. Saladin allowed the dowager queen and Sibylla to leave Jerusalem, to eliminate a potential rallying point for defenders of the city. The freeing of Guy was delayed until July. Sibylla and her husband were finally reunited at Nablus.

Saladin, who wanted to arrive at Jerusalem to celebrate Muhammad's Night Journey to the city, concluded that Tyre, a highly defensible strongpoint jutting out into the sea, could be left to be captured later. This was a mistake. Surviving aristocrats had taken refuge there, demoralised because of the Hattin disaster and awaiting the inevitable surrender. A stray pilgrim arrived, totally unaware of Hattin and its sequel, and galvanised them all into resistance. This was Conrad of Montferrat, son of William V, marquis of Montferrat of the former Lombard dynasty, long resident in the Holy Land, who had been captured at Hattin; Conrad had sailed from Constantinople to Acre and was puzzled to find Acre in Muslim hands; pretending he had arrived to trade, he used the next favourable wind to sail back to Tyre. Saladin tried to bargain his way into Tyre, presenting the old marquis as a hostage, his freedom to be given in return for surrender. Conrad, a hard man, would have none of this.

Saladin moved on. By siege and parley he had secured Acre and the strongpoints of Gaza, Ascalon and Latrun, which might threaten his rear as he besieged Jerusalem. He commenced action on 20 September. Jerusalem had pitifully few surviving defenders, and mining gave him entry. He planned a massacre to avenge the deaths of Muslims in July 1099 and was only foiled by a leading baron, Balian of Ibelin, whom he had earlier released to travel to Jerusalem to collect his wife and family, with the promise that he would stay for only one night. Balian had lingered, organised defence and then conveyed an effective answer to the threat of massacre – Saladin might attempt to do his worst, but Balian still had enough men and time to kill 5,000 Muslim prisoners in the city and destroy their sacred sites. Saladin stayed his hand. Christians were to be allowed forty days to pay ransoms, 10 dinars for a man, 5 for a woman, 2 for a child. They could take possessions, excluding horses and weapons, and be given safe conduct to places of refuge. The numbers were very great as the city had been crammed with refugees. Some of the poor were accommodated as Balian paid a lump sum for 18,000 to be released and Saladin's brother pleaded for others. There were cases of corruption and scandal: notably Eraclius, the unworthy patriarch, paying a tiny fee for his stores of wealth. Saladin preferred not to intervene. Emirs who had fought with him and scholars who had supported him were generously rewarded. His intimate circle lamented his open-handedness, but it was his style: he rarely kept adequate reserves.

The fate of some Christians was sorrowful: there were still many enslaved, the men to work as labourers on Muslim works, older women and children to serve at the will of others, younger women to be concubines. Pleas of individuals were heard. Christian womenfolk of men who had served at Hattin sought information about them – those made prisoner he released and to those who had lost their men he gave gifts. Saladin was, as in this case, capable of acts of compassion beyond the conventions of the day. The traditional code of conduct in which the true Muslim kept his word, served Saladin well in many of his dealings in his last years. It was not just a political device.

On 1 October the keys to Jerusalem were handed over. It was, as Saladin had hoped, the eve of the annual festival of Muhammad's Night Journey. There followed a tempestuous Islamisation, as the cross was dragged off the apex of the Dome of the Rock to great cries of '*Allahu akbar*' and beaten through the streets. Guards were set to ensure homes were not looted but the sacred vessels of the church were swept away, some shrines and churches were closed and others suffered change of use, as in the case of Melisende's foundation, the church of St Anne, which became a *madrasa*. Byzantines replaced Latin clergy; Armenians and Jews were invited back. The fate of the Church of the Holy Sepulchre was debated: the memory of the caliph Umar, conqueror in 638, was cited and after being closed for three days, the church reopened for Christian worship. Bells were silenced: only the *muezzin* was to be heard and Christian services announced by clappers or cymbals. Churches and a Christian presence remained, albeit a modified one. Saladin's family thoroughly cleansed the Dome of the Rock from the pollution of the polytheists, as they saw the Christians, scrubbing, dowsing with rose-water and using incense. Nur al-Din's *minbar* was installed in the al-Aqsa mosque, the *mihrab* in the wall of the al-Aqsa mosque unblocked and the *khutba*, the Friday prayer, pronounced by Saladin's supporter, the *qadi* of Aleppo.

Mercenary, usurper, warrior against Muslims, Saladin as liberator of Jerusalem gained imperishable renown. The young man, who had learned by heart extracts from the 844 Arabic poems compiled in the ninth-century *Hamasah* of Abu Tammam, had come a long way from his wandering days as a Kurdish mercenary. Then, no doubt, he had occupied his mind reflecting on the ancient pre-Islamic world from which the poems sprang – a simpler world than that of the twelfth century, a desert society where riding skills, heroism in battle, the duty of hospitality to friend or foe, submission to fate, reigned supreme – repeating to himself words in what was, from the time of Muhammad, the language of angels. Now Saladin had himself become a worthy subject for praise and reached a position unthinkable at the start of his long, chequered career.

His feat in cleansing Jerusalem from crusaders' pollution and making it ready for the Last Judgement and the heavenly reward of just Muslims is commemorated in cursive script on gold mosaic in the Dome of the Rock, comparing him to Moses and poignantly citing *sura* 20 on the End of Time, verses often read at Muslim funerals.

Jihad against the Franks came of age in the twelfth century and restored Jerusalem as a Muslim city and pilgrimage centre. Two Turks and a Kurd in their different ways brought this about. There were bogus, opportunistic *jihadis*, true *mujahidin* determined to secure Jerusalem, and a third form of *jihad* which emerged in the course of the century. The last was *jihad* against heresy, which led to the abolition of the Ismaili caliphate at Cairo in 1171, and would have been the achievement dearest to the heart of Nur al-Din.

7

SALADIN AND THE
LIONHEART

Richard the Lionheart took the cross in November 1187, making his vow just as soon as the news of Hattin and the fall of Jerusalem reached the West. As a child of southern France, crusading was part of the air he breathed; the pilgrimage route to Compostela passed the great churches of the region, where pilgrims prayed at the shrines of their saints, recounted stories of atrocities inflicted on Christians by Muslims and talked of holy war against the Muslims of Spain. Warfare beyond the Pyrenees, which had once engaged French aristocrats merely in pursuit of booty, by Richard's time had become a true crusading movement, and St James (Sant'Iago) of Compostela had become the patron of warfare for the cross under vow against the Moors.

The familiar story of Roland's heroic rearguard action against the Basques had been transmuted over time. The Basques had become Muslims and Charlemagne's commander, Roland, a crusader. The episode became the subject of one of the finest and best-known *chansons de geste,* a prime example of epic vernacular literature, its themes widely illustrated in art and architecture. Roland himself lay in a tomb at Blaye on the Gironde river and his horn was reverently preserved in an abbey church at Bordeaux. This would have been familiar to the young Richard, who developed into a practised composer of *chansons.* Its concepts shaped his attitudes. Bertran de Born, a poet from the Limousin, though not always sympathetic to Richard, understood very well the driving force of his life. 'Richard', he said, 'desires honour (*pretz*) more than any man, Christian or infidel. He seeks honour and success so intently that his reputation constantly grows and improves.' Honour was to be earned most of all in battle in the Holy Land, and it was this which impelled him to make his crusading vow in 1187 at the earliest possible moment.

When Richard went to take the cross from the archbishop of Tours in his cathedral, he would have been mindful of his great grandfather Fulk V of Anjou taking his vow as the chosen husband of Queen Melisende. He would have been conscious, too, of the spiritual benefits of going on crusade, of the indulgence for those who by papal decree were granted remission of their sins and delivered from the pains of hell; death on the battlefield opened the gates of heaven to the fallen who became martyrs and Richard was not lacking in belief. By the casual, volatile standards of a princely fighting man of his epoch, he was a devout man, aware of his transgressions. Contemporaries honoured Richard as the first leading aristocrat in the West to take the cross at this juncture.

At the time Richard took the cross, he was in a state of suspicion and hostility towards his father, Henry, count of Anjou and king of England and would no doubt have been aware that, if he had followed correct procedure and asked his father's permission, it would have been refused. When Henry in his court in Normandy heard the news, he shut himself away for several days, so great was his fear for his realms, as crusading would necessarily take Richard away for a very long time and his absence was likely to upset the balance of power within the kingdom of France.

The Hazards of Aquitaine

Fourteen years of marriage to Eleanor of Aquitaine had produced only two daughters, so Louis VII had had his marriage annulled; disconcertingly, Eleanor made a dynastic union with Louis's most powerful vassal and greatest rival, Henry, count of Anjou, eight weeks later. It was a disaster for Louis, compounded when Henry added to his sprawling Angevin Empire both the kingdom of England and the duchy of Normandy by inheritance from his mother, Matilda. Western France was thus in effect lost to Louis. He knew he could do nothing about it and made it into a joke, telling an English chronicler how the king of England 'has men, horses, gold, silk, jewels, fruit, game and everything else. We in France have nothing but bread and wine and gaiety.' It was said 'merrily', the chronicler reported, but the joke was nothing but the truth. Like any medieval alliance, Eleanor's marriage to Henry was one of convenience to a man twelve years her junior, but it was remarkably fertile, issuing in eight children living into adulthood, of whom four were sons.

Relations between Henry and Eleanor soured as Eleanor came to realise that the duchy of Aquitaine, the centre of her life and interests, was in danger of being subordinated to the Anglo-Norman and Angevin interests of her new husband. In a manner unusual in high aristocratic society, and which created shock among English clerical observers, she became actively hostile to Henry and incited her sons against him, plotting rebellion with the complicity of Louis VII. Henry, a skilled and resolute manoeuvrer of immense energy who deployed great revenues and was thus able at will to hire many professional mercenary soldiers, overpowered them all, forced Louis to make a truce, captured Eleanor, supposedly clad in male clothing and caused Richard to accept defeat and in 1174 prostrate himself in homage. Thereafter Richard devoted himself to warfare within Aquitaine against recalcitrant vassals of Henry, ravaging, skirmishing, castle-breaking and honing the military skills which he later deployed against Saladin in the Holy Land. These were shown in his siege of the apparently impregnable castle of Taillebourg on the River Charente in 1179, which revealed his characteristic blend of cool calculation and reckless personal courage in the tradition of Roland. It was the fruit of cunning following a close reconnaissance of his target. This built him an unrivalled reputation in Aquitaine and beyond.

The art of war was Richard's prime interest and occupation, in contrast to his elder brothers, who were in comparison dilettantes. Handsome and eloquent, yet addicted to tournaments, his elder brother was known as the Young King Henry because Henry crowned him king of England to secure the succession, but he lacked Richard's decisiveness in war and diplomacy.

Geoffrey was silver-tongued and a treacherous manoeuvrer rather than a warrior. Chance removed them both from the scene, as the young Henry succumbed to illness in 1183 and Geoffrey was trampled to death in a tournament in 1186. Eleanor remained in close captivity for a year, in effect a hostage for the good behaviour of Richard, who was his mother's favourite son.

Henry never let Eleanor out of his custody, whether close or open. At the end of her life she depicted herself on the walls of a chapel at Chinon going into exile as a captive, riding behind her husband towards England, looking back at her sons, but especially at Richard, to whom she had just given her falcon as a symbol of princely power. In him, pre-eminently the child of Aquitaine, she reposed her greatest hopes. Henry was enmeshed in his lifelong practice of deceiving his rivals. He saw his sons as such and they were constantly offered honours, castles and loot and then had them withdrawn. Richard finally became exasperated.

The sense of honour which had led him to devote himself to Henry's service was affronted when Henry insisted on treating him with deceit. He underestimated Richard's resolute character and sense of honour and, ageing as he was, failed to notice that he had to deal with a new king of France, a formidable opponent. Louis had solved the problem of succession by entering into a third marriage one month after his second wife's death in childbirth. This at last gave him a son. As a student in Paris, Gerald of Wales remembered the clamour of bells, the lighting of candles and the mass of bonfires, making him think the city had caught fire, as the citizens celebrated the birth of Louis's son, who reigned as Philip II and is known to history as Philip Augustus, because 'he enlarged the kingdom'. After his accession in 1180 he showed himself much more ruthless and cunning than Louis had ever been and adept at exploiting the divisions between Henry and his sons. If Richard went on crusade, it was very dangerous to Henry for Philip to stay behind.

Events settled the problem. A groundswell of popular enthusiasm for capturing Jerusalem swept over France. Troubadours and preachers transfixed their hearers with searing images of Christ being hit in the face by an Arab and a mounted Saracen above the Holy Sepulchre, his horse urinating on the sacred site. Henry and Philip at Gisors in Normandy in 1188 were confronted by the stirring preaching of the archbishop of Tyre. In the face of all this Philip felt he had no alternative but to take the cross.

Yet after Gisors there were considerable delays, as Henry still intrigued and Philip was moved by a deep hostility to the Angevins because of an ancient childhood betrothal of Richard to Alice, Philip's sister, who for many years was in Henry's household while disputes recurred over her dowry. Richard never did marry her, having a justified suspicion that she had been deflowered by Henry, but to be reconciled with Philip he professed himself ready to do so. They made peace, and Richard did homage to Philip. A sick man, Henry at his last Christmas court was deserted by many of his strongest supporters and died in July 1189. Richard came once to stand at his father's corpse, then paid him no more reverence but moved at speed to put his stamp on Aquitaine, establishing his own distinctive resolutions of ancient problems of loyalty, then going on to his coronation in England.

The taking of the cross by men who wished to follow him, the granting of money, the selling of offices, the adherence of leaders in society (including his archbishop of Canterbury and Ranulf Glanvill, his justiciar) ready to travel to the Holy Land, all followed easily from the spontaneous zeal for Jerusalem. The crusading movement was smeared yet again by the anti-Semitism that had followed the call ever since the days of Adémar of Chabannes and Raoul Glaber. Jews bringing gifts to the new king at his coronation banquet were set upon and killed; there were pogroms elsewhere and murder and betrayal at York, most poignantly as Jews who escaped their killers fled to the castle. Despairing of holding out, however, some killed themselves while others, believing in the promises that they and their families would be spared if they accepted baptism, came out only to be massacred. On returning to the continent, Richard made necessary appointments to secure his lands. He arranged a dynastic marriage for himself to Berengaria, daughter of King Sancho of Navarre, in order to secure the Pyrenean frontier against hostile moves by a rival, Raymond, count of Toulouse, while Richard crusaded.

At the abbey church of Vézelay, associated with the thunderous power of St Bernard launching the Second Crusade, the two kings made their solemn compact on 4 July 1190, precisely three years after Hattin, agreeing to meet again at the deep-sea port of Messina for their voyage to Outremer. To take whole armies by sea, with all the difficulties of providing so many suitable vessels and allowing for provisions, water and fodder for horses, was without precedent. Philip and Richard brought vital prestige and manpower to reinforce the armed men who had spontaneously gone ahead, together providing a formidable threat to Saladin.

Saladin Prepares for the Coming of the Crusaders

Saladin's position was like that of an amateur chess-player who seeks to remove as many of his opponents' pieces from the chessboard as he possibly can before a Grand Master comes to take over play. He knew that his capture of Jerusalem would inevitably stimulate a major response in the West and the problems of raising money, troops, arms and transport would be bound to delay the arrival of substantial armies, as opposed to small contingents and freelances. So it was, and in the years 1188 to 1190 he took many pieces off the board. He and his brother al-Adil had effectively captured most of the Frankish coastland in the south before the fall of Jerusalem. Then, soon after conquering the Holy City, Saladin had moved to capture Tyre and taken the crucial action of neutralising Conrad of Montferrat. From 25 November onwards he bombarded the garrison with siege engines and pinned Conrad's ships in harbour with galleys from Acre. But Tyre was always a tough nut to crack and Conrad had reinforced its defences. It all went wrong when a surprise early-morning sortie by the Franks from within the harbour knocked out five of the galleys and their crews, leaving too few to sustain the blockade. Saladin's emirs became restive. Sweeping successes after Hattin had made them expect further victories. They knew Saladin's financial weaknesses only too well and suspected that, as money ran out, he would turn to them to finance *jihad*. They wanted to go home. Finally the weather broke. On 1 January 1188 the sultan lifted the siege, released the emirs and went into winter quarters.

So here he failed, but as weather improved in May 1188 he resumed operations, using a small force with a siege train to take as many ports and towns from the Franks in the north as he could within a limited time frame. He needed to keep his own armed men busy and have loot for his supporters, and was aware of the recommendations of Islamic military science for commanders after a major victory – attempt no long sieges, maintain momentum of action, give the impression of an irresistible force, wage war by psychology. The major advantages he had were the absence of any field force that had a good chance of bringing relief to the garrison and his own reputation for sticking to his word when he made a treaty. He took the port of Latakia and besieged or received the surrender of a series of strongpoints within the Principality of Antioch, isolating the great city itself but deciding not to attempt an attack on its formidable perimeter. Sahyun in a remote countryside fifteen miles from Antioch remained a menace so long as its garrison continued and blocked the route from the coast to the Orontes valley. Saladin took it in three days in July 1188, distracting the defendants with a fierce bombardment with mangonels across the ditch while another force broke in at a weak point in the perimeter behind. The garrison then fled to the Byzantine keep and sued for terms. Baha ad-Din related how, as Saladin's men swept in, they ate the food the garrison had cooked for themselves. Saladin decided to settle a truce with Prince Bohemond III of Antioch who handed over Muslim prisoners and promised to surrender in eight months. Beirut had surrendered, so he had gained much of the vital coastline. Tripoli was too well defended, and at Tortosa he had only partial success, destroying its defences and burning the cathedral but being compelled to leave Gerard of Ridefort with his Templars in possession of a tower in the north-west corner of the city.

It was at Tortosa that he made the momentous decision to fulfil his promise made before the fall of Jerusalem to release Guy of Lusignan. He extracted the promise from Guy that he would not bear arms against him and that he would go overseas. Guy had himself absolved from his oath, and joined up with his brother Geoffrey, freshly arrived from the west, together with other cavalrymen and troops from Tripoli which had become a refuge for released Frankish prisoners. He requested entry into Tyre. Conrad was not going to surrender his rich prize to a man who, he believed, had lost all right to call himself king of Jerusalem and to hold command in Outremer. At first refused any chance to join Conrad's force and wait in Tyre for a crusade from the west, Guy nonetheless prevailed, forcing a degree of acceptance from Conrad. He then surprised both Franks and Muslims by leading a force along the coast road, aided by friendly Pisan ships.

Receiving intelligence of this strange and apparently foolhardy move, Saladin, still confident that he could eliminate it at leisure, cautiously shadowed Guy's mini-army and allowed him to take up position in August 1189 outside Acre on a tell, an artificial hillock in the plain, half a mile to the east of the city which had been fortified and garrisoned by the Muslims.

Guy had amassed a sizeable force and then in addition Pisans landed other troops on a beach south of Acre. Guy's men set about harassing the city, while Saladin, with extensive forces spread out around it, was able to attack the besiegers and of course, encourage his own Muslim garrison. One surprise for the Muslims was the coming of ships with supplies and reinforcements: Danish, Flemish, Frisian, German. On 4 October a Christian attack went wrong and was beaten back with heavy losses. Corpses were piled high, and there was every prospect of pestilence, so Saladin withdrew some 7 miles to the south-east to escape contamination. Medical knowledge of the time had no understanding of the origins of disease but was aware of 'miasma' associated with corpses which could kill, and that bodies could contaminate water. This move gave the chance for Saladin's opponents to reinforce their trenches, to build palisades and to make themselves much more dangerous in front of Acre. The scene was set for many months of debilitating warfare in which neither side could win. Whatever the reasons for Saladin's release of Guy, it was a decision he lived to regret.

The Coming of the Third Crusade: Barbarossa's Attack

In 1189 Saladin had news that the Emperor Frederick Barbarossa was to be the leader of the first wave of the great crusader armies to arrive in the Holy Land. In his mid-sixties, Barbarossa was an old man by medieval standards, a veteran fighter who knew conditions in the Near East and had served on the Second Crusade. As a ruler, he stood at the opposite pole from Henry II who alienated his great men by his slippery diplomacy. Despite defeats in Italy, Barbarossa had never lost the trust of his leading aristocrats and brought together an army of high calibre to travel along the traditional landward route through the Byzantine Empire and Anatolia. Isaac II, the Byzantine emperor, a feeble and superstitious holder of the office, consumed by an unfounded fear that Barbarossa's true aim was to destroy him and his empire, imprisoned German envoys and attacked the army. Barbarossa kept his patience but was delayed over the winter and then had to endure attacks by the Seljuq Turks in Anatolia, but still he beat them off and won plunder. His host was not seriously disturbed. Then disaster struck. Travelling across Anatolia in the oppressive heat of July 1190, Barbarossa took a dip in the cold water of the River Saleph and suffered a fatal stroke. Without him his army disintegrated. Although his son Frederick persevered, he brought only a remnant army to reinforce the Franks in the Holy Land.

It was an immense relief to Saladin who had lacked troops even to act as a tripwire to Barbarossa advancing through the north as he still had too many men scattered in small numbers besieging major inland fortresses in the south. The sites were so formidable that, if garrisons were determined, only starvation could force surrender and a minimum number of soldiers was needed to hold the enemy down and stop supplies getting through. Now worries over that were over.

More important still was the effect on Muslim morale. The sudden end of the chief enemy was widely hailed as a sign of God's favour: striking Barbarossa down was a sign of divine approval for Saladin and his army and this mattered greatly for Saladin's inner security. He never wholly lost his sense of inferiority as one of the despised Kurds and as a man who, try as he might, could not assume the attributes of the Arab aristocracy.

The Third Crusade Resumes: Richard and Philip at Messina

On 23 September 1190, at the head of a great armada of ships, Richard made a ceremonial entry by galley into the port of Messina, standing on a specially constructed platform in a manner befitting a great prince, heading a flotilla adorned with varied painted and colourful shields while the trumpets pealed out and the townsmen hurried forward to catch sight of the great man. By contrast, Philip had slipped in unheralded a week earlier with his much smaller fleet and throughout the proceedings felt like a shabby poor relation. Late in 1189 the premature death of the Norman William II, ruler of both southern Italy and the fertile island of Sicily, created a dynastic crisis necessarily affecting Richard as his sister Joan's marriage to William had been childless. There was a general agreement that this vital kingdom should not pass to the Germans and so an amicable general conspiracy to cut them out made the heir Tancred of Lecce, an illegitimate cousin of William II. Tancred at first refused to give up Joan's dower, which was very considerable and needed for crusade finance, and kept her in confinement. Richard dealt firmly with him, released Joan and the dower and obtained for the crusade a legacy from William II, finally soothing Tancred by the munificent gift of Excalibur, the sword of King Arthur.

Richard headed an armada of 219 ships with an immense complement of warriors and sailors, possibly as many as 7,000, which imposed intolerable strains on food supplies. Food riots were a consequence, made more acute by hostility between Richard's men and the Greek population in Messina who took a sharp dislike to each other. Attempts at peacemaking foundered. In a skilled operation, Richard's men swiftly took the city, looting, destroying galleys and planting his banners on the walls, implying total rights for Richard over the citizens and defences. Affronted, Philip insisted that the banners be replaced by neutral ones, those of the Templars or Hospitallers, and Richard felt obliged to do this but nevertheless took hostages and, with a notable absence of tact, built a tower dominating Messina called Mategriffon, 'Kill Greeks'. Tensions were not assuaged but the kings contrived to work together to impose a price freeze on provisions and create a crusade discipline, while Richard in the long wait for sailing weather eased problems by largesse.

The natural procedure for a leading crusader would have been to visit the pope, but Richard chose to ignore him and instead went to consult the aged Cistercian abbot in Calabria, Joachim of Fiore, with a reputation for prophecy. He had heard of Joachim's compelling painted image of the seven-headed dragon, based on Revelation, Chapter 13, the heads representing all the great persecutors of the Church from Nero onwards to the sixth figure, the ravaging head of Saladin. Richard put the question: would he, Richard, slay this deadly dragon's head? Joachim believed he would and urged him to persevere, confident in God's providence. In Joachim's scheme the killing of Saladin by Richard and the return of Christians to the Holy Land would be followed by a period of peace and joy in which old problems simply disappeared – an age of saints. But this joyful interlude was but a prelude for the last and greatest persecution of all, in which the seventh head, that of Antichrist, would wreak terrible havoc for three and a half years before the End of Time and Christ's return. The seventh dragon's head, the greatest of all persecutors, had, Joachim believed, already been born in Rome. Could this future Antichrist be the current pope, Richard asked? Joachim was not going to follow Richard in this speculation, characteristic of the anticlericalism of leading princes. Higher churchmen came from the same class as they did and, while respecting their doctrinal role and their guardianship of relics which played so vital a role in contemporary religion, they were determined to ensure that they did not overstep the line and usurp power that properly belonged to the secular arm. Richard made his own spiritual preparation. Going on crusade was his act of devotion to God and he was well aware that the rightful preliminary was to confess sins. In a ceremony in the presence of bishops and archbishops, Richard stripped naked, confessed his sins and publicly scourged himself.

Escorted to Sicily by the indomitable Eleanor, then given into the protection of Richard's sister Joan, Berengaria of Navarre travelled on with him towards the Holy Land. The armada travelled via Crete and Rhodes before reaching Cyprus, making sure that ships took on fresh water frequently for men and, above all, horses. Richard's last act before making landfall at Acre was to capture Cyprus, ruled by a former Byzantine governor, Isaac Comnenus, who had usurped the island from the emperor in Constantinople and was therefore vulnerable. Manifestly underestimating Richard, he believed he could block the beach at Limassol and use his superiority in numbers to sweep Richard back into the sea. Nothing of the kind occurred. Richard stealthily landed war-horses by night, well fed and watered, and made a sudden charge, leading from the front as he always did. His clerk Hugh de la Mare was aghast at the risk, only to be told, 'Sir clerk, you get on with your writing. Forget about fighting and leave the chivalry to us, by God and Saint Mary.' Richard overwhelmed Isaac's camp, captured rich booty and soon took the allegiance of major landholders. Guy of Lusignan landed to seek Richard's support in his continuing battle for power against Conrad of Montferrat – Richard agreed, endowing him handsomely and using Guy and his men to complete the capture of Cyprus. Isaac tried to buy time by fleeing to the mountains but, intimidated by the capture of his daughter, surrendered. Richard promised that he would not clap him in irons and kept his promise, but with sardonic humour put him in silver chains instead. It was an acquisition of great strategic importance with rich, well-cultivated lands, prosperous after centuries of Byzantine rule. With Joan and Berengaria anchored off Limassol and the island safe, Richard and Berengaria were married in the chapel there, and on the following day she was crowned queen of England by a Norman bishop. At last, after sinking a massive Muslim sailing ship laden with equipment and troops for the relief of the Acre garrison, Richard arrived at the muddy battlefield of Acre in June 1191.

The Siege of Acre

The armies of Saladin, the crusader force and the Muslim garrison had been battling since August 1189, fed spasmodically by newly arrived crusaders or by Muslims responding to the call of *jihad*, fighting bitter but inconclusive battles that relapsed into stalemate, beset by rain, cold, hunger and illness. There was a heavy death toll – Sibylla, the archbishop of Canterbury and Ranulf Glanvill all succumbed to disease. Loss of life was much greater than in the fast-moving encounters with Saladin (aside, that is, from the catastrophe at Hattin) and had much in common with the trench warfare of the First World War, as damp and mud brought on trench foot and both sides bombarded each other periodically with siege engines and arrows. Saladin received pitifully little help from the caliph.

For all his great wealth, he sent two loads of *naphtha*, spear hafts and a letter of credit authorising borrowing, in effect resourcing no more than a day's fighting. It was all the more galling as, since his conversion, Saladin had felt it his duty to support a caliph's rulings.

Both sides were near exhaustion. Philip with the French contingent arrived first, amid both hymns and tears, which checked crusader desertions. He used siege engines to step up the pressure. Richard's reputation preceded his arrival with massive resources in June and morale rose with the unpacking of Mategriffon, sections of the wooden structure that had intimidated the men of Messina and been carried on his ships for use in the bombardment of Acre. But he succumbed to arnaldia, a disease that had some likeness to sheep mange, well known to English farmers, and was forced to lie behind silk curtains on his bed, albeit still on the battlefield, from where he directed operations. He followed the crusader convention, which laid down that a crusader who fell ill must stay at a battle site and, if need be, die there as part of his devotion to the cause and not be tempted to draw off for better medical care. Philip chose to depart for France on 31 July: he too had suffered illness and felt the need to deal with new problems in his kingdom and recover his health. He lost prestige by his decision. It left Richard in undisputed command.

Blockade in the end brought defeat to the Acre garrison, the crusader forces having a naval superiority that squeezed the defenders. Terms were agreed on 12 July, sparing the garrison in return for payment, handing over prisoners and surrendering the city and Muslim ships. Richard and Philip before his departure had arbitrarily divided spoils, cutting out rewards for fighters who had suffered from the long battles which had led to the victory of July and creating anger in the camp. Saladin delayed settlement: whether through a wish to fatigue his opponents and simply win time or through an oriental bargaining tradition is not clear. Some 2,700 prisoners were held hostage for the fulfilment of the treaty and on 20 August Richard, determined to cut delay and march towards Jerusalem, brought them out and massacred them in sight of Saladin. This act created great bitterness and led Saladin to counter with torture and killing of prisoners as campaigning continued. Richard seems not to have been easy in his mind about it, as he wrote a letter in defence of his conduct to the abbot of Clairvaux. Did he fly into a rage in this case? Or had he coolly concluded that it was impossible safely to hold the prisoners and yet march on?

Travelling some 5 miles per day, there followed an 80-mile march along the coastal road from Acre to Jaffa to recapture the littoral, while making full use of crusader naval power. Ships kept station, providing food and protection while infantry marched on either side of a column of cavalrymen, acting as a carapace for the vital Frankish weapon – their battle winner – the armed and fully trained war-charger. Saladin travelled in parallel. His light horses darted in and out, firing arrows; the tunics of the crusade infantry after such attacks could look like pincushions. To relieve the pressure, the columns alternated, one column enduring the enemy assault and the other marching between the cavalry and baggage train and the sea. Some died from heatstroke. There were casualties in a series of minor clashes. The high purpose of the crusade was recalled by chants at night of the prayer 'Sacrum sepulchrum, adiuva nos', 'Holy Sepulchre, help us'. The military orders had a key role to play in maintaining discipline, the Templars forming the vanguard and the Hospitallers warding off attacks on the most vulnerable point, the rearguard. Horses as well as men suffered.

Saladin held the initiative. He was free to attack and retreat at will but had to avoid pitched battle, in which his archers and light cavalry could be mowed down by the classic Frankish cavalry charge. Only once in the long march, as Richard's army emerged from the forest of Arsuf, near Jaffa, did Saladin come close to suffering the kind of defeat which could have destroyed him. His forces advanced too far and the Frankish cavalry, in such close packed conditions, succeeded in inflicting heavy casualties. Saladin had a shock. Thereafter he kept his distance and shadowed Richard as he marched on.

At Jaffa, the traditional point of disembarkation of warriors and pilgrims for Jerusalem, the army halted. The failure at Acre and the loss of so many soldiers had depressed Saladin and his emirs. Fighting for ports and stopping Richard was a natural instinct, but fear of fresh disasters led Saladin and some of his entourage to prefer destruction as the safer alternative. So Saladin destroyed the defences of Jaffa before the arrival of Richard's army, which in consequence was forced to camp outside in the orchards while men set to work rebuilding them – Jaffa mattered too much for the future. Meanwhile Saladin went on to destroy the defences at Ascalon, to the dismay of the inhabitants, and put obstacles in the way of a possible march by the surviving crusaders on Jerusalem.

Diplomacy for Richard was spasmodically an accompaniment to military action. Before the battle at Arsuf, Richard had attended an interview with Saladin's brother al-Adil. Both sides could find negotiations profitable, Saladin hoping to delay or distract the onward movement of a well-led and equipped army, Richard probing for possible advantages that came to nothing. In October he launched a scheme for an apparently outrageous marriage between al-Adil and his sister Joan: the two would together hold the kingdom and bring peace. It was a tactical move in order to gain up-to-date knowledge of his opponent's thinking; Joan was indignant and did not understand her brother's half-joking diplomacy as messages went up and down and Richard got what he really wanted: valuable intelligence about the Muslim camp.

Marriage and the kingship of Jerusalem continued to play a background role. Intrigue brought a marriage between Conrad of Montferrat and Isabella, the half-sister of Sibylla by Amalric's second marriage to Maria Comnena. Maria and others had bullied Isabella into abandoning her happy marriage to Humphrey IV of Toron and marrying the grizzled veteran in November 1190. Sibylla's death from disease at Acre had removed Guy's claim and after the Conrad marriage Richard recognised he could no longer support Guy and generously made arrangements to compensate him with the lordship of the island of Cyprus. Conrad came to a dramatic end, stabbed to death by two Assassins in the street at Tyre in April 1192, and the luckless Isabella was married off to another candidate, Henry of Champagne.

In late 1192 both sides were becoming exhausted. Saladin, who had had to release some emirs from their military service over winter, wanted to play for time and used the ambition of Conrad of Montferrat to split his opponents, while Richard was pulled to and fro between genuine crusading passion for Jerusalem, his wish to keep his own troops and survivors from Philip's expedition on board and his strategic sense, which understood that any attempt on Jerusalem was highly risky because of the lasting problem of water supply and the lack of troops to keep a worthwhile garrison once the crusaders had fulfilled their vow and gone home. His powers of cool assessment led him to accept that Egypt held the key to Palestine, and only taking power there would preserve the Holy City in the Christian interest in the long term. He negotiated with Italian cities to back an Egyptian foray and refortified Ascalon but time and money ran out and reports of the actions of John against him in England forced him to think of leaving. However, in November 1191 he moved troops forward, preparing supply lines, repairing strongpoints and enduring both Muslim harassment and relentless rains. The prospect of at last attacking Jerusalem sustained morale and the decision in January 1192 to turn back dashed the hopes of many and there were desertions. Saladin's army was still depleted and he could do little. Then, in May, French great men and their troops, with some of Richard's own men swept on into another move up to Jerusalem, carrying Richard willy-nilly with them. They paused in June at Bait Nuba, 12 miles from the city, and during this time Richard captured a major caravan passing over the Negev desert. But the hazards of occupation after the crusaders had gone home remained, and in addition Saladin had poisoned wells, and so on 4 July Richard gave the order to withdraw. Yet Saladin had been taken by surprise by Richard's second move towards the city and it is just possible that a sudden coup then could have succeeded.

Here Richard had missed an opportunity. Inevitably in Near East conditions his intelligence about the Muslim side was inferior to theirs about him, his followers and rivals. No one informed him of Saladin's acute dilemma in June 1192, at the time of the second projected attack as the army halted at Bait Nuba: what would happen if Richard bottled him up in the city? He was well aware how much the drive to *jihad* rested on his personality. If he withdrew from the city and Richard took it, would he then be discredited? If he were captured, on the other hand, his life's work would be ruined. He spent a night praying in the al-Aqsa mosque with tears and groans, then withdrew in early July. The moment for Richard had been lost.

Richard had moved to Acre to prepare for his departure from the Holy Land when, late in the same month, Saladin descended to snatch Jaffa: in two moves Richard first pushed out the Muslim occupiers, then defended ground taken against wave after wave of cavalry far outnumbering him and intent on recovering town and harbour. He ordered his men to plant their spears in the ground and take post behind, protected by their shields. Archers were placed between each pair of spearmen. As Muslim cavalry charged, they were first disconcerted by pegs in the ground, then baulked by the line of spears. As they faded back, archers stepped forward to fire volleys, retreating before the next cavalry charge, only to shower the cavalry again as they turned around. Finally, as the Muslim horsemen crumbled, Richard, with only fifteen horses, led a charge to push Saladin's force away and end the attacks. It is widely accepted that it was the greatest feat of arms of his career and recognised by Saladin with the gift of a charger. But alone, it could not redress the Frankish weakness at his campaign's end. In September he made a treaty, accepting a three-year truce, the right of the settlers to hold Acre and Tyre and the land between – but also, a grievous clause, that the fortifications at Ascalon were to be demolished, undoing much painful and expensive work.

After much resolute soldiering Richard had recovered a coastal state, with a secure all-weather port at Acre and a town and harbour at Jaffa. He had made an agreement for pilgrims to continue to go peacefully to Jerusalem, which, for all it weaknesses, lasted for another century. His galley left Acre on the morning of 9 October; he promised to return and prayed to God for time to do so.

Forced ashore on his way home, Richard paid a penalty for his high-handed treatment of Leopold, Duke of Austria, to whom he had denied a share in booty after the port of Acre fell, despite the Duke's endeavours during the siege. Trying to reach friendly territory, Richard was captured on the lands of Leopold, who sold him to his enemy, Emperor Henry VI, who in turn exacted an immense ransom before releasing him. Richard returned to England with the intention of settling his realm and returning to Jerusalem. It was not to be. Characteristically admiring a display of courage by a solitary crossbowman shooting at him from the ramparts of the castle at Châlus, near Limoges, while improvising his own defence with a frying pan as a shield, Richard lowered his own shield to applaud his enemy. He raised it again a fraction too late and the bolt embedded itself in his left shoulder; the wound turned septic, causing his death on the evening of 6 April 1199. Saladin had died at dawn on 4 March 1193 in his beloved Damascus, worn out by the campaign. In effect Richard had killed him, albeit not in the manner predicted by Joachim of Fiore.

The immense sums of money raised for his crusading and ransoming were not begrudged in England and in his time the crusading impulse remained as vital as ever it had been and Richard himself a devoted crusader. Richard was deeply flawed, a passionate fighter who could not bear to be beaten even in games and tournaments, subject to fits of rage and capable of spite and partisanship, but a regular attender at Mass, accustomed to walk about the royal chapel telling his clerks to sing with greater vigour. His Latin was distinctly shaky but he was a master of contemporary vernacular poetry. He had a sincere devotion to the Cistercians and he respected holiness and courage in St Hugh of Lincoln, but took substantial revenues from the Church. The passion for Jerusalem was a central point in his life and he did much to transform the way in which Western Christendom viewed it. The naval dimension became important and Cyprus an asset for the future. The First Crusade had never understood how many Muslims there were in the world and succeeded because they did not know how great the obstacles were to their taking the city. Richard's strategic sense and his long professional campaigning began to change that view. His authority gave new impetus to the search for land in Egypt and was reinforced by the insistence of Saladin on the renewed dismantling of Ascalon's defences in the final treaty. It was clear just how much the sultan feared an attack on that front. The Western world was becoming aware that the obstacles against capturing and retaining Jerusalem on its waterless plateau were so great that only calling on the source of power in Egypt or providing some kind of counterweight would suffice to win it and keep it. Richard was one of the great commanders of history:

it is not always realised what a massive jump was needed from commanding limited forces, skirmishing and castle-breaking in Aquitaine to taking charge of over 200 vessels and a composite force of French royal, German and Anglo-Norman infantry, cavalry and sailors and other ships from varied quarters. If so eminent a commander felt he could not take the city, a new approach was needed.

Saladin had risen from obscurity by a mixture of great resolution, diplomacy, tireless manoeuvring and well-chosen acts of violence. He became a master of propaganda: Imad al-Din was sending 70 letters per day to the Muslim world announcing the capture of Jerusalem. As a commander he was not in the same class as Richard and tended to be very cautious. His successes were marked by reasoned tenacity, although there are exceptions. Hattin and the trap he set for the Franks were masterly and he showed great skill in capturing Burzey in the Nusairi mountains in the northern campaign of 1188.

Arabic poetry remained a support throughout his life. It was a curiosity of the contest with Richard that both were masters of the vernacular poetry of their day: Saladin with his memorisation of the *Hamasah* of Abu Tammam and Richard with his mastery of the *chansons de geste*. Love of poetry brought Saladin into contact with Usama ibn Munqidh, born in 1095 in the castle of Shaizar, who lived till 1188 and so received the news of Saladin's capture of Jerusalem.

Usama was a poet of the highest calibre in a genre which has resonances in twentieth-century Welsh poetry, with ancient, rigid structures demanding great ingenuity in its practitioners. He was a prolific author and it is natural to surmise that composition formed a compensation for many years of exile from his beloved home, to which he never managed to return. He eked out a living by giving diplomatic and military services to an incongruous series of masters, proceedings which led him into doubtful acts. He was not a political success but he was a great poet, and Saladin valued contact with him. Saladin gave Usama a pension, consulted him on military tactics and made one of his sons an emir to serve in his army. This would have been gall to Usama. A perceptive modern observer with knowledge of the whole output of Usama has spotted a strange deficiency.

He never ever uses the word *jihad*. He had the blend of qualities befitting an Arab gentleman: mastery of hunting and fighting, deep knowledge of the animal world, a capacity for Arabic poetry and a skill in rhetoric. He had *adab*, and Saladin did not. For all the friendly contact between the two men, it is clear that Usama belonged to a different world, alien from the uncompromising pursuit of *jihad* and the 'thick-fingered Turks and Kurds' who pressed on with plans to destroy the Christian presence and expel them utterly.

To his faithful supporters, his secretary and his chronicler Saladin was a hero. Some historians, aware of the traditions of Islamic praise-poetry and the tendency for highly partisan history-writing, have been suspicious of their accounts of their master – but surely unjustly. They were aware of his deficiencies in administration, his weakness for his family members and his careless financing, and were ready to criticise him but still manifestly held him in high regard. He could surely not have dissimulated when in such long contact with them. He was in essence a conventional man, not a broad thinker, a partisan of the Shafite law school rather than an ecumenical Sunni. Still, he changed the Muslim world.

Between 1188 and 1192 crusade came close to defeating *jihad* for Jerusalem. The capture of Jerusalem unleashed a massive response in the West. Barbarossa led many war-experienced aristocrats and war-chargers and by July 1188 was bringing his army with its battle-winning powers down to Syria. Saladin had too few troops to hold the line against him and in his campaigning in 1188 had been unable to eliminate the County of Tripoli and its port facilities. King Philip and Richard the Lionheart transported their men by sea and Richard's armada accommodated a major force of war-chargers, kept fed and watered for action. The unexpected deaths of Barbarossa and William II changed this, forcing both Philip and Richard to remain in Sicily in 1190 and miss the sailing season. An earlier arrival in the Holy Land, and one that followed swiftly on the appearance on the scene of Barbarossa, would have presented a grave threat to Saladin. His campaigning in the Frankish north between May and September 1188 was a model of skill and speed, but he became distracted in 1189. His generosity in releasing captives and his habitual caution as a general allowed Guy and his men to build up a formidable attacking position before the walls of Acre. Although it led to the deaths of many crusaders, the siege lost Saladin many men and put strains on his emirs.

By capturing Cyprus, Richard added a naval dimension to crusading. His tenacious campaigning in 1191–2, although it did not recover Jerusalem, created a coastal kingdom based on Acre with continued opportunities for the coming of crusaders and pilgrims by sea. Damaged by his deficiencies in administration and failure to keep financial reserves, Saladin nevertheless hung on with grim determination. For good or ill, he had become the one vital figure for sustaining *jihad*, and he continued to avoid being killed or captured, however often defeated, and being drawn into the decisive battle which Richard desired. He saw off Richard, who needed to return home but who in turn left a legacy to all future crusaders – the belief that to recapture Jerusalem it was vital to win power in Egypt or find some counterweight to Muslims outside Jerusalem itself. Saladin indeed had won, but could fairly have expressed the same sentiment as the Duke of Wellington after Waterloo, that it was a damned close-run thing.

8

STRATEGIC CRUSADES
AND THE COMING OF
THE MONGOLS

Jerusalem and the Ayyubids

Saladin's legacy crumbled. He had intended to leave behind him a confederacy with territories apportioned between his sons and his brother, al-Adil. But in the years after Saladin's death in 1193 the coldly calculating al-Adil through his superior diplomatic talents, outmanoeuvred the sons and by 1202 had made himself master of the Ayyubid world. Even he lacked security though, for he had enemies among the Seljuqs, in Mesopotamia, in Christian Georgia and in Armenia and troops under his command in Syria and Palestine were widely dispersed. As sultan in 1202, he set about apportioning territory: to his son al-Muazzam, Damascus, and to his son al-Kamil, Cairo. This resulted in weak successor states eyeing each other with suspicion and jockeying for supporters and strongpoints, none being in a sufficiently secure position to carry Saladin's *jihad* to its conclusion and expel the surviving Franks from the Holy Land.

Titular kings of Jerusalem continued but resided in Acre, the true capital of the Crusader States, the monarchy descending through Isabella, Queen Sibylla's half-sister. In 1197 her third husband, the capable warrior Henry of Champagne, fell to his death from the balcony of his palace in Acre with his pet dwarf beside him. She then married Aimery of Lusignan, ruler of Cyprus and brother to the deceased king, Guy, thus uniting Cyprus to the Holy Land in a way advantageous to both. By 1205 both were dead.

Maria, Isabella's daughter by her marriage to Conrad of Montferrat, succeeded and John of Ibelin, lord of Beirut and holder of wide territories in the Holy Land, became regent. Maria came of age unmarried, as she was not a great catch because the state was now so frail. Finally John of Brienne, a Champagne knight of good crusading lineage but limited resources, came forward and they married in 1210. After two years Maria died, having given her husband a daughter, known as Isabella II or Yolande. Thus John continued as king of Jerusalem, regent to an infant daughter.

The Ayyubids, with their economic links to the remnant kingdom, had another reason for not wishing to pursue *jihad*. Acre boomed, benefiting from a growing Western interest in exotic luxuries from the Levant. A network of commercial links from the city as far as the well-established colonies of Western merchants in Alexandria benefited from intimate connections between Muslim-occupied lands which supplied raw materials to craftsmen and fuelled the traditional spice trade between East and West. Peaceful contacts brought advantages in dues to Ayyubids, especially al-Adil, and favoured stability.

The weakness of the Ayyubids coincided with a lack of confidence within the crusading movement. A new breed of crusader not only looked for some means of unlocking the riches of the Nile delta and altering the balance within the Muslim world so that Jerusalem would fall back easily into Christian hands but also sought some counterweight to Muslim power. Mission could make little progress where Muslims were concerned, but it might draw other hitherto neutral powers onto the Christian side. Novel approaches to crusading coincided with the reign of Innocent III, who in a dynamic pontificate developed the indulgence system further to raise money for the Jerusalem crusade and gave new impetus to non-Jerusalem crusading. They were heady days.

The Fourth Crusade: The Role of Dandolo

Over ninety and blind, Doge Dandolo of Venice led with shrewd tenacity and crusading zeal what was, in effect, an independent republic and the greatest sea power in the medieval world. 'In the name of God and profit' was a phrase commonplace on the flyleaves of merchants' account books, and for Venice and Dandolo it meant just what it said. The Venetians had been at pains to obtain papal permission to continue trade with Muslim powers; they had their churches and their patron, St Mark – they were crusaders in their own way. Not only did Dandolo build war galleys but, at great financial risk, he also commissioned a set of fifty expensive specialist galleys, *huissiers*, craft for transporting horses, with stern-posts for embarking and disembarking on beaches where there were no port facilities. Sailing ships with massive holds were more efficient, but the horses had to be disembarked in ports using smaller boats. Dandolo wanted to take the master-arm of Western crusading – the war-charger – combine it with trained men, navigate the Nile delta, fight off local resistance and at a stroke capture the lucrative spice trade of Egypt. The wealth and power of Egypt would recover Jerusalem and they would also give Venice an overwhelming advantage over rival Italian cities. It met the prevailing sentiment that Egypt held the key to Jerusalem; it needed only capable Western cavalrymen to ride the chargers and demolish Muslim resistance. The way forward for Venice was made easier as the other great Italian powers, Pisa and Genoa, were in conflict.

Innocent III (1198–1216), the youngest of the cardinals in the conclave, succeeded at the age of thirty-seven, having lived through the shock of Saladin's capture of Jerusalem and the disappointment in the West at the failure of both Barbarossa and the Lionheart to recapture the city. He adapted and renewed the crusading indulgence to attract more men, allowing non-combatants to take the cross and commute their vows for money. So much did he care for the crusade to Jerusalem that he first thought he would lead it himself. But step by step, disaster unfolded. He was unable to check the disputes over land and rights within the kingdom of France; death removed the Lionheart; Philip was no crusader; the emperor Henry VI, who had imprisoned the Lionheart, had collected a fighting force, co-ordinating his action with Jerusalem, before Innocent came on the scene but he had died of malaria. The pope would have wanted leadership from crowned heads, with their financial and regal powers, but could not get them; instead, it was his powerful actions and preaching over the winter of 1199–1200 which provided the nucleus of a new crusade.

Penitential seasons were the setting for well-connected, rich aristocrats with impressive crusading pedigrees and devoted vassals. On Advent Sunday in November 1199 a tournament at Ecry-sur-Aisne, near Rheims, brought together the counts of Blois and Champagne for a solemn, collective taking of the cross and a similar action was staged at Bruges by the wealthy Baldwin, count of Flanders, in February 1200 on Ash Wednesday. Six plenipotentiaries went from the aristocratic group to negotiate terms with Venice. The landward route was discredited. It was natural for them to look to Venice as the master-transporter for horses and men and to aim for Egypt; the difficulty, they felt, was that the appeal would be blunted if they revealed their true objective, as the magic of the name Jerusalem still reigned supreme for rank-and-file volunteers and they dared not disregard it. The agreement to sail for Egypt was kept secret by the leaders: it was the beginning of troubles.

The Treaty with Venice and the First Diversion

The fatal contract with Venice, which was agreed in April 1201 in a solemn gathering at St Mark's and accepted by plenipotentiaries for the committee of aristocrats, made massive demands on both parties – the crusader leaders and the doge himself. Dandolo would provide fodder for the horses, food for the men, sailing ships and the stern-post vessels, the *huissiers* for horses plus war galleys, while on their side the Christian leaders agreed that they would provide astonishing numbers of troops: 800 knights and their horses, 9,000 squires and 20,000 foot soldiers. Departure was scheduled for June 1202 – an ideal month, allowing for arrival in early July, before the Nile began to flood and while prevailing winds were favourable. Crusader commanders suffered from the perennial optimism affecting medieval leaders. Their numbers for the appointed rendezvous fell short of those scheduled in the treaty and thereafter they were in the hands of the doge: he expected and needed half-shares in conquest and booty to meet the massive shipbuilding outlay for his galleys and specialist vessels. Moreover, while he built his *huissiers*, ordinary commercial activity was much hindered and he sought compensation. The official prospectus claiming that the crusade was setting out for Jerusalem had awkward consequences. Crusaders using their own resources arrived in the Holy Land and asked the titular king of Jerusalem if they could fulfil their vows and attack Muslims. King Aimery, who had made a truce with the Ayyubids, did not want them.

Venice's expedition deliberately avoided Outremer. While other crusaders, paying their own way, took advantage of the transport arrangements, still numbers and payments were not enough and the doge insisted they should meet the shortfall with an attack on Zara, a port on the Dalmatian coast which had previously escaped the control of Venice and put itself under the protection of the king of Hungary who had taken the crusader vow. Encamped on the Lido facing the lagoon of Venice, the crusaders were at a major disadvantage as food ran low. On the one side, there was a passionate wish to do something for the cause, having made sacrifices to go crusading; on the other side stood the doge's demand, but as the king was a declared crusader, an attack on Zara meant a grievous breach of crusading law. Some crusaders, unable to accept the rightfulness of the attack, left for the Holy Land. Struggles with consciences continued. Peter Capuano, the legate representing papal authority, had some qualities as a crusade preacher but very few as a moral adviser. He told crusaders that the pope would prefer to overlook whatever was unbefitting in order to avoid the great crusading pilgrimage disintegrating. It was not so, and Innocent wrote a letter of condemnation after the capture of Zara.

The Turn to Constantinople

Pragmatism ruled. The season over, the true objective of Egypt could be resumed in the following year. Venetian naval power had a free hand, for Byzantine naval forces had fallen prey to rot and worm in their vessels and galley oarsmen were no longer being trained. It was part of a massive decline in Byzantine power after Manuel's defeat by the Seljuq Turks in 1176 at Myriokephalon and his death four years later. Factions struggled in

1. The Church of the Holy Sepulchre was reconsecrated by the patriarch on the fiftieth anniversary of its capture by the First Crusade, its interior skillfully adapted to allow the passage of a multitude of pilgrims through the Holy Places.

2. The *Kaba* (cube), the 'House of God', stands 43 feet (13m) high, constructed of granite masonry, covered with the *kiswa*, a black silk cloth embroidered with Quranic texts in silver and gold thread, replaced annually. The black stone (see Glossary) to be kissed or acknowledged by the pilgrims is not visible.

3. In a Persian text Ali, veiled and with his holiness symbolised by flames behind his head, is shown on the roof of the *Kaba* destroying the pagan idols in 630, aiding Muhammad below him, similarly veiled and with symbolic flames.

4. Before Muhammad achieved his overwhelming authority he had to face stone-throwing enemies and is here being defended by Abu Bakr.

5. The winged horse Buraq with a woman's face in the Night Journey of the Prophet transports Muhammad, accompanied by winged and crowned angels, upwards from the Temple Mount in Jerusalem to the highest heaven.

6. The Dome of the Rock, a masterpiece of architecture and decoration, was the work of Caliph Abd al-Malik, asserting Muslim power over Herod's Temple Mount and dominating the Church of the Holy Sepulchre below.

7. The *minbar* of Nur al-Din was designed by him to be placed at the end of the Temple Mount in the al-Aqsa mosque once it had been recaptured from the Christians.

8. The Janissaries, seen here on ceremonial parade, were the vital supporting arm of the Ottoman sultans. They were recruited from Christian parents in the Balkans and were as skilled with weapons as the Mamluks had been.

9. The Hospitallers as a naval power are on display in front of their port at Rhodes in Caoursin's history of the great siege of 1480. Pierre d'Aubusson, the Grand Master and the hero of the defence, is shown on the right of the carack while the Ottoman Prince Zizim on the left, feasts and drinks wines as a pensioner of the order.

10. King Louis Philippe of France distorted history to support colonialism.

11. Kaiser Wilhelm II sought Germany's economic advantage by declaring himself the friend of all Muslims.

12. Sultan Abdul-Hamid II of Turkey accused Western powers of being nothing but crusaders.

13. The statue of Saladin in Damascus was commissioned by the late President Assad of Syria to honour Saladin's triumph.

14. A statue now in the Belval Abbey church in Lorraine shows the cloth cross crusaders pinned on their clothing. Is the crusader's wife welcoming him home or saying farewell?

15. The fragment of a tower in the Turkish township of Antakya, recalling the array of towers in the massive Byzantine fortifications of Antioch which delayed the crusaders in 1097–8.

Ramped entry hidden
from view of the camera

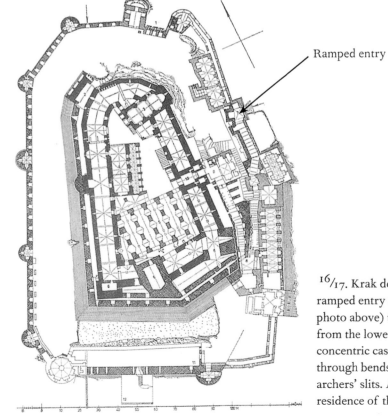

Ramped entry

16/17. Krak des Chevaliers: the
ramped entry (on the far side of the
photo above) took cavalrymen up
from the lower level of the
concentric castle to the upper level
through bends dominated by
archers' slits. At the top lay the
residence of the Grand Master.

18. The 'bone in the throat of the Muslims', the castle and garrison town of Kerak sat on a rocky spur ten miles east of the Dead Sea and dominated the vital Muslim caravan route. Starvation alone forced its surrender after eight months of blockade in 1188.

19. The ascent to the great mound, once the powerhouse of Nur al-Din at Aleppo, was built by an Ayyubid governor, culminating in a guardhouse to check the entry of enemies.

20. Twists and turns within the guardhouse exposed intruders to the defenders' weapons of spear and bow. The Ayyubids built a new mosque but retained the mosque of Abraham, used by Nur al-Din for his private devotions.

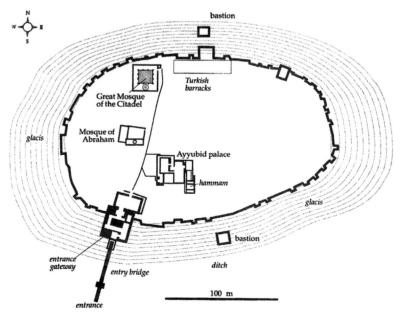

bastion

Turkish barracks

Great Mosque of the Citadel

Mosque of Abraham

glacis

Ayyubid palace

hammam

glacis

bastion

entrance gateway

entry bridge

ditch

100 m

entrance

21. In rugged terrain the castle and town of Masyaf in Syria was an Assassin strongpoint. Saladin, seeking vengeance for two attempts on his life, besieged it in 1176 but failed to capture it.

22. At the Horns of Hattin, Saladin's masterly plan to destroy the Christian army reached its triumphant climax in July 1187. It turned out to be the end of Christian hopes of taking the Holy Land.

23. Sahyun is a striking example of the lengths to which settler-barons were willing to go to create near-impregnable castles. Forced labour dug out a massive ditch in the rock, leaving a needle to support a drawbridge. T.E. Lawrence in 1909 called it 'the most sensational thing in castle-building I have seen'. Nevertheless it fell to Saladin in three days in the aftermath of Hattin in July 1188.

24. A pillar of another kind with intricately interwoven stonework, the Ablution Tower on the Haram was the work of the Mamluk Sultan Qaitbay in the late fifteenth century. It reminds the observer that warriors who superseded Saladin's heirs were capable of sponsoring fine artistic work.

25. The Latin cathedral dedicated to St Antony built at Famagusta in Cyprus between 1308 and 1315 was a sign of continued Western vitality in the Mediterranean after the fall of Acre. It fell into ruin after the Turks took the island in 1571.

26. Bodrum on the mainland of Anatolia, now Turkey, with a port and fortifications, was a high point in the expansion of the Hospitallers. The engraved slab, dating from 1472, has the arms of the Grand Master, supported by the Virgin and St Peter with the arms of the Captain of the castle below.

27. King Ibn Saud

28. Sultan Atrash

29. Sir Mark Sykes

30. François Georges-Picot

Twentieth-century personalities, Western and Eastern. Sykes and Picot were determined that the interests of Britain and France should prevail, whatever the fate of Ottoman lands. Sultan Atrash and King Ibn Saud were inspired by Islamic movements from the past – Atrash leading Druze fighters to defeat the French regular army during the mandate, Ibn Saud rescuing Wahhabism on the brink of death under his father.

the Empire; fragmentation began and the breakaway provinces defied the emperor. Murder and intrigue wrecked central authority. Isaac Angelus, deposed and blinded by his brother, who reigned as Alexius III, had a son, Alexius Angelus, who escaped from prison, sought help against the usurpation and rescue for his father. Envoys for Alexius Angelus arrived at Zara and made a tempting offer to the encamped crusaders to facilitate their objective, Egypt. Angelus's case appealed to the crusaders' sense of honour and the will, so fundamental to medieval aristocracy, of ensuring rightful succession. If they would back him to become true emperor, as he deserved, he would accept obedience to Rome, the schism between two great Christian powers would be ended, just as Gregory VII had wanted, and he would both endow the crusaders with rewards from Byzantine resources and use his forces to make the attack on Egypt which they sought. They succumbed to the offer. It was just the massive addition to the crusading cause of the troops and money needed to turn the key in the lock and recover Jerusalem.

So the crusaders moved to Constantinople. But Prince Alexius carried no weight and was jeered by crowds. His uncle and rival Alexius III rallied the populace, feeding their patriotism with memories of Western pressures on Byzantium, but made a major tactical error when he retreated behind the walls of the city rather than take on the attackers. Disgraced, he took money and fled. Desperate to fend off attackers, leaders in the city brought out the blinded and mentally frail Isaac Angelus and made Prince Alexius co-emperor, to reign as Alexius IV. For a time this worked. Alexius toured round, while Isaac worked hard melting precious objects from church treasuries to satisfy the crusaders' desire for payment. But then skirmishes created tension, a Western attack on a mosque led to brawls and the burning of parts of the city; fireships were launched by the defenders against Venetian vessels and skilfully parried; in a coup, Murzuphlus, 'heavy eyebrows', from a rival family made himself emperor and killed Alexius IV. Isaac died.

The end was a violent crusader takeover, much looting, especially of relics, and on the ruins of the old empire the setting up of a Latin successor state, frail and needing support from the West. Nothing more was heard of the move to Egypt. Murzuphlus was captured and killed. Innocent, at first excited by the prospect of healing the schism, was saddened as he learned of the true sequence of events. The crusade was run by a joint-stock enterprise of mainly French nobles, unlucky in the early death of Theobald of Champagne, who had displayed the charismatic qualities of an outstanding leader. No one was quite able to take his place, and the whole crusade was blighted by the absence of a crowned head with the ability to command the resources of a whole state and discipline troops in a tricky maritime expedition. Innocent's ebullience and subtle lawyer's skills, valuable for church reform, were not well suited to remote control of often confused crusaders. This left a bitter memory for Greek churchmen.

The Fifth Crusade: Preparations

The pope was not going to give up on his grand design. He picked out what he saw as the reasons for the failures of 1203–4: the lack of sufficient finance, the dominance of one maritime power, the lack of a determined, well-equipped single commander and the sins of the West. Patiently from 1213 he set out to remedy these weaknesses for a new expedition. His Bulls *Quia maior* and *Ad liberandam* set the conditions for obtaining the crusade indulgence for the rest of the Middle Ages. Central control was key: there was to be one authority to direct preparations in each country and a legate on the ground with sole authority to deploy finances. Finally the crusade was to go to Egypt, without equivocation or secrecy.

How intimately Innocent linked the progress of reform with crusading victory, averting the wrath of God against the sins of the believers, is shown at the culmination of his rule by the Fourth Lateran Council, of 1216. The greatest council of the Middle Ages, this brought together 400 bishops, 800 abbots and high ecclesiastics, agreeing a series of reforming, pastoral and doctrinal measures.

The elective monarchy of the Empire was in dispute between two rival dynasties: the Welf and the Hohenstaufen. The pope steered a course between them, eventually accepting as rightful emperor the Hohenstaufen child Frederick II, commended to the pope's care by his mother, Constance, the widow of Henry VI, before her own death. Contrary to some historians' views, it was with Innocent's blessing that Frederick, when he came of age in 1212, took the cross at Aachen, redolent of the memory of Charlemagne and his soldiers' anti-Muslim campaigning. He was to be the single commander with prestige and finance needed for a new expedition.

Reform to bring God's blessing, the raising of more money (especially the direct taxation of the clergy), the setting into action of distinguished preachers for the 'negotium Jesu Christi', the business of Jesus Christ, new procedures for action against unsatisfactory bishops, the recognition of grassroots evangelical movements looking to the early Church for inspiration – all were inextricably intermeshed in the pope's mind. 'We ought to fight', he wrote, 'not so much with physical arms as with spiritual ones.' The great Council was also a launching point for the crusade itself. Part of the inspiration for the First Crusade had sprung from the institution of the Peace of God: Innocent now instituted a general Peace and in his legate to France, Robert de Courçon, chose a man with skills to persuade quarrelling great men to accept the Peace while still salvaging their honour. Tournaments were forbidden for three years. Finally a date was set in 1217 for the launch of the crusade, and Brindisi in Frederick's territory of south Italy, was selected as a mustering point.

Assessment of the achievement of a pope so consumed with the passion for the Sepulchre has to be nuanced for, while he had no doubt about the primacy of Jerusalem, he was uninhibited in encouragement or passive acceptance of non-Jerusalem crusades. He accepted the Baltic crusades against the Slav inhabitants, the indigenous Prussians. The Albigensian crusade which he declared against Cathar heretics and those who supported them in Languedoc gave the crusading indulgence for forty days service to all who enlisted – largely northern Frenchmen. He miscalculated, attributing the murder of an aggressive papal legate to the Count of Toulouse. He exaggerated, probably unjustly, the degree of complicity of the aristocracy of the south in the heresy and lost control of the civil war stirred up by the crusading army under the elder Simon de Montfort. In Spain a defeat by the Moors of the king of Castile at Alarcos in 1195, coming so soon after the fall of Jerusalem in 1187 to Saladin, began to shake the popes in Rome and the hierarchy in Spain. Innocent did well by staging a fasting procession in Rome dedicated to the victory over the Moors in Spain and putting pressure via legates and archbishops on kings, which quenched their quarrels long enough for them to present a united front in 1212 at the battle of Las Navas de Tolosa, where a fortunate quirk on the battlefield produced an overwhelming victory which, coupled with their own dissensions, shattered Muslim power in the peninsula.

Another action, however, was in the long run a damaging one. In 1199 Innocent had become nervous about the intentions of the marshal of Henry VI acting on behalf of the Hohenstaufen and, he had believed, manipulating the position he then occupied as regent to the child Frederick. The perennial fear of popes of being squeezed in Rome and the papal states by a hostile power holding lands and authority in Germany, northern Italy and Sicily, had come into his mind. It led him to select a papal champion against the marshal and to declare that the crusading indulgence would be given to those who fought against this marshal because his actions were 'impeding' the crusade for the Sepulchre. Use of Muslim troops by the marshal gave a little colour to this declaration but it was in truth a political crusade: that is, one which in reality only served the secular landed interests of the papacy and not the Jerusalem crusade. 'Impeding' was a dangerous doctrine. All fizzled out. The marshal and the papal champion died, the threat faded, but a precedent had been set.

Innocent never lived to see his work fulfilled. Choosing to act as the supreme authority for preaching the cross in Italy, in April 1216 he exhorted a gathering in Orvieto, where he stood after his sermon in torrential rain, personally pinning crosses on the clothing of all men who made their vows. He caught a chill; fever followed; he died the following July in Perugia.

The papacy as Innocent left would hardly have been recognised by Gregory VII and Urban II as it had become an institution with a formidable bureaucracy, an underpinning of canon law and a wealthy body, due largely to the rise of crusading taxes. But for all his great talents, his quick and subtle mind and his shrewd assessment of character, the task Innocent had set for his papacy as the decisive reforming power in the Church was too much and failures outran successes, above all in his relationship with rulers. Perhaps Innocent's most important legacies for the future were his recognition of St Francis and his poor companions, who sought with a Rule largely based on Scriptural texts a fierce poverty that seemed beyond men's powers and the support which he gave to the Castilian St Dominic and his Order of Preachers. Both orders of friars were to become major forces.

The Expeditions and Their Fate

Two expeditions set out: one to the Holy Land in 1217–18 and the other in 1218–21 to Damietta in the Nile delta. Both were preceded by the strange affair of the Children's Crusade of 1212, in which adolescent apprentices – the *pueri* of the sources, not in fact children – joined with poor peasants, girls and old men in processions for the sake of the Holy Land. They got nowhere but they were an indication of dissatisfaction with the progress of the warrior class in the task of taking Jerusalem. Forces under the duke of Austria and the king of Hungary led troops in a foray to Acre, encouraged by John of Brienne, titular king of Jerusalem, who supported crusading to Egypt. He believed Acre could be in danger of a sudden coup by Muslims in the light of al-Muazzam's fortification of Mount Tabor in western Galilee in 1213, menacing Acre and insulting the Christians by occupying one of their most sacred sites. The troops brought supplies to mitigate the famine which had devastated Syria and boosted the morale of the garrison. The military orders played a decisive role as castle builders, suppliers of dedicated and trained fighters and bankers. Innocent enlarged their numbers by recognising the Teutonic Knights, who originated caring for sick and wounded Germans at the siege of Acre during the Third Crusade. But the military orders quarrelled and the baronage became a byword for anarchy and instability. The arrival of crusaders in the autumn of 1217 had its achievements and revealed in a flash the weakness of al-Adil, the leading Ayyubid, for as the crusaders marched over the Jordan and around the Sea of Galilee he kept out of the way, knowing his forces were too widely dispersed to make it feasible to challenge the incomers. All co-operated in re-fortifying important staging posts on the route to the south at Athlit (Château Pèlerin), near Haifa and Caesarea. Athlit was a Templar fortress and the strengthening of the castle with the latest concentric wall plan and ingenious use of water defences to obviate mining made it a masterwork. It was never conquered.

For the Egyptian target, the crusaders selected Damietta, at a key point on the eastern estuary of the Nile. It was a very well-fortified strongpoint with a massive population which, once conquered, would give a safe baseline for the advance to Cairo some 100 miles south on the Nile, while riverlanes to Damietta provided easy access for vessels. It was a great wilderness of sandbanks, islands, marshes and mud, home territory to part of the audience of the preacher Oliver of Paderborn, the true hero of the Damietta crusade. He talked to Frisians, men from the Netherlands and South Germans, some of whom were used to marshlands and canals and were at home in the desolate landscapes of the delta.

Army and ships arrived in May 1218. There followed a long sequence of fighting over access to river passages towards Cairo, shifting camp sites, scuttling vessels in the river channel by Muslims and fresh dredging of an old canal by the Christians. A peak of achievement was reached in August 1218, when Oliver of Paderborn, by devising a floating fortress with a drawbridge, enabled troops to seize the Chain Tower, a garrisoned strongpoint on an island controlling iron chains which prevented vessels sailing towards Cairo. It was followed by the death of al-Adil, and more insecurity in the Ayyubid camp as al-Kamil succeeded his father as sultan. He knew how the crusaders had suffered through winter storms and scurvy caused by food shortages but was nervous of rivals in the fluid Ayyubid world. To ensure the Christians left Egypt, he presented a deal in the summer of 1219 in effect exchanging Jerusalem for Damietta and offered to pay tribute in return for keeping the castles of Kerak and Montréal, vital to safeguard his route to Damascus.

It was during this period that the crusaders received unexpected visitors: St Francis of Assisi and one of his fellow friars who had come to preach to them, fulfilling the commands of Jesus in the Sending of the Seventy, who dispatched His followers to go two by two to preach the coming of the kingdom of God with a greeting of peace. They were to be defenceless 'as lambs among wolves'. Francis exhorted the crusaders in words available to all, 'virtues and vices, heaven and hell'. There would have been no dogmatic preaching, which was reserved to the priesthood. With his companion and dressed in a dusty habit with holes in it, the sign of his vocation to live as the poorest did, he crossed the lines to preach to the Muslims as well. The risks were great. Brothers who had preached in Morocco had been executed. 'Now I have five true brothers' was Francis's reply when he heard the news. They were brought to the open-minded al-Kamil who, unusually for a caliph, was happy to sit in on a debate between Muslims and the Coptic patriarch at a later date. He received Francis courteously, heard him speak and had him escorted back to the Christian side, seeing Francis as a Christian version of the poor, wandering Sufis he knew.

It is hard to find a precedent for Francis's actions: it was a parable for peace, forming part of a strand in thinking about Muslims and crusades that grew in importance in the thirteenth century. Force was not wholly abandoned. Francis, himself once a knight errant in his romantic youth, referred to Roland and his doomed expedition as 'martyrs' and, during his stay in the crusader camp, tried to deter Spanish fighters from an attack, not because he thought it was wrong but because, with his gift of prophecy, he knew it would fail. Nonetheless, Francis's simple action for peace was potent, a forerunner of new and more humane personal attitudes to the Muslim enemy.

As a preacher, James of Vitry had affinities with Francis for he shared a calling to an evangelical, spiritual way of life, inspired by a women's movement led by Marie of Oignies – who as a woman could not preach, but who found in James a man who could. James toured preaching with a relic of Marie, a finger bone, round his neck and on the strength of his preaching power was invited to be bishop of Acre. He was an unyielding supporter of the rightfulness of crusading, but he had preached in the Holy Land to the Saracens, and begged at Damietta to receive Muslim orphans, who were normally sold into slavery and baptised them before finding volunteers to instruct and nurture them. It was another straw in the wind – for mission to convert Muslims and not simply attack them. James nonetheless was not a Francis to risk martyrdom: he only preached to the Saracens when he had an armed escort.

The offer of al-Kamil to exchange Jerusalem for Damietta divided the crusaders. Their expedition was a joint enterprise of individuals and contingents making communal decisions leading to the same problems which had beset the Fourth Crusade. John of Brienne, as titular king and resourceful warrior, soon emerged as leader. But he had been thought of only as a stopgap till the arrival of Emperor Frederick II with imperial troops, who would dramatically alter the balance of power. He wanted to accept terms, but the legate expected the arrival of the emperor and was not prepared to do so. Frederick would have wished to take the lead but was preoccupied with the pressing needs of his own territories. While the crusader leaders debated, al-Muazzam made his own deductions from the weak state of the Ayyubids, and over 1219–20 dismantled fortifications at Jerusalem, Mount Tabor and other strongpoints, believing that the Christian forces would be less likely to intervene if their targets were unprotected and correspondingly unattractive. After al-Kamil made a last attempt to relieve Damietta, the city, its inhabitants and garrison destroyed by starvation, fell easily, and al-Kamil retreated up the Nile. There was panic in Cairo. Rich booty was collected in Damietta, and again John of Brienne and the legate clashed. Who was to hold the city? John of Brienne claimed it as the king's; the legate claimed it for the Church. The army remained immobile for an extraordinary length of time, staying in Damietta debating their next move. John of Brienne went off on other ventures while the legate was beguiled by omens and prophecies passed off as ancient texts, leading him to wait for help from mysterious Christian forces in Africa and India. In Africa, the existence of a Prester John drew its origins from the ancient Christian Coptic kingdom of Abyssinia, also called Ethiopia; his citing of a 'King David of the Indies' had some basis in the belief that Thomas the Apostle had in early days brought Christianity to India. Preaching from such apocryphal works consoled the crusaders. The legate was the more able to hold sway because of the extensive finances he had at his disposal and he continued to reject all offers made by al-Kamil.

Then, in a swirl of hopes and fears, under the leadership of the legate the crusade moved towards its disastrous end in 1221. The efficiency of the maritime delivery of warriors and the equally efficient departure mechanism had created much coming-and-going, with crusaders serving for a year to earn the indulgence and then departing, so that the crusade lacked the *esprit de corps* which came about when warriors served and suffered together continuously, overriding national and personal rivalries. The remaining forces went towards Cairo with their ships and with troops on the eastern bank to attack al-Kamil's fortified camp at Mansura. In vain John of Brienne urged withdrawal, fearing they would be caught by the flood waters of the Nile; the legate refused to listen. The waters rose; other Muslim forces blocked landward retreat to Damietta; troops seized wine supplies and got drunk. They had to sue for peace, and al-Kamil allowed the remnants to leave without ransom. Prisoners were exchanged, and there was a truce for eight years. Al-Kamil had got what he wanted, the departure of hostile troops from Egypt. The crusade had suffered ignominy.

The Coming of the Mongols and the Revival of Jihad

Patterns of power, especially in the Islamic world, underwent profound change under the pressure of these attacks. Behind the story of King David of the Indies lay a muddled awareness of a movement in the depths of Inner Asia under a chieftain of the Mongols (also known as Tartars). A ferocious warrior of the steppes was born about 1167. His father had been murdered by a lesser chieftain when the boy was twelve, leaving him to provide for his mother and younger siblings. Steeled in adversity, he avenged his father and assembled a coalition of tribes, abandoning minor squabbling over pasture rights and sporadic raiding to aim at world power. As he came to maturity, he reigned as Ghengiz Khan ('universal ruler') till 1227, assembling under his dictatorship an extraordinary number of horsemen, exploiting the traditional nomad skill and their austerity of life, also benefiting from a period of more humid climate, revealed recently in a study of tree-rings in the Siberian forests in Ghengiz's epoch, which enriched normally barren pastures and allowed for the breeding of stronger and more resilient mounts.

The nomads drew in and terrified peoples from the forests and oases in the steppeland, conquered part of China and under Ghengiz set new standards of terror, demanding total submission to the will of the ruler. A vast host of cavalry unencumbered by infantry or equipment had overwhelming mobility and a will to total massacre of all opponents. Human life meant nothing and the stacks of corpses and utter destruction intimidated all victims and led to surrender after surrender. Patterns of power, especially in the Islamic world, underwent profound change under the pressure of these attacks. Booty from the capture of cities was immense and could be used to hire miners to bring down walls and, with tight discipline, to reward warriors or employ Chinese siege engineers. Alternatively, captives were forced into labour.

Attitudes to this new power in the world fluctuated from indifference to both the Mongols and their Muslim victims to interest in Mongols as a counterweight to Islam or, finally, to seeing them as, at least in part, Christians who would emerge to help the West. Those who began to investigate the Mongol-dominated territories did indeed discover Christians who had long existed unknown to the West, but they were Nestorians who held dissident views on the Incarnation and had been condemned as heretics. Ambassadors or missionaries seeking souls to convert misunderstood Mongol attitudes. They tolerated men of religion and gave them privileges but were primarily interested in the present life, in obtaining longevity for their leaders, better health and fertility for themselves or their stock. They insisted on the observance of their ancient folk religion and its taboos but were generally pluralists, unwilling to accept any religion exclusively, and thus hopes of conversion to Christianity were dashed.

Long-term, the effect of the Mongol irruption into history was negative for the crusading cause. True, it devastated some Islamic lands, and, as we shall see, a Mongol army ended the Baghdad caliphate; on the other hand, resistance to the Mongol menace brought into play a great force within Islam, the Mamluks, who destroyed Outremer.

The Sixth Crusade

One strange episode brought Jerusalem back to the Christians by a diplomatic manoeuvre of the Emperor Frederick II, who entered Jerusalem in 1229. Frederick's interest in the Holy Land was a sincere one; his original taking of the cross in Innocent's lifetime was no flash in the pan and its renewal in 1220 on the occasion of his crowning by Pope Honorius III was a continuation of his long-standing commitment. It was reinforced by association with King John of Jerusalem who had come to believe that his position as titular king would be strengthened by association with Hohenstaufen imperial power and accepted a marriage for his daughter Isabella II to Frederick II, which took place in 1225.

John had imagined that he would continue as regent for his daughter but was outsmarted by Frederick who swept aside his residual claim and thereby created an enemy for life. Isabella died after childbirth, leaving a son, Conrad. John of Brienne campaigned against Frederick in south Italy, while Frederick for his part made extensive grants, assembled troops and made ready for action. For the sake of papal support in Germany and Italy he bound himself by treaty to a time frame for setting out but in 1227 was afflicted by disease. Close to death, he returned to port only to find himself excommunicated for having failed to go on crusade as he had solemnly promised. In Gregory IX he was faced with a more steely personality than Honorius III. Gregory's real anxiety lay in the perennial papal fear of being stifled in Rome by an imperial power. Frederick's advantage lay in his inheritance from his Norman predecessors and their international culture in Sicily; he spoke Arabic, had a representative to deal with the sultan al-Kamil and was more in touch than any Western ruler with the realities of diplomatic and military relationships among the Ayyubids, who, he knew, were very much more concerned with their own Islamic world than with Jerusalem and the Holy Land. Al-Kamil, wishing to ward off competition from his rival al-Muazzam and an implicit threat of freebooting Khwarazmian Turks, resurrected his earlier projected deal with the Fifth Crusade leadership.

The death of al-Muazzam in 1227 relieved al-Kamil of one source of anxiety. When Frederick finally sailed to Acre in June 1228, preceded by his marshal, Richard Filangieri, he used his force as a bargaining counter to threaten al-Kamil and press him to surrender Jerusalem. There were local military achievements, despite the tensions which inevitably came with the local baronage and which sprang directly from Frederick's over-bearing personality, revealed when he clashed with John of Ibelin, acting as a regent for the young King Henry I in Cyprus. Nevertheless, after hard bargaining Frederick succeeded and in the Treaty of Jaffa of February 1229 recovered the Holy Places of Jerusalem, Bethlehem and Nazareth with corridors for access from the coast, as well as some other strongpoints and a ten-year truce. Jerusalem lay unfortified; Muslims were left free access to their own Holy Places in the Dome of the Rock and the al-Aqsa mosque, but their resident population was evacuated and the Christians left free to occupy the city. The Frankish occupiers of Jerusalem set about rebuilding the fortifications. On 18 March 1229 Frederick crowned himself in the Church of the Holy Sepulchre. Nervous of his position under attack in south Italy, aware of interdict and excommunication and foiled by a united force of Templars, the patriarch and Italian merchants against his attempt to impose his *bailli* to rule over the Holy Land in the imperial interest. He slipped away from Acre on 1 May, his entourage pelted with tripe and offal by butchers. He never returned, but did not forget Jerusalem and left instructions for the cross that he had taken in 1215 to be affixed to the covering of his corpse in the great porphyry tomb which still stands in the cathedral of Palermo. A great reader, he picked up Joachimite doctrines and came to believe that he was destined to return as emperor and retake Jerusalem as a final move preceding the Second Coming of Christ. Despite temporary reconciliation, from 1239 under Gregory IX and his aggressive successor, Innocent IV, papacy and empire moved into a long conflict, ending in Frederick's death in 1250.

The Seventh Crusade

The last of the great strategic crusades, the apogee of French commitment to the recovery of Jerusalem led by King Louis IX, was better prepared than any other. It was sparked off by two catastrophic events, the fall of

Jerusalem to the Khwarazmian Turks, who desecrated the Sepulchre, and the overwhelming defeat of the field army of the surviving Crusader States. The response to these events of Louis IX was that of a king who represented all the conventional virtues of his age and who commanded for that reason the total loyalty of his fighting men.

Two minor crusades in 1239–41 led independently by Theobald of Champagne of the well-known crusading dynasty and Richard of Cornwall, brother to Henry III of England, demonstrated that the time for individual, small-scale crusading was definitively at an end. Although Theobald made a treaty recovering Galilee and Richard built a new fortress at the citadel of Ascalon, these achievements were in reality dependent on the will of scions of the crumbling Ayyubid dynasty whose decisions could be predicted by neither the incoming Westerners nor the resident fighting men of Acre and its territories. Jerusalem was occupied over the winter of 1239–40 by al-Nasir of Kerak whose command of the fortress left him dominant in southern Palestine; he withdrew peacefully. The walls had been rebuilt but the insecurity of the city attracted too few Christians. Minor expeditions such as those of 1239–41 did not meet the vital need for a garrison of warriors willing to reside permanently. Richard Filangieri lived on at Tyre representing the imperial interests; Templars and Hospitallers adopted different strategic objectives; the Italian cities had their own preoccupations.

Meanwhile al-Salih Ayyub emerged as the master of Egypt and the holder of a winning military force, his own slave soldiers, the Mamluks. In 1244 he launched a two-pronged attack, letting loose the bandit Khwarazmian Turks, remnants of a kingdom in Persia and Iraq demolished by the Mongols, assured of pay and land to maraud into the Holy Land while he moved from Egypt with his Mamluks. Christian residents fled from Jerusalem to the coast and were massacred on the way by Muslims: few survived. The fighting garrison staying on in Jerusalem were too few to man the defences, despite the restored walls, and were overwhelmed by the Khwarazmians. The invaders demolished the tombs of the kings, destroying memorials to Godfrey of Bouillon and Baldwin the Conqueror; priests saying Mass in the church of the Holy Sepulchre were beheaded. The Sepulchre was set on fire. An exclusively Muslim occupation was established and lasted until 1917.

The warriors of the coast determined to fight and allied with Ayyubids opposed to al-Salih Ayyub. With characteristic Latin impetuosity they rejected advice to hold back and thus allow the undisciplined Khwarazmians to break up and leave the field; instead, they attacked al-Salih Ayyub's combined Khwarazmian and Egyptian army and were almost annihilated in battle at La Forbie, near Gaza, in 1244.

In December 1244 Louis took the cross when recovering from a near-death experience as a result of a fever. His mother and advisers wished him to abandon his plan because of the dangers from baronial revolts threatening the kingdom during a long absence and from conflict with Henry III of England. He insisted. His mother, Blanche of Castile, had ruled as regent after the early death of his father and his own succession at the age of twelve. He was thirty when he took the cross and there is little doubt that an undeclared factor in his decision to go crusading was the will to escape from this capable but overpowering woman. He took with him his devoted wife and three brothers.

No crusade had ever been planned so carefully, with awareness of past sources of failure. Louis's grandfather Philip Augustus had built up the resources of the kingdom and he drew on immense sums to finance the expedition. Both in France and in England crusade levies were the basis for heavy taxation. He took a minor shallow-water base at Aigues-Mortes in the Rhône delta and at great expense turned it into a deep-water port, with a mole to embark horses and a pure water supply so as to be independent of existing cities which would strike bargains for the use of their facilities. He assembled a large fleet with entry points in vessels below the water line caulked over on embarkation to contain his horses, and he put together an enormous mass of provisions, stockpiled in advance on Cyprus. The preparation of his kingdom spiritually to earn God's favour included the unprecedented appointment of *enquêteurs-reformateurs,* peripatetic inquirers into abuses of tax collectors. Military preparations were also meticulous, restricting his crusaders to capable professionals and including a strong body of crossbowmen.

There was never any doubt of his total control of events and preparations and the first day in Egypt began with a resounding success when he chose, like the Fifth Crusade, to assault Damietta. Louis and his cavalry took the risk of crossing the Nile to the shore in front of the city: horsemen facing them were deterred by lances thrust into the ground and slithered on the rough terrain. Panic and rumour of the death of their sultan led to evacuation of the city. On 5 June, Louis had achieved more in a day than the Fifth Crusade had in seventeen months. He was not prepared for this and delayed. The enemy harassed his army, and they became restive. Only in November, when Alphonse of Poitiers arrived with more troops, did he begin to move up the Nile but he fell foul of the intricacies of the waterways. The attempt to build a causeway over the Ashmun Tannah delayed his army as his men were subjected to a storm of missiles. Ships' timbers were used to build high wooden walls manned by his crossbowmen, but attrition of his troops continued.

Stage by stage Louis's army diminished, for he had to leave a garrison at Damietta; skirmishing during his earlier delay there lost more, and the battle over the waterway led to heavy casualties. Then, bribing a Bedouin revealed the existence of a ford higher up the Ashmun Tannah and enabled a cavalry force to wade across and move directly to attack the enemy outside Mansura. Louis's brother Robert of Artois charged but over-excited at surprising the enemy, he took his own men, the Templars and William Longsword, the cousin of Henry III and leader of an English contingent, on into Mansura. It was fatal.

Since the Fifth Crusade Mansura had become much more than a camp. It was an inhabited town, with winding narrow streets and houses and there the enemy's Mamluks held all the advantages, showering the cavalry with missiles from all sides as well as from the tops of the houses. Nearly all were lost. Louis was in trouble. Relying on his naval superiority, he had sustained supplies to his army with ships travelling up the Nile but had left no caches of provisions for his men as they marched up the bank. Neatly, the enemy had segments of boats carried overland on the backs of camels, and, once reassembled, these blocked the way upstream for Louis's ships. Under blockade the army began to starve and were afflicted by dysentery and scurvy. Against heavy counterattack, they held out in an improvised defensive camp in front of Mansura, then retreated across the river successfully. Louis's courage and tenacity never left him, but the situation deteriorated and became a struggle for survival as the enemy killed wholesale, sparing only those who looked wealthy enough to be ransomed. Retreat degenerated into massacre. A pontoon bridge, left unguarded after the crusaders had retreated, enabled their enemies to cross and harass the fleeing Christian remnants. Earlier there had been opportunity to strike a bargain, offering total withdrawal in return for ceding of Jerusalem to the Christians. That moment had passed. Thus, when Louis was ready to seek terms, he had no bargaining power left and in consequence found that his enemies made impossible conditions. He no longer had a viable force and early in April 1250 was forced to surrender.

Left in Damietta, Louis's queen, Margaret of Provence, played a heroic role, using the money she had for her ransom to induce the Pisan and Genoese merchants to stay with their vessels, allowing for escape and provisioning. She made the elderly knight who guarded her promise to kill her if she was in danger of being taken by the Muslims. An immense ransom was demanded for Louis, imprisoned in harsh circumstances and threatened with torture.

Jean de Joinville, close to the king, observed all his actions and recalled them at the end of his life. He never wavered in his appreciation of the king's heroic virtue, his prayers, his austerities and his flagellation. But he tells us also that Louis had no gifts as a battlefield commander. His personal courage commended him to his followers, just as the Lionheart's had done, but he lacked Richard's skill as a diplomat and his ability to anticipate the enemy's moves. He could not read a battle; above all, he lacked the sense of timing crucial in war.

Damietta was surrendered, Alphonse of Poitiers was kept as hostage, much money handed over and an agreement made for the balance to be paid. Margaret and Louis sailed to Acre where Louis, in hopes of recovering some advantage from Muslim disunities and in the determination to wait until his imprisoned followers could be ransomed, stayed on, acting as the effectual king of Jerusalem and refortifying Acre, Jaffa, Caesarea and Sidon. The scriptorium at Acre produced one of its finest works, the Arsenal Bible, as a compliment to Louis's faithful queen, giving emphasis in illustration to the decisive female figures in Scripture, such as Esther and Sisera.

The Flemish friar William of Rubruck reported to Louis during this stay in the Holy Land on the council of religious representatives he had attended at Karakorum, in the presence of the Great Khan. Louis had long been disillusioned about any prospects of enlisting Mongols as allies after an earlier emissary of his, taking with him a tent with Christian symbols as a present for the Khan, had received a dusty answer. William's report, however, added to the West's knowledge, providing accurate information on Mongol practices and attitudes and making the first mention of Buddhists, hitherto wholly unknown in the West.

Despite Conrad being the titular but absolute king of Jerusalem since the death of his father, the emperor, in 1250, barons welcomed Louis as the *de facto* king. Louis had no thought of formally taking the role. Disregarding Innocent IV's dramatic decree of deposing Frederick II, he had always treated Frederick as emperor and so accepted Conrad as his lawful successor.

Even though his army was now small, Louis hoped to wring concessions from the Ayyubids, profiting from their dissensions and the threat of allying his army to one faction or another. That failed as the contestants perceived the danger to Islam. He stayed on, in fear that without him the remnant kingdom could easily founder and when he sailed for home in April 1254, left behind a small salaried contingent of a hundred warriors under Geoffrey de Sergines, commander of his bodyguard, who served in Outremer until his death in 1269. Despite disasters, Louis's unswerving devotion to his ideal won hearts and the spontaneous popular movement of *Pastoureaux*, shepherds, agitated for him while he remained in the East.

Pilgrims now had to make the best of Muslim domination of the city. The resolute could make their way to Jerusalem, but the occupiers made them enter furtively by a side-gate and pay a heavy fee. Less venturesome travellers were catered for with sanctuaries and reliquaries in the forty churches of Acre. The barons and the Italian cities remained anarchic. In

1257–8 rival sides fought each other on land in the streets of Acre and on sea as the Venetians reacted violently to an action of the Genoese, suddenly seizing a strategic point, the hill overlooking Acre on which stood the monastery of Saint-Sabas, and all the quarrelling factions piled in. The Hospitallers began sending crucial documents to Cyprus for safety, and individual settlers attempted to make deals with the Mamluks.

Louis's Last Crusade and its Sequel

In 1267 King Louis once again took the cross. Joinville refused to support him, saying he was too frail and that the kingdom needed him. Fleet and troops assembled and were directed in 1270 not to Egypt or to Jerusalem but to Tunis, where the presence of Dominican friars, who kept a language school and were allowed to ring their bells and minister to Christians, led the king to believe that the emir of Tunis was ready to convert to Christianity. He was responding to a vision which recurred in the strategic crusades of the thirteenth century, that somehow an additional force, a counterweight, could be called into being to bring Jerusalem back to Christian hands. It was a false hope. The emir turned on the Dominicans, and Louis died of dysentery in the camp before the gates of Tunis with 'Jerusalem' the last word on his lips. The fleet dissolved. Some ships attempting to go on to the Holy Land were lost in a storm; others went back to Europe; arriving late, the Lord Edward, Henry III's son and heir, who had beaten rebellious barons in England, went on with his galleys to the Holy Land. He was a true crusader, unwilling to let tensions with France spoil co-operation with Louis. Charles of Anjou, Louis's brother, arrived to make peace and succeeded in extracting tribute for himself in Sicily from the emir.

There followed the pontificate of Teodaldo Visconti, elected when he was still in the Holy Land, who reigned as Gregory X from 1271 to 1276 and was the last pope to be devoted, above all, to crusade for Jerusalem. He summoned the Second Council of Lyon in 1274 and called for judgements on the reform of the Church, reunion with Byzantium and the way, militarily, to pursue the crusade – themes which in his mind all interlocked.

A treatise submitted to the pope by Humbert of the Romans, formerly master-general of the Dominicans, was designed to defend the use of force to recover Jerusalem and in scholastic fashion surveyed all the criticisms known to its author before dismissing them, a proceeding too often misunderstood as implying that during the thirteenth century rejections of crusading had grown in number and vehemence. This is not so, but at one point one may suspect a new factor, brought into play by Louis's sanctity and his failures. If he, with his heroic virtues, could not win through, might it be that the recovery of Jerusalem was not the will of God? Significantly, no submission to the Lyon Council spoke for crusade to Egypt. Instead, there were interesting developments in ideas about professional, even mercenary, small-scale crusading, involving regular reinforcement of the Holy Land garrison, to provide freshness in warriors to confront the Muslim enemy, and the launching of a *passagium particulare,* again small-scale and highly professional with no stray accompaniments, to back the garrison and begin to turn round the military situation. Trade boycott was advocated, followed by a *passagium generale*, a general crusade to exploit damage done to Muslims and bring about a reoccupation.

Crusading had not died, but it was beginning to run in different channels. The pope hoped to discuss projects face to face with kings. It was not to be. Gregory was still working towards a new crusade when he died in 1276. No one of his calibre and determination succeeded him, and no general crusade was ever again launched to recover the Holy City.

Crowned heads could still achieve victories against Muslims and the thirteenth century saw decisive advances by St Ferdinand III of Castile (1230–1252), with the expulsion of the Moors, territory gained and cities taken. *Mudéjars* were made second-class citizens. James I of Aragon (1213–1276) took the Balearics from the Moors.

When Acre at last fell in 1291, it was still not clear that a rescue of the Holy Land was impossible and there were still attempts made, with varying degrees of credibility, to recover it. But to the perceptive it became clear that a shift was taking place, away from Jerusalem and towards crusading inside Europe.

9

THE VICTORY OF
THE MAMLUKS

Baybars, a Kipchak Turk from the South Russian steppes, a victim with his family of the irruption of the Mongols into their lands and forced into slavery, was a short, swarthy, barrel-chested man of powerful physique and extraordinary energy – the greatest of the Mamluks and the destroyer of the crusaders' residual hopes for the Holy Land. A boy slave in the second half of the thirteenth century, he was accursed of God in the eyes of contemporaries because of the white spot in his eye. His first purchaser returned him to the auctioneer because of the flaw; the mother of the second, seeing the eye, said, 'Have nothing to do with that swarthy fellow, he has an evil eye' and persuaded her son to give him up. He was then chosen as a bargain by an emir who subsequently got into economic difficulties and finally he passed from the emir into the hands of al-Salih Ayyub, the dissident son of al-Kamil who had achieved some success in the fighting and manoeuvring of the Ayyubid heirs after the death of al-Kamil and had captured Cairo. Al-Salih was distinguished for his habit of collecting Mamluks whom he trained to a high calibre of fighting and kept as an elite force for his disposal on an island in the Nile, Bahr al-Nil: hence their name, *bahriyya*. Al-Salih's decision to take him launched Baybars on his career.

Slave soldiers were not new in Islamic history, for the development of their selection and training went back to the caliph al-Mutasim in the ninth century: wearied at the cost and volatility of Arab troops, he had spotted the opportunity in Islamic law to recruit pagan boys as slaves to be trained as soldiers and form a praetorian guard. Boys they had to be. Puberty was the best time to recruit, when muscles were still forming and minds could be shaped. No Muslim could be enslaved but a pagan or Christian could, and nomad peoples on the fringes of Islamic lands were easy prey for slave dealers. Nomads were cheap to acquire: dealers could act as substitute parents. Al-Mutasim was one of the great Muslim generals but had reigned for only eight years, before dying in 842; however, the concept of the slave soldier that he developed was a vital one for the future.

Al-Salih's army depended on the superb horsemanship of his troops, bred in the steppe. Once recruited, a boy would be given years of exacting military training, building on horsemanship to achieve a mastery of the bow, lance and sword, accompanied by induction into Islamic beliefs. They were wholly in the hands of their masters and had only one loyalty and one interest.

The master guides for the techniques of the cavalryman and the care of horses, the *furusiyya*, gave detailed information on the making of skilled professional fighters out of raw recruits. The master would take the novice right back to the first principles of riding and the manipulation of weapons, including both balance and manoeuvrability. Central to the equipment of the Mamluk was the bow – but not a bow of the type usual among invading crusaders. It had an ancient origin on the steppes and was adjusted to dry climates, not to the humidity of the West, since it was composed of horn and sinew brought together on a wooden frame. This powerful weapon needed more pull than the classic Western longbow but had much more penetration. Extensive training was needed to master the pull, using the thumb, protected by rings, to draw the bow right back to the ear. The whole manoeuvre was carried out on horseback, the knees controlling the horse and the archer adapting to the rise and fall of his mount. Only a supreme mastery of riding would make possible the classic achievement of the horse-archer, in which the retreating horseman could swing his body round to fire at his opponent without halting.

The Mamluk expected to take with him on his mount a substantial collection of weapons: generally a second bow for security, a quiver with arrows varied for different purposes, and a lance plus a sword, dagger and mace for close-quarter fighting. To aid this carriage of weapons there was a tendency to breed heavier horses than the steppe ponies, fodder-fed rather than reliant on casual grazing on the thin Middle Eastern grass. Exercises built up specialist skills: endless slicing at lumps of clay on horseback to produce exceptional arm muscles, or shooting at a gourd mounted on a pole. The skilled use of the short sword was developed by exercises using the right side and arm while the left held the reins.

Islamic instruction, no doubt emphasising the remarkable conquests of the early caliphate, led the recruit to feel he was being taken out of the darkness of heathenism into a new light of true and conquering belief. *Jihad* fitted admirably into the Mamluk ideology: Mamluks were shock troops for the holy war. Recruitment from Turkish speakers and the predominance of one ethnic group, the Kipchak Turks, from which Baybars derived, gave an additional coherence and unity to al-Salih's quality Mamluks. Turkish was the language of command and conversation and this tended to cut soldiers off from Arabic-speakers. Eunuchs were commonly given command positions in order to obviate the dangers of pederasty; there were heavy penalties for sodomy.

Within this competitive military society, as developed by al-Salih Ayyub, Baybars flourished. The *bahriyya* survived the death of al-Salih and played a crucial part in the failure of Louis's crusade to Egypt. Joinville ruefully records how Mamluks harassed him and his colleagues with the skilled use of tubes to loose off fire darts. Baybars was a junior emir in the subsequent episode in which the king's brother Robert of Artois charged into the streets of Mansura, opening the French army to the skill of the *bahriyya* in fighting at close quarters. Success against the crusade won fame, but it did not lead to a Mamluk supremacy. Instead, for years they were troubled by squabbling, assassinations and political manoeuvring while the Mongol menace, unchecked, threatened both the Christian Eastern world and the great area of the conquests of the early caliphs. In 1241 Mongols won battles in eastern Europe against Teutonic Knights and Poles at Liegnitz and against a Hungarian army at the River Sajo, spreading great fear across Europe. Meanwhile, al-Salih Ayyub had insisted on leading the fight against St Louis, even being carried towards the battle on a litter while a dying man. He succumbed to his illness while his son and successor, Turanshah, was still far away in northern territory; installed in power, his son showed himself sluggish and dissolute; moreover, he set about replacing members of the *bahriyya* by his own men. Baybars, bursting into the tent where Turanshah was dining with his emirs, attempted to assassinate him; bleeding, Turanshah escaped, only to drown in the Nile. It was a controversial action, resented by other Mamluks; some of the *bahriyya* even attempted to murder Baybars himself.

There followed an eccentric episode in which Shajarat al-Durr, al-Salih's widow, was elected queen of the Muslims but then was forced to abdicate in favour of a leading emir, Aybeg. In 1254 Aybeg made use of the emir Qutuz as his agent to kill off Aktay, the leading figure in the faction which included Baybars, who never forgave the killing and withdrew with 700 of the *bahriyya* to Syria and Anatolia. There they engaged in casual violence before finally trying to storm Cairo and seize power, only to be beaten off by Qutuz, who killed any leaders he could capture.

Over a decade the Mamluks so forcefully collected and trained by al-Salih Ayyub had shown both their outstanding military skills and their inability to exercise power. Baybars had backed the wrong side and remained an outsider. This began to change only when the fear of the Islamic world before the menace of the Mongols pulled him out of the shadows.

The Battle of Ain Jalud and the Defeat of the Mongols

Genghiz Khan, the great destroyer, had died in 1227, but the threat of the Mongols to both the West and Islam had not abated. After Liegnitz, victories continued. The Assassins, the supposedly impregnable dissidents of the Islamic world, had been eliminated and the Abbasid caliphate ended. Cracks within the Mongol empire began to appear when rivals manoeuvred for the great inheritance of Genghiz Khan, but not swiftly enough to undermine the terrifying power of the Mongol cavalry, their mounted archers and their reputation for utter destruction of those who resisted. Hulegu, the brother of the Great Khan Mongke, defeated the army of the last caliph of the Abbasids outside Baghdad in 1258, skilfully using a combination of his horsemen and the marshy land near the battle site. The caliph still resisted but was forced to surrender as the Mongol siege-engine specialists set about reducing Baghdad's walls. Hulegu, influenced by his Nestorian wife, spared her fellow Christian believers but no one else. Avoiding the direct shedding of blood, the Mongols rolled the last Abbasid in a carpet and trampled him to death under the hoofs of their horses. Damascus surrendered: there too the Mongol command humiliated the Muslims and gave favour to the Christian minority. When cross-bearing processions were arranged, they were forced to stand in respect and Christians offensively showed their contempt for Muslim practices by drinking during Ramadan.

Christians elsewhere surrendered to the Mongols and the last great Muslim city of Syria, Aleppo, was devastated. There remained Egypt and the seat of Mamluk power and to Qutuz, recently made sultan without restrictions, Hulegu sent the habitual Mongol demand for surrender without any reserve. Qutuz executed Hulegu's envoys, cut their bodies in half in the horse market and put their heads on the gates of Cairo. He now made a major decision, responding to an astute offer by Baybars to come over to him. It was agreed that Baybars should join him, bring his own formidable force from the *bahriyya* and stand together with him against the Mongols. Witnesses remembered the icy hostility of the two men as they met in March 1260. But they made a deal. Baybars in the event of victory was to receive the governorship of the ancient Syrian fortress at Aleppo. It was agreed that they would not stand and fight in or near Cairo but choose terrain well forward suitable for deploying cavalry skills. One fortunate chance aided their decision. The Great Khan Mongke had died in August 1259 and dissension between two brothers of Hulegu caused him to draw off part of his army to Maragha, at the edge of modern Iran, to await events; alternatively Hulegu may have thought that, in the long term, the Levant could not support the Mongol mass of horse. He left behind him his lieutenant, Kitboga, and a diminished Mongol force.

Thus the Mongols lacked their usual overwhelming superiority of numbers. Still, Qutuz was aware that his troops were facing the greatest warriors of the age, with a remarkable record of victories. Even Mamluks could waver facing them. Qutuz appealed to *jihad* and the great days of Nur al-Din and Saladin.

The Mongols set out from Damascus and the Mamluks from Egypt, while the Franks remained neutral and even received Baybars in Acre. Battle was joined in Palestine. Baybars played a helpful part at the beginning of the campaign, skirmishing with a reconnaissance force of Mongols, narrowly escaping encirclement and giving Kitboga the impression that the Mamluk army was smaller than was the case. There were probably 12,000 on either side. Straddling the Jezreel valley, the Mongols encamped at Ain Jalud, Goliath's Spring, where there was ample watering for their troops, spare mounts and animals kept with the host to slaughter en route. The location had resounding biblical echoes. Ain Jalud was the site of David's encounter with the giant Goliath and Mount Gilboa, on its flank, was where the Philistines killed King Saul's sons and he and his armour-bearer fell on their swords.

Baybars quickly warned Qutuz of the Mongol position and the key decision for victory was made. In the darkness of the night on 2 September 1260 a massive Mamluk force slipped into position behind the Mongols on the northern foothills of Gilboa, gently sloping and at that time devoid of trees.*

At a key point in the battle the reserve force from the foothills of Gilboa moved against the Mongols, with devastating effect. Even then the manoeuvre almost failed as the rest of the Mamluks' front line had been so weakened by the detachment to Mount Gilboa that it came close to giving way in the face of the Mongol hail of arrows. Qutuz kept his nerve and by a narrow margin rallied his troops. Then, on the flank, al-Ashraf, an

---

* A masterly analysis of the site and sequence of events is in P. Herde, *Gesammelte Abhandlungen und Aufsätze* vol. 2, pt 1 (Stuttgart, 2002), Chapter 14, with map. I am indebted to Professor Herde for information from his work, both on Hattin and on Ain Jalud.

Ayyubid leader and his Muslim auxiliaries, whom he had brought to the Mongol side, kept their promise to Qutuz to desert and turned on the Mongols, who collapsed and fled, some to be killed on the slopes of Gilboa by local men, others caught in reeds, others fleeing towards Damascus and cut down by Baybars, others flying to take refuge with Hetum of Armenia. Kitboga, courageously resisting, was killed. It was a major event: it broke the legendary invincibility of the Mongols. They could be defeated; the Muslim world took heart and the Mamluks gained massively in prestige.

It is a good surmise that a new sophistication of the Mamluk archers' weaponry also played a part. For all their effectiveness, Mongol arrows were of one kind only. Mamluks took to carrying at the hip a splayed quiver with as many as sixty arrows – some for armour-piercing, some very light for creating a storm, shower-shooting from above, others for long-range, direct attack. The usual Mongol technique of combining movement with rapid firing could still be devastating – it nearly prevailed at Ain Jalud – but the Mamluks had gained an edge in weaponry.

Despite playing an exemplary role, Baybars was not given his promised prize of Aleppo and the enmity with Qutuz continued. Qutuz feared Baybars and dared not let him far from his sight. Uneasily, with their entourages, the two travelled through the desert to Cairo. Baybars hatched a plot with other Mamluk emirs to be rid of Qutuz, making use of his passion for hare-coursing to divert him from their line of travel and strike him down on 24 October. The emirs conferred with Baybars and would only accept his leadership in return for promises of their security and power.

Unaware of Qutuz's death, the army carried on. The conspirators had calculated that the vanguard would have believed he was with the rear-guard and vice versa. Meanwhile, Baybars and a small party galloped ahead to Cairo, made fair promises to the vice-regent and took the citadel. When morning prayers bade the people pray for the dead Qutuz and the new sultan, Baybars, Cairo was astonished. Baybars acted swiftly to allay adverse response by removing Qutuz's emergency taxes levied to pay for the Mongol campaign, avoiding the ceremonial ride that should have followed his enthronement and burying Qutuz in a secret site. Rapid removal of inconvenient witnesses to Qutuz's murder led Mamluks to support him as a strong man who would look after them. He reigned for seventeen years.

The Mamluk Sultanate

Installed in power, himself an assassin and executioner, Baybars was determined never to fall victim to murder and so patiently created a structure designed for his own protection against conspiracy and built himself an administration with a firm financial core, of a kind which had entirely eluded Saladin and his Ayyubid successors. He increased Mamluk numbers. Under him there flourished the finest and most professional army of its day, still recruiting from the steppe and numbering many thousands. Within the army he developed a core of Royal Mamluks, the most rigorously trained of them all and firmly linked to him. Training and long-term support cost a great deal and the Mamluk army was feasible only because Baybars had built up a massive, stable income.

As he began developing his support in devoted soldiers and administrators, so he also looked to ideology and to ceremony, to attract both literate and illiterate. Promoted Mamluks took an oath of allegiance to the sultan by the tomb of al-Salih Ayyub, Baybars's quondam master. Saladin and his *jihad* were cited and revered. Baybars presented himself as the leader who would fulfil all their plans. He was illiterate and thus vulnerable to a scheming hermit-soothsayer, Shaykh Khadir, whom he endowed richly, allowed to seize the property of Jews and Christians and consulted over and over again. When he was found guilty of multiple sexual offences, Khadir said his death would be followed by that of the sultan, so Baybars spared him execution and put him in prison. Khadir's hold may also have been aided by Baybars's adherence to Sufism.

Despite many vicissitudes in the history of the caliphate, believers still had an inveterate attachment to the ancient office, which had some juridical importance, and Baybars followed the lead of Qutuz in appointing a puppet caliph to succeed the line which had once reigned in Baghdad. A candidate, al-Mustansir, claiming relationship to the Abbasids, emerged, was vetted by experts and duly installed. He fulfilled his function by issuing a diploma in favour of Baybars as sultan of the whole Muslim world, after which he, Baybars, promised his allegiance to the caliph to rule justly, to protect the true faith of the Sunnis and to pursue the *jihad* against the enemies of the faith. Baybars and al-Mustansir rode through the streets of Cairo, with Baybars displaying symbols of power, including the sword of the great caliph Umar; when al-Mustansir perished in an attempt to recover Baghdad, Baybars selected a kinsman of his, who had survived. The practice of appointing such shadow caliphs continued under Baybars's successors.

His military achievement was made possible by the peculiar nature of the slave aristocracy which he inherited. They have been described as a one-generation nobility. The successful individual could expect to be rewarded in his lifetime, to be given higher commands in recognition of his talent and courage and to be emancipated from slave status. He could have wives, whom he could readily divorce, and concubines. The link to his biological father, far away on the steppe, had long been lost. His loyalty was to his fellow Mamluks, joined in a military comradeship to his sultan, and above all to his patron, who manumitted him. It was understood that he could not transmit land, power or wealth to his sons. He was in no way subject to the pressures of a wife seeking to advance her son at the expense of others. He could engage in trade or perhaps join the reserves. But that was all. The system prevented the build-up of appanages, which often in medieval states generation by generation reduced the land and revenues available to rulers, as leading nobles provided for their families. In addition to the advantages Baybars gained from the Mamluk system, his dictatorship took firm charge of the lucrative Egyptian seaborne trade.

Baybars faced two Mongol powers to east and to west: the Ilkahnate of Persia and Iraq and the Golden Horde's settlement in southern Russia. After various manoeuvres he came to hold al-Bira, on the Euphrates, as a forward post against the Ilkahnate and benefited from the decision of Berke Khan of the Golden Horde to convert to Islam. Berke Kahn was fêted on a trip to Cairo, flattered by being included with Baybars in the *khutba*, the Friday prayers, and provided vital collaboration with Baybars by giving unchallenged passage to victims of the slave trade, so allowing a steady flow of young boys for his army, while the Genoese kept their lucrative role as middlemen.

Meanwhile the combination of Mongol power and the Mamluk ascendancy under Baybars reduced the role of the Assassins. They paid tribute to the Hospitallers, then wisely shifted their tribute to placate Baybars himself. The Mongols had destroyed Alamut. Other castles fell; Baybars appointed Grand Masters at his will and forced remnants to live at his court. By 1273 their strange power, which had issued in over fifty assassinations, frightening Sunnis and Franks alike, was over. Yet there remained the Ismaili beliefs, originally born of a combination of anger over the appointment of a caliph by improper procedures in 1094 excluding the more than capable son, Nizar, of the aged Fatimid caliph in favour of the inadequate candidate al-Mustali as a cat's-paw. The Assassins had never accepted the choice of 1094, continued to back Nazir, and were inspired to support him as the true caliph and fight against what they saw as the marginalisation of Shiism. In obscurity the sect lingered on in Syria and Persia, shorn of its murderous capacity but still retaining an intense devotion to its imams as religious leaders. The two branches drifted apart; nothing more was heard of the Syrians, but effectively only in Iran the sect continued to exist.

Baybars was aware of the continued threat of the Mongols. His plan was both to keep them apart – aided in this by their mutual hostility – and to prevent them linking up with the remnants of the Crusader States. After the disaster of La Forbie in 1244 the settlers had no effective field army but still had the dedicated forces of the military orders. Baybars knew that an appeal from the East could yet start off a crusade. He had to keep an eye not only on the Mongols and the Holy Land Christians but also on individual adventurers and the remnant of the Ayyubids, meeting these threats with a mixture of diplomacy and force administered with terror. Only once did he attempt a direct major attack on the Ilkhanate and that was one of his rare failures. He still held the inner lines of defence against his Mongol enemies on the north and east and could easily switch his forces from one front to another.

The sources depict Baybars as a serious *jihadi*. He intended to enforce obedience to the Quran, to forbid alcohol, to stop pederasty among his young Mamluks and to look after Muslim Holy Places. When opportunity offered, he made the *hajj* pilgrimage in secrecy for fear of assassination and had repairs undertaken in Mecca and Medina. In Jerusalem he restored the Dome of the Rock and the al-Aqsa mosque. In 1263 he sent a high-level delegation to Mecca, bearing the *kiswa,* the black silk veil with a band of gold-embroidered Quranic texts, to cover the great cubic shrine of the *Kaba*. Freshly manufactured in Egypt each year, it established Baybars's effective claim to succession to the rights and powers of the Abbasid caliphs.

The Destruction of the Christians

Baybars's ferocious zeal for *jihad* was made manifest in his attacks on the Christians and his systematic demolition of their coastal strongpoints. He was aware of Mamluk naval weakness and concluded that while the Christians kept their superiority at sea, pulling in by the maritime route both pilgrims and warriors, Islam would never be secure against their Holy Land presence. The solution was to destroy all the ports and fortifications on which they relied.

To siege warfare he brought subtlety, secrecy and intense attention to detail. If the Christian fortresses lay inland, he could devote ample time to the siege because it was unlikely that a Christian army could come to its relief; the fortifications could be severely damaged, notably by mining, but then built up again in the Mamluk interest. There was always enough finance to do it. Castle-breaking was Baybars's most notable military achievement. Techniques differed. In an early coup against Kerak, the fortress on the caravan route to Damascus, Baybars invited its Ayyubid governor, al-Mughith, to his camp; what appeared to be a mere courtesy call turned sharply into a court set up to judge and condemn al-Mughith for treasonable correspondence with the Mongols; forged papers proved the case, he was removed to Cairo and there killed. His sons gave up the castle, thereafter kept in trim by the Mamluks. He also ensured Mamluk control at an early stage of Shawbak (Montréal), the other fortress dominating the caravan route.

Secrecy helped: sealed letters were given to his generals to avoid leakage of information. The counterweight trebuchet had a key role for siege warfare. Baybars developed a technique of assembling massive blocks of stone for the counterweight, brought by oxen over great distances to ensure that his machines could throw projectiles weighing up to 500 lb. It was an expensive but devastatingly effective procedure, and here again his mastery of finance was crucial. *Naphtha* could secure the torching of vulnerable buildings. After storming the outer walls at Caesarea, he faced a citadel that had been reinforced by St Louis; he did not attempt to undermine it but used his trebuchets to devastate the defenders with stones and *naphtha*. A church tower was also used to project hails of arrows. The defenders surrendered, went to their ships and the site was razed to the ground.

At Arsuf there was a hard-fought battle over the moat, with Baybars filling in a passage over it and the defenders mining beneath and destroying his infill materials. Eventually the defence was overwhelmed by trebuchet and the entire strongpoint destroyed, captive Christians providing labour. Safad was an inland fortress in Galilee and had a Templar force commanding Syrian Christian auxiliaries to defend it. Baybars built up tension by promising amnesty to the auxiliaries if they surrendered. Aware of the immense shift of power in the Holy Land, auxiliaries did leave, putting a strain on the Knights' ability to man the walls. Allegedly the Templars failed to meet conditions imposed on them, so that when they surrendered they were massacred and a Mamluk garrison took over.

At Beaufort uncompleted improvements had left a level space outside the walls, thus providing a base for Baybars's trebuchets, which destroyed the defences in ten days. An attack on Antioch ruined the quondam buttress of crusader strength in Syria. Bohemond VI, heavily compromised with the Mongols, was based in Tripoli; Baybars left him there and moved on to Antioch. On the First Crusade it had stood siege for eight months; Baybars and his superior equipment took it in little more than a day, then locked the gate and massacred the inhabitants, writing to Bohemond to describe the scene of 'flames running through your palaces, your dead burned in this world before going down to the fires in the next'. A scanty littoral was now left to the Crusader States.

In part, Baybars had been aided by the Mongol irruption. They were a menace he never failed to emphasise. They also had created a vacuum in the Muslim northern lands, assisting his attempt to make Cairo the true and only capital of the Muslim world. There was no longer tension between Syria and Egypt, and complicity with the Mongols enabled him to eliminate Christians more or less at will. Abbasid errors, combined with Mongol destructiveness ruining the irrigation systems, had destroyed the economy of Iraq, which had become a backwater. Baybars's mastery of the express postal system enabled him to have control of Syria and crush dissidence. Relays of horses, postal stations and efficient riders enabled messages to pass between Damascus and Cairo in four days and in grave emergency three. Dispatches were taken directly to the sultan wherever he was, even on occasion received in the bath. A network of towers kept the traditional pigeon service in being.

The sultan himself was relentlessly in the saddle. Not for nothing was the symbol of Mamluk power gold cloth on a saddle. Baybars loved horses, had an extraordinary energy and insisted on personal supervision, even turning up secretly in disguise to spy on his subordinates and see what was happening. Fear of his enemies gave him chronic insomnia and indigestion. Intelligence was gained through merchants acting as spies in the West to inform him about the doings of popes, kings and would-be crusaders. They came to the sultan in deep disguise, worked as individuals, were never allowed to meet up with each other and, in the manner of intelligence services at all times, collude in serving up agreed information to their masters. Terror backed intelligence and kept his power in being. Conspirators and the recalcitrant were subjected to impaling and crucifixion. A massive hippodrome was constructed in Cairo for riding exercises and the endless training requisite for his army. Here he would inspect his men, ensuring by a grand parade that all present had with them the full equipment. Polo was a passion and encouraged as a sport, for it practised the swift turns which were so much a part of Mamluk military skills.

Attention to detail was incessant, as in the case of the lime blocks he obtained for supporting the bridge at Lod, which survives to this day. Krak des Chevaliers fell to him late in his reign, in 1271. Needing a month to batter at the outer walls, his troops would have been dismayed at the great slope of the glacis guarding the inner fortress, where the knights held out – once climbed by the young T. E. Lawrence in plimsolls – but a ruse got his Mamluks over the obstacle with the delivery of a forged letter from the Grand Master, instructing the Hospitaller Knights to seek terms. They were too few and had no prospect of relief and so, whether they had their suspicions or not, they duly surrendered and marched out. Krak was repaired and kept as a stronghold in northern Syria.

The last serious intervention from the West to save Acre came from England. The Lord Edward, long blooded in fighting rebels against his father, Henry III, brought with him to Acre in May 1271 a skilled fighting force a thousand strong with thirteen ships and – a rare event in crusader history – his beloved wife, Eleanor, who gave birth in the Holy Land. He took the risk of exposing her to a dangerous climate because of his fear of breaching his crusader vow by falling to the temptation of adultery.

Baybars saw in this intervention by Edward, who was expecting to link up with an attack from the north by the Mongol Ilkhan Abagha, just the type of crusading irruption into the Near East that he always feared. The Ilkahn was too far away and the combined attack never came off. Baybars made peace, but he was still wary of a capable general from the West and, just to make sure, hired an assassin to stab Edward with a poisoned dagger while he slept in his chamber at Acre. Edward lay unconscious and only just survived to take ship for home, leaving a small English garrison behind.

Thereafter, Baybars was occupied elsewhere and delayed the final attack on Acre, which would have completed the expulsion of the Christians. On 1 July 1277, in a rare moment of relaxation watching a polo match in Damascus, he met his end drinking *qumiz*, fermented mare's milk, a drink which just skirted the Quran's prohibition of alcohol. It had its hazards: notoriously when over-fermented, it could kill. So it was for Baybars.

The Fall of Acre

In their prime the Mamluks stopped hereditary succession but sometimes nonetheless the inveterate wish of fathers to hand over power to sons prevailed. Baybars tried to pull it off and associated his son Baraka with him in rule in his lifetime. Succeeding, Baraka showed he lacked competence. His father-in-law, a fighting general, Kalavun took over and Baraka was packed off to a gilded seclusion in Kerak, where he died later after a mysterious fall from a polo pony.

In the second battle of Homs in 1281, Kalavun had to face a Mongol army which included Georgians, Turcomen, Armenians and probably some Hospitallers, and in consequence was larger than the army that Baybars and Qutuz had defeated at Ain Jalud. He was outnumbered and weakened by the presence in his army of Mamluks whom he had promoted in preference to the *bahriyya*. Good generalship, Mongol carelessness and some good luck won Kalavun the victory, but at a cost of heavy losses, which delayed the final showdown with the settler Christians. The honour of destroying them fell instead to one of Kalavun's sons – no favourite of his – called al-Ashraf Khalil. Kalavun died on the way to the final attack on Acre, which he so much desired, and his son took over, surmounting grave difficulties in deploying a total of ninety siege engines, including the monster trebuchet, a counterweight catapult which needed a hundred carts pulled by teams of oxen so as to provide for assembly on the site of the siege. In bitter weather oxen died of exposure but still the materials for the monster were carried through.

Jihad brought in volunteers. On the Christian side disputes over kingship faded. It was accepted that Henry II, ruler in Cyprus, was also king of Jerusalem and he came to fight, leaving by sea only when the situation became hopeless. Sea power brought in supplies to the garrison and reinforcements gave the opportunity to make attacks on the besiegers. The great double walls led civilians to seek safety within the city but the throwing-machines inherited from Baybars battered walls and towers and created entry points for Muslim soldiers, while the sewers opened the way for their mines.

There was a multiplicity of different, often conflicting, forces within

Acre; nonetheless, in the last resort the military orders, Templars and Hospitallers, despite past quarrels, all fought on with great courage, matched by the Teutonic Knights, latecomers though they were on the Holy Land scene. After the fall of most of Acre in 18 May 1291, the Grand Master of the Hospital, severely wounded, was carried away against his wishes by his men to Cyprus, whence he wrote 'in great sadness of heart'. The beautifully illuminated Burdett Psalter, which depicts him in worship before Christ, was thought to have been lost but when it resurfaced in the twentieth century was sold at auction for a record price. A last stand by the Templars at their strongpoint on the extreme south-west side on 28 May ended in a collapse of walls, burying attackers and defenders alike. Al-Ashraf Khalil ordered Acre to be razed to the ground so that crusaders could never return.

By August all strongpoints and ports were gone. The Templars kept the tiny island of Ruad, 7 miles off Tortosa, as a springboard for a return, but were forced out of it in 1302–3. Cyprus was a refuge and there Lusignans went on ruling into the fifteenth century.

The Decline of the Mamluks

Plague in the fourteenth century devastated the Mamluk state and its soldiers, while lasting damage was done to the agriculture of Upper Egypt by greedy and oppressive measures. The Mamluks lost discipline. Enslavement of boys continued as Circassians from the Caucusus replaced Turks, but too many sultans were unsatisfactory.

Ottomans evolved from Turkish war bands in Anatolia and gained prestige when they captured Constantinople in 1453. They defeated the Mamluks of Egypt in 1517. The legend persists that Ottomans defeated Mamluks because they knew how to use gunpowder while their more hidebound opponents declined to keep up with the times. Robert Irwin has demonstrated that this is untrue. The curved bow was superior to the handgun for Mamluk cavalry. If the horsemen were well trained, their bows could fire off six shots per minute while handguns of the time could only achieve one to two shots. Handguns were useless to men in the saddle;

they might, in contrast, be handed out to low-grade infantry who lacked horsemanship and the training needed to draw back the curved bow. Both sides at various times used cannon and handguns, but they were not in themselves decisive. Ottomans won because Mamluk leadership had grown decadent and because they had developed one military technique, the defensive chained wagon, which the Mamluks never mastered.

One harsh military dictatorship based on slave soldiers, the Janissaries, succeeded a previous such dictatorship, to the detriment of Islam. The breakdown of Iraq's irrigation system ruined the civilisation based on it. Baghdad ended as a dull provincial town, shorn of intellectual life. It is true that the cultural life of the Mamluks can be underestimated. They were willing to use a great historian, Ibn Khaldun, as a tutor to a boy sultan. They were ultimately responsible for a wide range of Arabic writing and were patrons for one work of world literature, the *Thousand and One Nights*. They left their mark on Jerusalem, and architecturally it was a good one. Christian sites were not demolished because they brought in pilgrim traffic and Islamic ones were cherished. Sultan Qaitbay, who reigned from 1468 to 1496, was responsible for a masterpiece of intricate stonework, the ablutions tower placed west of the Dome of the Rock, which still fascinates tourist and pilgrim.

Yet military success was purchased at a high price, and in this respect Mamluk and Ottoman dictatorships were alike in that they were similarly systems of arbitrary rule, stifling any developments in the heartlands of Islam similar to the effects in England of counsel and consent on kingship, and the emergence of bargaining power on the side of the Commons to mitigate the power of kings. The message of Mamluk and Ottoman alike was that only despotism paid, to the great detriment of Muslims down to modern times.

10

THE LONG AFTERMATH

Response to the Loss of Acre

The fall of Acre in 1291 moved the West. The reaction was not as strong as that which followed Saladin's capture of Jerusalem in 1187 but it was noteworthy just the same in that it influenced the most committed advocates of mission to Muslims to think again about the need for crusade to rescue the Holy Land. The reason lies in disappointment that God had deserted His people and given victory to the Mamluks. A sense of divine purpose had run through crusading history, and now almost every foothold had been lost in the Holy Land and the associated states. Other strongpoints had already gone, but Acre was the very last of importance, being well known due to its size, its massive walls, its burgeoning population and its commercial and industrial life.

Appeals for money and warriors in the West had largely gone unheeded because of the growth of nation-states, their conflicts and the immense costs of up-to-date warfare. Edward I of England, before he came to the throne, was a notably committed crusader; when he became king, however, he was too preoccupied with problems at home to consider going to the Holy Land.

The New Force: Philip the Fair (1285–1314)

Popes in the late thirteenth century were terrified of a renewal of the Hohenstaufen threat to exert power and to put intolerable pressure on the independence of the papacy in Rome through co-ordinated action from Germany, northern Italy and Sicily. One French pope decided to back a safe ally, Charles of Anjou, brother of King Louis, to take south Italy and Sicily and destroy the last of the Hohenstaufen 'brood of vipers'. This Charles proceeded to do, killing Frederick II's bastard son Manfred in battle and ruthlessly executing Frederick's sixteen-year-old grandson in Naples but his dictatorial attitude angered rebels in Sicily, who called in the maritime power of Aragon against him. Peter III of Aragon, married to Manfred's daughter, took up the Hohenstaufen claim and was accused of 'impeding' the Holy Land crusade, in the phrase once deployed by Innocent III at the start of his pontificate. A French army, equipped with the crusading indulgence under King Philip III of France, embarked on a disastrous venture overland against Aragon, only to find its supplies ruined by Peter's fleet. Beset by hunger and disease, the French were forced into a humiliating retreat over the Pyrenees. Philip III, who had to be carried in a litter, succumbed to illness at Perpignan in 1285. His son Philip, called the Fair because of his good looks, had accompanied him in his humiliation and in consequence bore a deep hostility towards the political crusading of the popes. Despite being the grandson of St Louis, he only played with the notion of a Holy Land crusade and his reign damaged both the papacy and the traditional crusading ideal.

The pontificate of the eccentric Celestine V, who resigned after nine months, was followed by that of a highly capable administrator and canonist, Boniface VIII (1294–1303). He brought about a workable solution to the long Sicilian crisis and called a Jubilee in Rome with attached indulgences and improved papal finances; but he had his dark side, manipulating a land deal for his family, the Caetani, and calling an expedition against their traditional enemies, the Colonna, a crusade. Coarse and self-willed, Boniface's casual remarks were damaging to the papacy's reputation and were ruthlessly exploited by Philip the Fair's ministers to discredit him and put pressure on his successors. A jurisdictional and financial conflict in

France escalated dramatically as Boniface used papal powers to excommunicate one of Philip's ministers, William of Nogaret, and issued the Bull *Unam Sanctam*, with the most extreme claims for papal powers ever made. William, with Sciarra Colonna, personally attacked Boniface, bursting into his private family palace in the hill town of Anagni, intending to arrest the pope and transport him by force to France to answer trumped up charges of corruption, simony, blasphemy and heresy. The pope met them with dignity and was liberated by his faithful townspeople but he had been profoundly humiliated and died within a month, probably from a stroke.

This was far from the end of Philip's campaign to subject the papacy to his will. He and his servants knew inquisition procedures well and were ready, it was clear, to exhume Boniface, put him on trial, convict him and burn his body as a heretic. The potential damage to the reputation of the papacy was one no pope could ignore.

Events split the cardinals. Some wanted to see a settlement with Philip; others supported the papacy and were unwilling to make a deal. After the short pontificate of a Dominican friar, an eleven-month interregnum followed with such deadlock that the only way to resolve the long crisis appeared to be to elect an outsider and so the Sacred College found a candidate in a Gascon, technically the subject of Edward I of England, Bertrand of Got, Archbishop of Bordeaux. Suffering from cancer, he was unable to work continuously, being overwhelmed repeatedly with incapacitating pains. He had intended to be crowned in Rome as Clement V but was not well enough to go there and instead was crowned at Lyon; thereafter he and his curia moved restlessly between Lyon, Poitiers and Bordeaux before finally settling in the small town of Avignon in 1309. Allegiances within the Sacred College were finally settled as he appointed Gascons as cardinals. The papacy came to be seen as French and every pope after Clement was French until the Great Schism in 1378. The papacy in consequence lost its international calibre.

James of Molay and the Fate of the Templars

James of Molay, last Grand Master of the Templars, a shrewd, straightforward military man and a good organiser, was elected after the death of his predecessor in Acre. He stemmed losses in finance and personnel, took up residence in Cyprus and combined with the Grand Master of the Hospitallers and the brother of King Henry of Cyprus to launch the last of the true Holy Land crusades, bringing into play the Christian enclave of Cilician Armenia and the Islamic convert and enemy of the Mamluks, Ghazan, Mongol Ilkahn of Persia. The deal was to recover Jerusalem and split territory between Christian settlers and the Mongol power using Armenia and the Mongols to expel the Mamluk garrisons. In an initial action in the winter of 1300–01, Cypriots, Templars and Hospitallers landed on the mainland at Tortosa from the island of Ruad and for some twenty-five days ravaged and took Muslims to be sold into slavery. The crusade project failed only when Ghazan, although he had taken Aleppo and all of Damascus bar the citadel, called off his attack, having grown uneasy about Mamluk strength and the lack of fodder for his horses. Templars retired to Ruad, holding themselves ready for another assault, but were overwhelmed by a Mamluk counterattack in 1302–3. It was the last Holy Land crusade to set foot on the mainland. Although Peter I of Cyprus contrived to take a substantial force in 1365 to capture Alexandria, he could not hold it and never got to Jerusalem.

Summoned by Pope Clement V to join with the Hospitaller Grand Master to discuss reform, economies and the merger of the two Orders, James left Cyprus in 1306. As a traditionalist, he feared that the Hospitallers would dominate the Templars and was wary of the potentially deadly hostile force of Philip the Fair. Clement had to put off seeing him for many months. It was at Poitiers that James of Molay approached Philip with his unease about rumours of accusations against his order and it was there that he spoke with Clement, who in September launched an inquiry of his own. Trapped in France by Clement's illness, James was lured to Paris by Philip on 12 October 1307 to act as pall-bearer at the funeral of Philip's sister-in-law. But all was swept aside in Philip's next, catastrophic move on Friday 13 October – a date it was said, so inscribed in folk memory as to make Friday the 13th in any month ill omened – when James and all the French Templars were arrested simultaneously in the early hours.

Philip made use of the inquisitor of France who had authority to investigate heresy and sorcery, while deploying his own men, often civil lawyers, propagandising against the Templars and using torture. A farrago of accusations emerged, corresponding to all the fears and tensions unleashed by the fall of Acre and lurking in a society under strain. Renegades, men with grievances, rogues set the ball rolling, and what followed was illogical and incongruous as well as gross exaggeration by scheming interrogators probing the suggestion that the Templars had betrayed Christendom to the Muslims.

Nonplussed by events, old by medieval standards, perhaps promised release if he confessed, James of Molay made a fatal mistake on 24 October, when he admitted sinful behaviour – probably no more than masculine horseplay – at an initiation ritual which got out of hand at his reception into the Order forty-two years earlier, and urged others to confess as he had.

The Chinon Parchment, recently discovered in the Vatican Archives, shows Clement's efforts over three days in August 1308 to rescue the reputation of James of Molay and leading Templars imprisoned in the castle of Chinon and thus free them from Philip's clutches. Contriving to infiltrate three of his cardinals into the prison to carry out a secret interrogation, he established the true nature of the initiation ceremony and acquitted James and the others of heresy. But Clement was too alarmed at the prospect of the exhumation of Boniface and the danger of the schism in the Church to make known the acquittal and absolution of James and the others. It stayed secret and the victims were left to their fate.

There followed a long wrestling match between Philip and Clement, who attempted to preserve his own control over proceedings and prevent Philip from exhuming and burning Boniface. Philip's motive was plain. He needed money: Templars were rich bankers, and Philip had engaged in expensive warfare compelling him to debase the coinage. Kings outside France where torture was not used, found the accusations unconvincing but did not feel able to intervene.

In the midst of the struggles Clement, a sincere crusader, attempted to maintain the call to rescue the Holy Land and summoned a General Council at Vienne, in Dauphiné, which sat between 1311 and 1312 in order to bring about church reform and launch a full-scale expedition. Popes before him had engaged too often in political crusading and the Council did not believe in Clement's motives, thinking his intentions mercenary. Some new thinking about crusades for Jerusalem emerged in Clement's time. Marino Sanudo Torsello, a member of the Venetian aristocracy, wrote the most thorough and expert analysis of the means required to destroy Egypt's economic power in preparation for a general crusade but it fell foul both of the unwillingness to cut off trade and of the preoccupations of Clement's successor, John XXII, who was devoted to restoring papal power in Italy.

Some Templars made a last heroic stand for their Order. In May 1310 fifty-four Templars in France withdrew their confessions and were promptly burned alive as relapsed heretics outside Paris by the Archbishop of Sens, an associate of Philip. That led the surviving Knights to accept guilt and receive pensions. Finally in 1314, James of Molay and Geoffrey of Charnay, former Preceptor of Normandy, also withdrew their confessions. In a rage and without authority Philip had them publicly burned alive for relapse on an island in the Seine. Their courage moved onlookers. But by that time Philip had won. In his attack on the Templars he was targeting rich bankers, smearing them and forcing Clement to suppress them, which the pope did at Vienne on the grounds that their reputation had been destroyed. Their possessions were transferred to the Hospitallers, from whom Philip extracted the money by charging massive 'expenses'.

Philip's actions caused major damage. By destroying the Templars he took away devoted manpower committed to the crusade and his ruthless propaganda discredited the papacy and created an atmosphere of fear of the Muslim world and of the inroads of Satan into Christendom. Political crusading was a morass which undermined popes and Philip made everything worse. The effects of his reign lasted long after his death in 1314. The public still cared about crusade and had a long tradition of popular agitation going back to the *Pastoureaux* working to rescue St Louis but a society lacking means of interpretation of natural disasters looked to conspiracy explanations and the general *bête noire* of the Muslims.

In 1321 in the south of France another alleged conspiracy was uncovered between Jews, lepers and Muslims said to be bent on poisoning water supplies used by Christians. Secret meetings had been held, it was alleged, and letters and magic powder sent by the Muslim kings of Granada and Tunis. The new king of France, Philip V, susceptible to such rumours, listened and Bernard Gui the inquisitor investigated. There were pogroms and burnings of lepers.

Damage to the papacy was also long-lasting. Popes had been the leaders and initiators of the crusade for Jerusalem, but now their reputation was gone. The papal residence at Avignon after 1309 was described as the Babylonish Captivity and there were long campaigns fought to bring order to Italy and a return to Rome. In the Great Schism (1378–1414) popes and antipopes were busy attacking and condemning one another and were distracted from crusading.

Crusade at Sea: The Naval Role of the Hospitallers

While the Templars underwent their long Passion, their sister Order secured a new role. An invitation to the Hospitallers from a landholder on the island of Rhodes to move there and help defend his interests against marauding Genoese corsairs secured the support of Clement V for its conquest, the nominal ruler being the Byzantine emperor. Relations between the West and Byzantium were poor and Clement authorised the Grand Master to make war, treating the Byzantines as schismatics and allowing him crusade subsidies. The Grand Master, Fulk of Villaret, nephew of the Grand Master who had collaborated with James of Molay, finally conquered Rhodes in 1309–10.

A rich, manageable territory with a deep-water port and old Byzantine fortifications, Rhodes had good agricultural land and ample food and water and lay 250 miles from Cyprus, within sight of the new, growing Muslim power in Anatolia. The Order adapted to a maritime function, harassing Muslim shipping and raiding the Anatolian coastline, combining naval warfare with their traditional land fighting. An indigenous population worked the land and valued the Order's success in bringing peace and treating the sick in their hospital. Knights, sergeants, mercenaries and slaves, together with the indigenous population forming a militia in emergencies, created a fighting garrison of some 7,500, strong enough to withstand a siege. Under the Hospitallers Rhodes distinguished itself as it fought off the fleet and army of the Ottoman sultan Mehmet the Conqueror, victor over Constantinople in 1453, when he attempted to end the Knights' raids and assaulted the island for eighty-nine days in 1480. Grievously outnumbered and subject to the monster cannon of the time, a last stand by the Grand Master, Peter d'Aubusson, on a walkway of the fortification called the Tower of Italy as it was on the verge of being taken, turned the battle. An early printed book with engravings by one of the Knights, Pierre Caoursin, recorded events of the siege and its aftermath, increasing the prestige of the order and boosting recruitment.

Crusade and Jerusalem

Philip the Fair's dramatic confrontations had been a kind of thunderclap warning to his world of a new situation. French popes, English kings, the Hundred Years War between France and England and other national conflicts put up near-impregnable barriers to the Jerusalem crusade; significantly, it was Edward III, the first of the English kings not to take the cross, who invented the chivalric ritual of the Knights of the Garter, overshadowing the traditional rites of crusading. The costs of war had grown and sucked in money which would otherwise have been donated to the needs of crusading. Major changes in feudal service, which increased the use of mercenaries, and new methods of waging war, which required time and investment, all worked against the continuance of crusading in the style of the past. It was not that all hope of Jerusalem had been put aside. When wars went well, victors were inclined to dream of Jerusalem's recovery, but practical difficulties always took precedence. The dream died, but only slowly.

For Mamluks who flourished on bribes and arbitrary fines, the pilgrim trade was a rich source of revenue and a reliable one as no one expected disruption from a Jerusalem crusade. Aristocratic pilgrims and some better-off bourgeois undertook the journey, while poor pilgrims were priced out. There was a change of attitudes. In Jerusalem the Franciscans occupied the Cenacle, the supposed site of the Last Supper on the Mount of Olives, and were allowed a role in escorting pilgrims but the pilgrims themselves no longer wished to be buried in the city.

The Franciscans maintained simplicity in worship, whereas previously the clergy in the Crusader States had provided pilgrims with a liturgy of the highest quality so as to leave them with a memorable experience. The friars were aware they lived on sufferance, at the whim of the Mamluks, who granted them rights at the basilica of the Nativity in Bethlehem and at the tomb of Mary but expected them to share these with members of the Eastern Churches. The keys to the sites remained in Mamluk hands. Under the Ottoman Turks the Franciscans were forced to leave their friary in 1551 but found another site near to the Church of the Holy Sepulchre and continued their long service to pilgrims.

Spanish Military Orders and Reconquista

The Hospitallers and Templars were so respected in the Iberian peninsula that two indigenous orders were founded along the same lines: that of Santiago in 1175 and that of Calatrava, approved by the pope in 1187. These had an advantage over military orders devoted to the Holy Land because of the shorter lines of communication during campaigns.

Two kings transformed the whole Christian future in Spain by breaking with the old traditions of raid, counter-raid and the levying of tribute. They were steeled by adversity, St Ferdinand III of Castile by his struggle till 1130 with the formerly independent kingdom of Leon and James I of Aragon by the conflicts he had to face between landlocked Aragon and the maritime ambitions of Catalonia. Ferdinand campaigned long and hard in harsh climatic conditions aided by dissensions among Muslims and tensions between successive Berber enthusiasts and settled *mudéjars*, winning

Cordoba and finally the richest prize, Seville. His archbishop, Rodrigo, was by his side to reassure him that the lands he was seizing could rightly be taken, for they had been Christian under the Visigoths. His history is much less well known than that of St Louis, who conquered no Muslim territory, but he was very like the French king in his austere devotion to the crusading cause. The sexual athlete James of Aragon was no saint, but he displayed a restraint especially unusual in the anarchic story of Iberian kings by handing over Valencia to St Ferdinand after he had conquered it and treating the conquered people of the Balearics, where there were substantial minorities of Jews and Muslims, with restraint and tolerance.

It was the context in which the Catalan Ramon Llull (1232–1315) began his career. A former troubadour in the court of James I, he had a vision and became a missionary to Islam. Studying Latin and philosophy in Paris and Montpellier, learning Arabic and reading the Quran, whose magnificent Arabic he admired, he followed the Franciscan ideal of poverty, believing in persuasion of Muslims and Jews to Christianity by exploring common ground. He devised a system of pictures and symbols based on the natural order of the universe to attract and persuade Muslims who did not accept and could not read the Gospels. The paintings associated with him – the system of persuasion central to his life's work – still move the observer. And yet, dedicated persuader as he was and tireless advocate for the learning of Arabic for mission, Llull could never emancipate himself from the use of force. Muslims should be compelled, he came to believe, to listen to the truth being preached, just as a child is compelled to listen to its lessons.

It was a view which corresponded to the decisions made by the canonist Pope Innocent IV in 1245, who accepted the universal doctrine that faith can never be imposed by force but also decreed that, since Christ as God had power over all men because of Creation, so the pope as His representative had responsibility for both Christians and non-Christians. He could thus require non-Christian rulers to admit missionaries to preach the Gospel and, in the case of refusal, call on Christian rulers to force them to do so. This looked like Christianity imposed by force and Innocent's judgement was used by the conquistadors to coerce submission in the New

World. A friar would be used to preach Christianity to the South American Indians in a language they did not understand. As they remained blank or, more likely, ran away, the ground was established for saying that they had refused missionaries the right to preach, and thus they and their rulers could be subjected to conquest. In this way Mexicans and Peruvians were exposed to tyranny and expropriation by Cortés and his fellows. Popes allocated spheres of influence between the Portuguese and the Spanish in lands occupied by enemies of the faith, providing these rivals with what was in effect a monopoly of trade. Montezuma defended his own beliefs, and it brought about his end.

Governments in Europe were solely interested in smooth transactions bringing rewards to them without dissidence from aristocrats. Europeans went to the New World, risking the hazards of the Atlantic to get rich quickly. Cortés and his fellows came from seaports attracting a mass of immigrants and in a maelstrom of bacteria acquired an unusual resistance to infection that their victims in the New World did not have. The indigenous population perished from disease in great numbers. Bartolomé de las Casas saw for himself what was going on, became a friar and, with others, devoted himself to denouncing what was happening – but without effect. It was a stain on Catholicism in the sixteenth century, the poisonous legacy of Innocent IV endeavouring to wrestle with relationships between the Church and alien peoples.

The Rise of the Ottoman Turks

The Ottoman Turks transformed the Muslim world. The early steps of their leaders in pursuit of power were so quiet and unobtrusive that they deceived both the ruling Mamluks and the West. Osman (1299–1326), the founder of the dynasty, an obscure border lord of the north-western corner of Anatolia, profited, as other emirs did, from the breakdown of the Seljuq sultanate. His son Orkhan, leader from 1326 to 1362, using the *ghazi* tradition of resistance to Byzantium and gathering adventurers around him, made remarkable and rapid advances, taking Busra across the Sea of Marmara from Constantinople in 1326, Nicaea in 1331 and Nicomedia in

1337; as early as 1333 the emperor of Byzantium was paying him an annual tribute. The Ottomans took Gallipoli in 1354, were pushed out but regained it. Thus early on, the Ottomans made a place for themselves both in the former Byzantine heartland of Anatolia and in Europe and so began the isolation of Constantinople. While the traditions of *jihad* and nomadism lay at the heart of their enterprise, the Ottomans' skill lay in moving from nomadism to pasturage, avoiding the temptation of going back to the steppe lands to make conquests and never forgetting the need to sustain military success as outsiders who had nothing but their arms to recommend them, having no title to consideration as descendants of Muhammad.

A further step in the consolidation of the Ottoman territories took place in about 1369, when Sultan Murad I (1362–89) established a working capital at Adrianople (Edirne), a key nodal point for travel and commerce. The town had succumbed easily after a well-placed massacre at nearby Chorlu led its occupants to choose surrender rather than suffer a similar fate. As rulers the Ottomans had real qualities but never shrank from ferocious action when crossed.

There were two reasons for the rapid advance of a distinctively Ottoman form of the slave-soldier, recruited from Christian boys within Ottoman lands who were removed from their parents at an early age, were converted to Islam and trained for military and state service. Called Janissaries (the 'new troop'), they carried all the advantages of Baybars's Mamluks and formed the cornerstone of the emerging Ottoman state. An infantry force, they had what initially no one else had – muzzle-loading muskets, powder and shot. Cavalry back-up was provided by *spahis*, feudal nobility who occupied a secondary role behind the Janissaries. The infantry's celibate life revolved round the Ottoman dynasty and they were rewarded according to their talent and success in performing the tasks set them. At the end of their service they were allowed to marry and were settled on the fringes of the empire, never at the centre where they could have caused trouble.

The second factor facilitating rapid expansion and success in retaining territory lay in the confusion which prevailed in the territories of the former Byzantine Empire. A shaky Latin Empire owing allegiance to the pope had been set up on the ruins of Byzantium as a result of the blunders of the Western troops and their leaders in the Fourth Crusade in 1203–4 and commanded no loyalty. It succumbed to an old Byzantine aristocratic dynasty, the Palaeologi, who took over the shattered city of Constantinople in 1261, expelling the Latins and promptly fell into the classic error of the emperors of the past, wasting money on elaborate ceremonial and neglecting their long-suffering peasantry. The papacy would do nothing to help the Byzantines because they insisted on emperors accepting their authority and their doctrine of the Procession of the Holy Spirit, before any military action was undertaken. In turn, the mass of people in Constantinople and the recovered Byzantine territories, the rulers and the Greek Orthodox hierarchy rejected any attempts at compromise made by emperors and aristocrats with the Catholics over papal authority and Trinitarian doctrine, remembering with bitterness the devastation inflicted on their city by the Fourth Crusade. Their intransigence was reinforced by a Byzantine mystical movement, Hesychasm, which led its adherents to accept passively their suffering as the will of God.

The empire remained weak; Western crusaders did not come to help the emperors; adventurers tried their luck. Statelets formed: a Villehardouin dynasty, Catalan merchants, Venetians, volatile and transient. In short, no force came into existence capable of standing up to the Ottomans in the whole area of the Aegean, the Balkans or the eastern Mediterranean. On the mainland in the Balkans the same weaknesses appeared. Bulgaria was passionate about escaping from the yoke of the Byzantines, remembering with tears the oppression of the Emperor Basil II the Bulgar-slayer in the eleventh century; trying to be independent, it was crushed. Belgrade, under a Hungarian garrison and galvanised under St John Capistrano, beat the Ottomans off in 1456, but it was the exception. Serbia struck out for its independence but, although it succeeded for a time, it was crushed at the battle of Kosovo in 1389.

Bayezid I (1389–1403) was the son of an Ottoman sultan and a Byzantine princess; a ferocious fighter, nicknamed 'The Thunderbolt', he overcame rival emirs in Anatolia. The defeat of a coalition of cavalrymen from the West – mainly Burgundian, some French, some Teutonic Knights

– recognised as crusaders by both the rival popes of the Great Schism, who travelled overland to aid Sigismund, King of Hungary, and were shattered at Nicopolis by the Danube in 1396, encouraged a great blossoming of ambition in Bayezid. The cavalrymen failed through their own impetuosity and their unwillingness to listen to advice from the Hungarians who were much more experienced in Ottoman warfare than they were. Charging full-tilt against the Ottomans, they were lured into an ambush, enveloped by Ottoman horsemen and cut down by their cavalry and Janissaries. Few survived. Nicopolis encouraged Bayezid to seek recognition as Sultan of Rum – that is, Rome – from the caliph at Cairo. This had great significance, because East Rome was an ancient title for the Christian Byzantine Empire and implied a new target for Ottoman conquest.

All plans of Bayezid, however, were wrecked by a shattering defeat at Ankara in 1402 at the hands of Tamerlane, the Tamburlaine of Christopher Marlowe's play, a Central Asian chieftain of Turkic descent with all the ferocity of Genghiz Khan. The Mamluks were ready to surrender Jerusalem, recognising a power greater than their own, but Tamerlane preferred to attack the Ottomans. Bayezid despaired and died not long after Ankara. Tamerlane's empire broke in pieces after his death and for a decade Bayezid's sons battled for the inheritance. It was one moment when a major Western intervention might have checked the rise of the Ottomans. It never happened. Popes were still the natural authority to summon into action residual anti-Muslim crusading impulses in the West, belatedly understanding what a menace the Ottomans were. But although recovered from the conflicts of the Great Schism, the papacy was preoccupied by political crusading, as a series of expeditions with the crusading indulgence were dispatched in 1421–31 to destroy the Hussites in Bohemia. They were contests widely seen as battles between Germans and Slavs over land and power. Byzantine emperors in the meantime were reduced to begging in vain for help in Western capitals.

Ottoman revival came from Murad II (1421–51) who, both as patron and as poet, celebrated Turkish history and myths and encouraged a new consciousness of the Ottoman past. He met and defeated a crusading army summoned by Pope Eugenius III, an advocate of reunion between the

Greek Orthodox and Catholic Churches, which combined Serbian and Hungarian forces under the heroic leadership of John Hunyadi of Transylvania acting in unison with the young king of Hungary, Ladislas. Venetian ships were to join with these land forces for an amphibious attack on the Ottomans at the Black Sea port of Varna in 1444 but the Venetians were unwilling to risk their ships and Murad split the Serbians from the Hungarians by offering peace proposals which the Serbians accepted and the Hungarians declined. The Hungarians were left alone to face Murad's troops; they fought all day and inflicted heavy casualties but had to withdraw.

In the Balkans, appeals for Christian unity often went awry when Ottoman rule was not seen as manifestly worse than that of Christian leaders making harsh demands on their peasantry. No doubt Murad would have wished to crown his sultanate by capturing Constantinople; he tried but failed. Finally, an ageing man, he abdicated, giving place to his son Mehmed II.

The Capture of Constantinople, 1453

In 1453 Mehmed II, the Conqueror (1444–6 and 1451–81), had at his disposal the power of the Janissaries and the wealth gained through rigid financial control and a competent taxation system. Constantinople's massive walls were still an obstacle and Mehmed sacrificed thousands of Janissaries in the assault, risking a backlash elsewhere because he had committed so much of his resources in men and materials to one objective, paying many specialist miners and obtaining at a massive fee a monster cannon which projected missiles of an unprecedented size. This cannon had been offered to the last Byzantine emperor, Constantine XI (1449–53), but he had not been able to afford it. Mehmed took an internal risk too, as he had been deposed, probably at the wish of a grand vizier who thought an attack on Constantinople too dangerous; for a time his father ruled in his place, but Mehmed made a comeback and, before long, eliminated the grand vizier.

No Western rescue came, only some individual Italians, and the city fell on 29 May 1453. Pius II, a pope of humanist background, tried hard to inspire a crusade to retake it, assuming a less common position about the importance of saving it by contrasting the barbarism of Turkish civilisation with the fount of Greek culture inside Constantinople. But in this he was mistaken: scholars had already fled and found new homes. He acknowledged the damage done to crusading by the 'greed' of his predecessors, and his attempt to enlist as leader the ruthless egoist King Louis XI of France got no response.

The capture had major effects. Mehmed's prestige soared as he had achieved a feat which had eluded the early Arab caliphate and his own father. After Constantinople fell, Mehmed not only felt himself heir to the traditions of world rule which the Byzantines had inherited from the Roman Empire but also withdrew from humdrum affairs, observing conferences from behind a lattice, half-concealed from view, while the grand vizier presided and the heads of the great ruling bureaucracies reported on their work. He was also influenced by the Arab caliphate of the early centuries of Islam and to the devotion to *jihad* of the *ghazis*. He began to build up Constantinople, renamed Istanbul. He had encountered a city shrunken and impoverished in population and proceeded to import Muslim craftsmen and their families with wares distinctive to the Turks, creating a luxury trade that attracted Western buyers. He also built mosques and schools to create a centre of Islamic teaching. From him stemmed a longlasting tradition of providing charitable foundations for the poor. A fortunate discovery in the district of Eyup of the tomb of an early Companion of the Prophet by Mehmed's spiritual adviser created a centre of Muslim devotion and drew the devout to seek places nearby for their graves. The site, together with the great dome of the Fatih mosque built as a rival to Hagia Sophia, gave a Muslim counter-balance to other districts inhabited strongly by non-Muslims.

Expansion was aided by the *ghazi* spirit but, once land was conquered, it was ruled with good sense and flexibility. Beyond the Danube the Ottomans had absorbed Romania by 1504; Belgrade fell in 1520; Hungary had fallen under Ottoman rule in 1529; Vienna was besieged in 1529 but not taken, exceptionally bad weather causing the attacking cavalry to lose their footing and creating problems over the positioning of cannon.

Central control and a notable lack of corruption were the keys to success. In a movement away from the Ottoman past, a powerful monarch dominated central institutions. High religious functionaries were given responsibility under the sultan and their fidelity to him over many years sustained the state. Communities were taxed and the responsible authorities, Muslim or not, gathered it, involving them closely in the system. There was no wish to convert Jews or Christians, as the *dhimmi* tax on monotheists played a vital role in sustaining Ottoman finances. Tax farming and consequent creaming of profits were stopped and taxes kept at a tolerable level. *Qadis* inspected army units and ensured rectitude in tax collection.

The *ulama* was kept under control. A chief mufti was appointed from 1433 to lead the body of *qadis* and scholars. Leading figures in *madrasas* served in a system which rewarded merit and loyalty. It was a controlled Sunnism, unwilling to allow the proliferation of groups under different schools of Islamic law disputing with each other. Leading Sufi brotherhoods were co-opted into the system, which made room for Jews fleeing from Spain and Portugal, using their administrative skills while giving them freedom of worship.

The wealth of the sultanate opened the way for artistic patronage: a grand theatre of ceremonial based on Constantinople and the Topkapi palace at its apex overlooking the Golden Horn, inheriting the tradition of Byzantium. Here were splendid rooms and decoration, a harem and opportunities for former slaves to rise to heights of power. There were indeed struggles for control within the family, exacerbated by the tradition of polygamy and fratricide to ensure succession – non-Quranic but defended on pragmatic grounds, to maintain stability. It was a practice disliked by the population. Generation after generation, a leading claimant murdered his rivals so that the children of his predecessors, whether by wives or concubines, could not be obstacles to succession. There was even an established technique for doing so, as deaf mutes with greased bowstrings had the regular task of throttling unwanted siblings.

The Western answer to this formidable power was spasmodic. The menace was understood but the defensive crusading which had evolved lacked the traditional verve. The magic of Jerusalem had long outlived the loss of the Holy Land and the liturgy recalled the Sepulchre and implied that it should be recovered. Western powers shuddered at the prospect of *jihad* being deployed by the Ottomans and resistance at times transcended the division between Protestant and Catholic. But Jerusalem generally had moved to the back of men's minds, a potent name still but no longer the target for military intervention. The cross, the vow, the indulgence, the traditional weapons of crusade were now most effective when they could be combined with the needs of the nation-state.

Revival of Crusading

Crusades revived in three areas, with failure in one and success in the two others. Two were launched against Muslims. Portugal strove to take the North African coast from the time of the capture of the port of Ceuta in 1415 to the battle of the Three Kings in 1578, when Sebastian, nephew of Philip II of Spain and grandson of John III of Portugal, with the flower of the nobility, was defeated by Abdul Malik of the Sharifian dynasty of southern Morocco. Disputing Muslim rulers had united in *jihad* in response to Portugal's crusading zeal.

The second area of crusading against Muslims, and a successful one, lay in Granada, where they were overwhelmed. The marriage of two distant cousins, Ferdinand of Aragon and Isabella of Castile, resolved the Christian tensions of the Iberian peninsula and put completion of *Reconquista* in the forefront. Under Ferdinand's leadership, military orders combined into one brotherhood, the Santa Hermandad, producing dedicated manpower. Other troops were provided by the great nobles and specialist gunners hired for high fees from far afield, while local minerals were exploited to provide 200 artillery pieces. The four-month siege of Malaga with its massive walls roused the determination of the Muslims but their defeat was a turning point. The ten-year war mutually stimulated the ideas of crusade and *jihad*.

The Genoese and Jews, sources of credit, were forced into making massive donations to Ferdinand's campaign. An order of 1492 demanded that Jews, numbering about 200,000, should either convert to Christianity or leave Spain. Some accepted conversion – the *conversos* – and were subjected to the harsh rigours of the Inquisition in which the rich were tortured, convicted and forced to forfeit their wealth; most were transported away and many were robbed in transit. This massive flight of Jews brought talent to the Ottomans. Thessaloniki, captured and deserted in 1432, was transformed by an influx of Spanish Jews to become a major commercial centre.

The third area of success stands apart from all others because it was directed against pagans rather than Muslims. When, after the fall of Acre, the Teutonic Knights left the Holy Land, they listened to the advice of their greatest Hochmeister, Hermann of Salza, who had a vision of a quasi-kingdom under the Knights' control on the east of Germany. The first attempt to realise this failed when the King of Hungary chased them out of the territory they held in Transylvania, but Hermann's vision came to fruition in the fourteenth century when the Order took power in heathen territory in eastern Germany and engaged in a species of perpetual crusade at the expense of the indigenous Prussians. This was a war of extermination in which the native peoples were reduced to serfdom and their language obliterated. A class of *ministeriales* from the German Empire were recruited and lived as fighting celibates in the manner of military orders in the Holy Land. But it was a harsh world. Captured Knights were put on bonfires in full armour and roasted like chestnuts. Here there was indeed heroism but nothing of the warrior understanding and ransoming characteristic of much of the Holy Land crusading. At the same time there were major economic gains as cogs, fat-bellied merchant ships, built up trade on the Baltic coast and German farmers advanced to settle under the shield of the Knights. The old traditions of crusading were maintained and warriors came out to fight in expeditions known as *reysen*, interspersed with feasts and hunting. It was genuinely felt to be a crusade and Bolingbroke, the future Henry IV of England, exiled by Richard II, gained prestige by his service with the Teutonic Knights.

Inner Weaknesses of the Ottomans

Movements of thought and practice within the Islamic world were more likely to destroy the Ottoman Empire than any Western attacks. Shiism, Zoroastrianism and the Bektashi Dervish movement all had major upsetting potential and the need was felt for drastic action to suppress them. Even the young Mehmed the Conqueror, living in Edirne before his accession, fell under the influence of a Sufi order with mysterious and whirling dances founded by Haji Bektash in Anatolia in 1337. These appealed to Shiites, Sufis and Christians alike, including Janissaries. When a Bektash preacher fell victim to orthodox Sunnis and was lynched, Janissaries reacted with anger, looting in the streets. Only the need for military action elsewhere and obedience to Sultan Murad, Mehmed's father, calmed the crisis.

At the death of Mehmed the Conqueror, his son Bayezid II (1481–1512) stemmed difficulties and neutralised the competition of his brother Zizim by paying a massive sum for the Hospitallers to keep him as a hostage until his death in 1495. A pious man, Bayezid disliked warring against fellow Muslims, welcomed victims of Ferdinand and Isabella and gave Jews and fleeing Muslims status and consideration, although he warily placed them in provincial cities, notably Thessaloniki, rather than in Istanbul. His major contribution was to build up the Ottoman navy and use it to strip away Venetian possessions in mainland Greece. However, he was complacent towards the Kizilbas, a Safavid Sufi brotherhood from Persia with the insignia of red caps, an ancient movement led by a gifted, charismatic and bloodthirsty Shaikh Ismail, who proposed to take over the Muslim world. Believing Ismail and his followers might be instruments of God to revitalise Islam, Bayezid gave permission for them to take an army across eastern Ottoman lands.

Selim the Grim (Caliph 1512–20)

Shocked by this, one of Bayezid's sons called Selim, governor of Trebizond, marched into eastern provinces in 1505 as a demonstration and was reprimanded by his father. Then in 1510 he defeated a Kizilbas army led by

Ismail's brother and was again reprimanded, after which he deposed his father in 1512 and took violent action against Ismail and his followers, whom he had rightly seen as a profound menace, not least because Ismail could claim descent from the Prophet. The leaders were hunted down while others fled back to Persia. Determined to destroy the Kizilbas, Selim instructed his ministers to make peace with his Western enemies the Mamluks, Venice and Hungary and asked for support from scholars in Istanbul to have the sect proscribed as heretical. His men identified suspects on the road travelled by troops marching towards Persia. They were then driven off to the borders of the empire, where they could do least damage. In 1514 he faced an army of Shaik Ismail at Caldiran, in modern Iran.

It was hard-fought, but the Janissary discipline held long enough to destroy the enemy. So uncertain was the fidelity of the Janissaries that, when Selim proposed to delay and seek additional advantage before battle, an adviser insisted that he should attack at once, and so he did. Shaik Ismail, although wounded, escaped and lived on till 1524 but Selim's victory destroyed Ismail's reputation for infallibility.

Next, having discovered a new Mamluk move to lay down high-quality cannon for the defence of Cairo, in the spring of 1516 Selim turned to attack them. Fellow Muslims they might be, and a slave-soldiery supporting Sunni orthodoxy, but Selim was not the man for finer points of ethics. Sooner or later he believed the Mamluk leadership would find it expedient to ally with Ottoman enemies. The Mamluks had little support: there had been too many greedy and incompetent sultans damaging the agriculture of Upper Egypt by their exactions and exacerbating effects of plague. Moreover, although they still recruited soldiers from the steppes – only now Circassians rather than Turks – they led them poorly. Battles in 1516 and 1517 defeated the opposition, bribery caused the defection of the governor of Aleppo, and Egypt fell. The last Mamluk leader was crucified, and the Abbasid caliph surrendered his powers, leaving the caliphal emblems, the sword and the mantle of Muhammad, to the Topkapi museum.

In a reign of eight years Selim had doubled the size of the Ottoman

Empire and brought about the surrender to the Ottomans of the three holy cities of Mecca, Medina and Jerusalem. Holding the sacred sites gave Ottomans further status. There was no succession problem, as relatives, siblings and nephews had been eliminated and Selim executed seven grand viziers. In 1520, after Selim succumbed, possibly to anthrax, his son Suleiman the Magnificent succeeded peacefully, rode through the streets of Istanbul and received the ceremonial sword of Osman.

Suleiman the Magnificent: Achievement and Flaws

Suleiman's reign (1520–66) saw the apogee of Ottoman power but also the roots of its decline. He knew the condition of Western Christendom well and had understood that Charles V and Francis I of France were fatally embroiled with each other and would not unite against him. After Charles's victory over him, Francis conveyed to Suleiman that he was open to offers of a discreet alliance and would welcome a move by Suleiman to attack Hungary and Turkey and weaken the Habsburg interest. Suleiman took the hint and at Mohács, between Buda and Belgrade, in 1526 killed King Louis of Hungary and his nobility. Despite their being thousands strong, he took no prisoners. With his backing corsairs came to dominate the North African coast and raided widely, benefiting from the use of a safe harbour in Toulon and overcoming the resistance of the Genoese admiral Roger Doria. In consequence Muslims were in the ascendancy in the Eastern Mediterranean.

His subjects remembered Suleiman as a lawgiver, codifying customary law on issues not covered by the Islamic *Sharia* code and doing justice to Jews by refuting blood libels directed against them and to Christians by liberating them from serfdom on lands he controlled. He was a poet of high calibre, echoing Mehmed II's combination of courage in battle with wide-ranging cultural interests. But there were moments which inspired fear in his non-Muslim subjects, as when in 1521 and 1537, in conflict with Christian powers, he considered killing Christians and destroying their churches.

Suleiman's forces ended a long-standing irritation with the great siege of Rhodes, the Hospitaller fortress, in 1522–3 when he avoided sea attack and concentrated instead on mining. The Sultan commanded in person. Heavily outnumbered, Grand Master Villiers de L'Isle Adam held out to the last possible moment, aided by a Venetian engineer who slipped into the island as a volunteer, aiding the defences against mining with a subterranean listening device that set bells ringing at the least vibration, so that enemy mines could be detected and destroyed. The effects of gunpowder were also mitigated by spiral vents inserted in walls. But Suleiman was too strong and could afford to keep his besiegers in action during the winter. The Grand Master accepted the vote of the garrison that Rhodes should surrender. Suleiman gave the Grand Master the honours of war, for himself, any Knights and any Rhodians who wished to leave, without ransom, and they took ship for Italy on 1 January 1523.

A remarkable reign ended in a defeat. The Hospitallers, in exile in Italy, still harboured the hope of a return to their offensive position in Rhodes, harassing Anatolia once again, but in the end felt obliged to accept an offer by the Western Emperor Charles V of the barren and unpromising island of Malta. As Suleiman moved to destroy another irritation and make an end of Hospitaller harassment, he assembled a host for attack, although on this occasion he did not command in person. He faced the Grand Master de la Valette, a man of iron resolution who had survived capture and a year's service as a galley slave and who in office proceeded to outmanoeuvre a Janissary attack by insisting on a defence of Fort St Elmo, their preferred landing point, at heroic sacrifice. The delay was crucial and a long fight continued in which the laws of war were certainly trampled on. When the besiegers cut the heads off Knights' corpses and fired them at their enemy from cannon, de la Valette responded by executing his Muslim prisoners and firing their heads back again. Somehow he held out from May to September, when Spanish relief arrived. The feat was welcomed as much in Protestant England as in Catholic Europe and bells were rung in celebration at the order of Queen Elizabeth. The harbour of Valletta in Malta celebrates the Grand Master's achievement. Meanwhile, Suleiman was engaged in warfare in Hungary, where he died and was thus unable to deal with the aftermath of the Hospitaller victory.

There was a sense in which the heroism of the Hospitallers acted as a conscience to the quarrelling kingdoms of Catholic Europe. At Lepanto in 1571, a fleet under the command of an illegitimate son of Emperor Charles V, Don John of Austria, surprised a Turkish fleet in winter quarters in the Gulf of Corinth and inflicted a shattering defeat. The galleys of the Knights were placed on an exposed flank in the attack, and deliberately so, because they could be relied on to fight to the end – as they did – and set an example for a much larger, miscellaneous and less reliable body of ships.

Lepanto gave a boost to the morale of the West, although the finances of the Ottomans were still equal to replacing ships lost – and yet a point of saturation was now approaching for defence expenditure, for the area controlled by the Ottomans was immense and the costs of sustaining and policing so much territory very high. Maintenance of ships and crews was costly, needing dockyards and arsenals for constant work and replacement as vessels succumbed to wood-boring insects. Campaigning sustained morale and kept Janissaries in fettle but it all cost a great deal: inflation caused by the immense inflow of gold and silver to Spain from the New World had a major damaging effect on both the West and the Ottoman Empire.

Suleiman failed to suppress the Safavid dynasty, patrons of a rich Persian literature. Twelver Shiism reigned, and the Safavids ruled a gun-powder empire. There were yet more conquests, which took the Ottomans to the Persian Gulf and overran Georgia and Armenia. Baghdad fell, but neither Selim nor his successors were able to destroy the Safavids totally.

Control and training of Suleiman's servants reached a high standard. His grand vizier presided over slaves who had demonstrated their skills and had been trained in palace schools, with the result that Istanbul became for a time a cosmopolitan Renaissance centre of learning, with secular subjects taught as well as Quranic instruction to shape Muslim boys to become teachers and imams.

Signs of future troubles nevertheless began to emerge. The Ottoman Empire was a vast free-trading area and the rewards for the dedicated commercial figures with know-how, contacts and linguistic capacity were immense. The Capitulations of 1536 were part of the deal made with Francis I and gave special privileges to French merchants, an unwise move as in less capable hands more privileges were given. The Ottomans had lost their vital hold on the spice trade when the Portuguese showed their mastery of the use of cannon on shipboard, creating the broadside, and dispatched Vasco da Gama round the Cape of Good Hope, making direct contact with the spice islands and with India.

There was a hardening of the arteries in the later sixteenth century and in the seventeenth, a loss of military pre-eminence, which combined with weaknesses in the sultanate to initiate a long period of decline. A decision by Selim the Grim in 1517 to decree the death penalty for those who engaged in the science of printing was a portent. Manifestly, it at once cut off literate and learned Muslims from an immense array of information and damaged their civilisation. Characteristically, Selim gave no reasons: it was an act of power, and one can only speculate on motives. Calligraphy was one of the glories of Islam and by tradition the act of copying the Quran was in itself meritorious. In Istanbul there was great expenditure on this act and a formidable body of skilled men deployed for the purpose. Examples of the calligraphy were also visible everywhere. Could it be that it was felt to be almost blasphemous for the uncreated word of God to be exposed to a mere mechanical, unthinking technique? Or had the influence of the *ulama* played a role? Their decisions, quietly circulated, had impor-tance. Ottoman authorities could glimpse what was emerging in Catholic Europe as the invention of printing gave the impetus to Martin Luther's challenge to the Church. Judgements by scholars within Islam could be made available to all who could read and might well shake the existing *ulama*'s authority.

The last and most significant of all factors damaging the Ottoman lands was the loss of quality sultans. Suleiman the Magnificent fell prey to the schemes of a favourite slave girl, Roxelana, who deceived him about his son, led him to have him strangled and then persuaded him to get rid of a capable grand vizier to ensure that her own son succeeded. He was Selim the Sot (caliph 1566–74), and his achievement was to lift the prohibition on wine-drinking and attack Cyprus to secure a share of its wine stocks.

Selim was fortunate in the high calibre of his grand vizier whom he was happy to leave as the effective power in the empire while he indulged himself. A Serb from Visegrad originally destined for the priesthood, he was pulled into Ottoman service and the Islamic faith through the *devshirme*, the military levy and rose steadily through the ranks by his great talents and fine manners and reigned as grand vizier under the title Sokollu Mehmed Pasha until his death in 1579. He exercised diplomatic skills, making peace with Western powers while never losing a gentle side-interest in his Serbian compatriots despite the barriers of belief between them: he revived the Serbian archbishopric of Pecs and built the bridge over the River Drina in Visegrad. His widow commissioned one of the most beautiful golden-age Ottoman mosques in Istanbul in his memory. Selim's grand vizier delayed decline but could not ward off the effects of unsatisfactory sultans and inner instability for the system depended on strong central leadership and sultanates of sufficient length for policies to be carried through. Statistics illuminate the position: from the founder, Osman, up to and including Suleiman the Magnificent there had been ten sultans reigning for nearly 280 years; from Selim the Sot there were thirteen sultans covering 140 years.

Sheer size created problems. The sultan's bureaucracy had to send out a multitude of orders and when control weakened, great families who had been clients, bound by ties of service to the sultan, made themselves independent, hereditary powers, only loosely linked to the sultanate. Queen mothers and harem favourites influenced sultans and foreign embassies learned to establish direct links with personalities. Western powers, preoccupied and only spasmodically concerned with Ottoman affairs, acquired a new vitality and challenged the Turkish war machine. The Portuguese ocean-going vessel, as we have seen, beat the Ottomans and eliminated their spice trade monopoly. Western powers with big ships – merchantmen with the broadside, such as caracks – came into the Mediterranean. The Habsburgs, with long-range cannon, musketeers and arquebusiers and the techniques of timed salvoes, changed battlefield conditions and forced Ottoman commanders to recruit much larger numbers of infantry and in consequence dilute the quality of the Janissaries, who ceased to be a highly specialised battle-winning corps. Cavalry diminished in importance. The view has been put forward that changes in warfare were the major driving force behind financial and institutional change in the seventeeth century.* Certainly two wars showed up Ottoman deficiencies, as campaigns against Iran between 1578 and 1590 ended in success but only after strain, and a long slogging match against Austria between 1595 and 1606 drained resources, lowered morale and caused food deficiencies in Istanbul. Contemporaries picked out moral failings, weak personalities and the withdrawal of sultans from battlefield command as the keys to decline.

The success of the Ottoman system had long depended on tight central control, a system above corruption and loyal, well-trained Janissaries with the *spahis,* the cavalry force not allowed to establish appanages for their families.

Ahmed I, the great-grandson of Selim the Sot, reigned from 1603. He had no military experience and the traditions of the past were abandoned. Appalled by the bloodbath in which his father, Muhammad III, killed nineteen sons, Ahmed felt it more humane to confine princes to special quarters with the harem, which had the consequence that many were terrified of taking responsibility. Hitherto Ottoman sultans had treated themselves as natural rulers of the world and all those who wished to make agreements were taken as supplicants who were due to pay tribute. Ahmed ended this and concluded a treaty with Austria in 1606 on terms of equality.

Still allowing heavy expenditure in a time of austerity, he made an impression on the skyline at Istanbul when his architect Sinan, himself a slave, designed one of the most beautiful of all late Muslim buildings, the Blue Mosque.

The judiciary, once respected, became corrupt. As time went on, Janissaries conspired to put in power sultans of their choice and insisted on financial deals with the harem. They abandoned celibacy and ensured that their sons inherited positions: the status of Janissary with privileges was sold; one young sultan who tried to bypass the Janissaries and raise a new military force was dethroned and killed.

---

*C. Imber, *The Ottoman Empire, 1300–1500: The Structure of Power* (Basingstoke, and New York, 2002).

Alien merchants took the place of an indigenous middle class which could have supplied stability and debt put the Ottomans in the hands of outsiders. A last effective crusade in 1683, in which a key role was played by Polish lancers rescuing Vienna, makes a natural endpoint. *Jihad*, the *ghazi* spirit, once an Ottoman inspiration, had died; crusade had won a victory, however precariously. Finally, in the eighteenth century decline had gone so far that it was found necessary to make a formal treaty recognising the special status of the Russian tsars as protectors of the Slav minorities.

While the Ottomans in decline lost their distinctive Islamic character, a new force, Wahhabism, sprang into life in the Arabian desert. Over and over again fresh impetus in the Islamic world has come from the bare expanses of the desert, the passion for monotheism which it inspires and the memory of Muhammad. So it was with the meditations of the scholar Muhammad ibn al-Wahhab based in central Arabia, a follower of Hanbal who insisted in the face of persecution that the Quran was uncreated and not open to commentary and interpretation. The Wahhabi viewpoint went well beyond Hanbal and propounded an extreme puritanism and an utter rejection of all compromise with other faiths. Al-Wahhab took time to study in Mecca, Medina, Damascus and Basra, incubating his drastic reformist ideas, then began to preach in 1740. It was not wholly an accident that his movement was launched just as the decline of Ottoman power was becoming manifest. Al-Wahhab was repudiated by his fellow scholars but rescued by the ruler of a small tribal principality in Najd, north-central Arabia, and thereafter his movement never lost its hold in the desert lands.

Al-Wahhab went well beyond Hanbal in his ferocious commitment to monotheism, rejecting the rituals of Sufism, all veneration of shrines, tombs and relics, even including those of the Prophet, and the most innocuous expressions of respect for other beliefs. Ibn Saud, the ruler of Najd, warred against rival tribes, seeking a super-tribal unification and followed al-Wahhabi's lead in using state power to enforce doctrinal purity. Riyadh became the Wahhabi capital. Wahhabis captured Mecca for a time, destroyed the birthplaces of Muhammad, Khadija, Ali and Abu Bakr, before being expelled by the Ottoman general Mehmet Ali, the reformer and revifier of Sunni Egypt. Wahhabism was never eliminated and in the view of its enemies lived on as a virus in the desert wastes of Arabia through the nineteenth century.

The Enlightenment

France was the key to this last development, inimical root and branch to crusading. Writers asked about the authenticity of the Christian Scriptures and speculated that hundreds of years had elapsed between the events and the writing of the Gospels. Diderot wrote scornfully and humorously about the Sepulchre, a fragment of rock which had led to the spilling of so much blood. The French episcopate was intimately bound to the army and often sprang from the same families: they sought obedience to faith and were not equipped to debate issues with intellectuals. The French Revolution had a strong anticlerical cast and involved pushing hapless clergy into blasphemous acts; the notion of a divine will requiring action for the faith, the vow and the indulgence were alien to such thinkers.

In England the fears of a Jacobite takeover by Catholic Highlanders created a panic and the Catholic Church, the source of crusading, sank to a low point with a recusant remnant subject to penal laws, remaining a quiet, patient group. Generally the climate of opinion was hostile. The Hospitallers were victims of the malaise and of aristocratic self-aggrandisement and their decadence opened the way to their collapse in 1798 in the face of Napoleon. In these circumstances it is surprising that there was such a revival of interest in crusading in the years following the French Revolution.

11

MODERN TIMES

Michaud and the French

Jean-François Michaud (1767–1839) began to publish his three-volume *History of the Crusades* in 1817, two years after the exiling of Napoleon and the return of the Bourbon monarchy. In 1829 a companion volume of text with translations appeared, revising Michaud's work before his death. It went on selling and reached a ninth edition in 1856, before culminating in a luxury edition of 1877 which traced crusading history from Peter the Hermit to the battle of Lepanto, with wonderful illustrations by Gustave Doré. Michaud's passionate views shone through. He believed in monarchy, Christianity and the superiority of the French nation and hated both the French Revolution and the Enlightenment which inspired it. The French were a crusading nation, he insisted, and they had won heroic victories: 'astonishing triumphs', he wrote, 'which made the Muslims believe that the Franks were a race superior to other men'.

The phrase 'astonishing triumphs' rings hollow when the facts are known: Jerusalem had been lost to the Muslims; the coastal strip had fallen in 1291; and Christian Orthodox Constantinople was captured by a crusading army. Michaud was aware of these events but, it seems, felt that they were outweighed by the gift which the Frankish crusaders brought to the Muslims, 'the victorious Christian law', which began 'a new destiny in those faraway lands which had first come to us'. The crusaders, he held, established 'Christian colonies' which would one day enable France to become the model and centre of European civilisation. The holy wars contributed much to this development, he believed. Michaud had a literary talent and the companion volume of texts made him seem like a researcher. It was not so: he was a jackdaw picking out facts to suit his thesis. The Crusader States were not colonies as the nineteenth century understood them and Christian law had made no impact on the Muslims.

Michaud's book and the attitudes which made it so popular were in effect a blueprint for the French colonisation of Muslim lands in the nineteenth century. Louis-Philippe, king of France from 1837 to 1848, took up Michaud with enthusiasm and commissioned a series of paintings, 120 in all, depicting the heroic acts of the French crusaders for five rooms in the palace at Versailles devoted to the crusades. The glorious past would underpin his rule and offset the unhappy impression of despotism and extravagance left by Louis XIV's building of Versailles; by contrast, Louis-Philippe's museum, devoted to the colonies, began with the Frankish conquests in Syria and Lebanon. A commentator viewing a painting of the French assault on Constantine in Algeria in 1837 made an uninhibited reference to the crusading past. 'We find there again, after an interval of five hundred years, the French nation fertilising with its blood the burning plains studded with the tents of Islam. Missionaries and warriors, they every day extend the boundaries of Christendom.' The conquest of Algiers in 1830 was described as a crusade, a Lieutenant Joinville served in the campaign to take it and the French intervention of 1881 in Tunisia was likened to St Louis's last crusade to Tunis. A statue of Joinville was erected outside Tunis.

Along with crusading scenes, Louis-Philippe's paintings included the arms of the aristocratic families whose ancestors had gone on crusade. Bourgeois families who had grown rich through entrepreneurship clamoured for inclusion. Their pleas were heard by Eugène-Henri Courtois, a forger of crusade charters who, with two accomplices, for good fees, obligingly provided evidence of crusading ancestors for his clients.

Walter Scott and the British

The romantic novels of Walter Scott on crusading, especially *Ivanhoe*, published in 1819, and *The Talisman*, published in 1825, added another dimension to crusading in the popular mind. Scott was a child of the Scottish Enlightenment, which regarded the whole crusading movement in the words of David Hume, as the 'most signal and most durable example of the folly of mankind in the history of any age or nation', and in *The Talisman* he is scathing about crusading leaders, describing a treacherous marquis and an evil Templar Grand Master and portraying Richard Lionheart as a man who was warlike but oafish. In the introduction he made a stark contrast between the Christian English monarch, showing 'all the cruelty and violence of an Eastern Sultan', and Saladin, displaying 'the deep policy and prudence of a European sovereign'. In the story a Scottish knight is befriended by an emir, Saladin in disguise, who subsequently enters the Christian camp to heal Richard Lionheart.

For his portrait of Saladin, Scott drew on a tradition established in medieval vernacular literature designed to appeal to aristocratic audiences who admired valiant warriors and loved good stories. A curious compensatory mechanism began to operate after the fall of the Crusader States in 1291. If God's will had allowed the crusaders to fail, might it not be better for defeat to have taken place at the hands of a man of true virtue who shared the chivalric ideas of his opponents? It was said that Saladin had been a child of a Western mother, daughter of the count of Ponthieu, and in a fifteenth-century account one of his aristocratic prisoners dubbed him a Western knight. He became a kind of honorary Westerner. Dante placed him in Limbo, the place of natural happiness reserved for those who had not received baptism, and in 1779 Gotthold Lessing, the German philosopher–playwright, made Saladin the hero of his play *Nathan the Wise*. Scott was heir to a long literary tradition which exalted Saladin – but he gave it an extra twist (and by implication a deeply anti-Muslim one) when he spoke of the 'deep policy and prudence of a European sovereign'. Here is anachronism indeed.

The British never quite made up their minds about the crusades. Writing about them oscillated between the view of Gibbon ('savage fanaticism'), part of his general denigration of the Middle Ages as 'the triumph of barbarism and religion', and a popular romantic storytelling tradition that admired crusades and included fictional characters to adorn their narrative in a genre much publicised in the sixteenth century by the Italian Torquato Tasso and his poem *Jerusalem Liberated*. The Victorian passion for the Middle Ages reinvigorated a positive interest in the crusades. The youthful Burne-Jones kept a handbook of chivalry, Kenelm Digby's *The Broad Stone of Honour*, by his bedside. The Pre-Raphaelites were moved by the Middle Ages altogether and a positive view of crusading was carried with it. Walter Scott's own Enlightenment view of Richard Lionheart was largely diluted by public taste for panoramas in the plays based on Scott's novels: the oafish warrior faded in the general diffusion of taste for all things medieval. Readers liked the sentimental impact of scenes such as Richard's first sight of Jerusalem and the wholly mythical depiction of Queen Berengaria catching sight of evidence of her lost husband's whereabouts after he is shipwrecked.

The clash of views is reflected in the discussions which took place over a proposed statue of the Lionheart. Baron Carlo Marochetti, a fashionable society sculptor best known for designing the tombs of Victoria and Albert at Frogmore, displayed his sculpture of Richard at the Great Exhibition of 1851 but found no takers. A commentator in the *London Illustrated News* thought it wholly inappropriate to associate a statue of 'that madcap fanatic sovereign' with the 'industrial triumphs of this age of progress'. After delays, a compromise was reached whereby public subscription amounting to £3,000 and a contribution of £1,600 from the Ministry of Works met the costs of the bronze statue of Richard in full armour brandishing a sword which was erected in 1860 near the entrance to the House of Lords, where it still stands. The statue represents the rehabilitation of Richard from Scott's harsh depiction. By contrast, Scott's description of Saladin as a generous, courageous and chivalrous leader has prevailed in popular understanding in the West and has effaced the Saladin of history, a man of great courage who grew in stature but who was more complex and more troubled than convention has allowed.

Kaiser Wilhelm II and the Ottoman Sultan

The assumption that Western powers in the Middle East were crusaders and that all Muslims (or at least Sunnis) had a duty to resist them goes back to the skilled manoeuvring of the Ottoman sultan Abdul-Hamid II, who reigned from 1876 to 1909. At the start of his reign he accepted a constitution which allowed for a representative assembly and was designed to pave the way for more profound reforms of the failing empire's stultified bureaucracy. The sultan, appalled when it was apparent that this was only the beginning and designed to lead to more far-reaching reform; also shaken by the Russian response to a rising by the Bulgarians, he abrogated the assembly and ruled thereafter as a dictator. Reform had been the work of the Tanzimat movement of Ottomans who loved the old empire but saw that it had to accommodate to the modern world to survive. It was their achievement to have abolished the Janissaries, replacing them with a modern trained army, and to have reformed the bureaucracy, trained diplomats in languages and put forward the principle of equality in citizenship, abolishing in effect the distinction between Muslim and non-Muslim. The last reform in particular was strongly opposed by Islamic scholars but nonetheless began to change the nature of the Ottoman Empire.

The Ottoman Empire was the sick man of Europe, unwieldy, yet controlling much land and having a major role in trade. As portions broke away and received virtual independence, the question exercising the Great Powers was, who was to control it – Russia, or Austria-Hungary, or even a Greek state formed out of early struggles for independence? Russia fought against the empire four times in the nineteenth century, seeking a warm water outlet for their fleet, and established what was in effect a protectorate over its Slav Christians. A Bulgarian rising in 1876 was put down with ferocity by the Turks and stimulated W. E. Gladstone in a white heat of passion in late August 1876 to compose a pamphlet on the massacres, *Bulgarian Horrors and the Question of the East*, which sold over 20,000 copies. At its heart was a demand that the Ottomans go away. 'Let the Turks', Gladstone wrote,

now carry off their abuses in the only possible way, by carrying off themselves. Their Zaptiehs and their Mudits, their Bimbashis and their Yuzbashis, their Kaimakans and their Pashas, one and all bag and baggage shall I hope clear out from the province they have desolated and profaned. This ... is the only reparation we can make to those heaps on heaps of dead, to the violated purity of matron, maiden and of child.

The massacres were not exaggerated: 12,000 victims, men, women and children were reported. In September Gladstone spoke to a crowd of 10,000 at Blackheath assembled in the pouring rain where in a great silence he repeated slowly the evocative description of the Ottoman officialdom, Bimbashis and Yuzbashis and the like whom he had exhorted to go. W. T. Stead, no mean polemicist himself, thought it one of the most memorable experiences of his life. But Gladstone never explained who was to take over to protect the Bulgarians; by implication, he was in the last resort prepared to accept Russia.

The Russians themselves were quite clear that it was their task. In command of their armies both the Tsar and the Grand Duke Nicholas called themselves crusaders and although the new Turkish army estab-lished under the Tanzimat reforms earned respect by its five-month defence of the town of Plevna against the Russians, losses to Russia elsewhere forced them to accept defeat. After victory, the Congress of Berlin in 1878 made a settlement allocating the spoils: Serbia, Romania, Montenegro and part of Bulgaria gained independence; Bosnia-Herzegovina was allocated to Austria-Hungary, France received Tunis, and Britain Cyprus. It all played into the hands of Abdul-Hamid's propaganda. In the Constitution of 1876 he had claimed the caliphate: 'His Majesty the Sultan, the Supreme Caliph, is the Protector of the Muslim religion.' Defunct as the caliphate was, it still carried an emotional significance as it recalled the days when great swathes of territory fell to caliphs' victorious armies. Some precedent existed for Abdul-Hamid – it was, for example, customary from the early nineteenth century for sultans at their succession to gird on the sword of the great caliph Umar. Abdul-Hamid went further, appealing to Muslims everywhere to accept his religious as well as political leadership. He moved skilfully and subsidised newspapers to proclaim his message in Muslim lands. If Western colonial powers came to be troubled by agitators questioning his right to rule Muslims, they would be distracted from dismantling his empire. He smeared the Western powers and the Russians and warned the Muslim world to resist these greedy interlopers, who were, whether they admitted it or not, crusaders. A series of revolts against colonialists involving Muslims gave colour to Abdul-Hamid's stand.

The leading nations of the time who assembled at Berlin in 1878 were not crusaders but statesmen attempting to secure a balance of power and seeking to prevent any one of their number establishing an overwhelming advantage. They included a resolution urging fair treatment of the Armenians, a very capable people who were scattered across the empire and much more difficult to protect than the Bulgarians. The precedent of the Bulgarian rising was dangerous to them and there were massacres, again denounced by Gladstone in his last years.

The sultan earned the title Abdul the Damned and was all the more moved when Kaiser Wilhelm II advanced in his flamboyant style to provide support for the shaky regime. Germany, throwing off its ancient divisions, had firstly established a customs union and later created an empire under the leadership of Prussia. They looked back to the Emperor Barbarossa, to Frederick II and the achievements of German crusaders to encourage them in their move to imperialism and, along with all the other powers in the scramble for Africa, in their will to establish colonies of their own. In his feverish rivalry with Britain, Kaiser Wilhelm saw opportunities to recruit the Ottoman sultan as an ally and worked hard to bring him on side. Business opportunities were of mutual interest: the sultan dreamed of a railway from Baghdad to the Black Sea and Germans began work on it. Wilhelm's own militarism, arrogance and anti-Semitism gave free rein to the worst elements in the late nineteenth-century German leadership. Wilhelm had an incurable defect to his left shoulder caused by an obstetrician's forceps and had been subjected to vain and humiliating attempts to cure him, a victim throughout of the notion that a German emperor could not have a major physical disability. Posturing and militaristic gestures were a response to this and to an unhappy childhood – his bluestocking mother, Queen Victoria's eldest daughter, being unable to express maternal love for him.

A visit to Jerusalem in October 1898 cemented the alliance with Abdul-Hamid. The Kaiser's talent for costume came into its own as he ceremonially rode on horseback into Jerusalem through a breach specially made in the walls, wearing a helmet surmounted by a golden eagle, in a costume designed by himself with Arab dress on his back and a cross on the front, recalling the crusaders and the Teutonic Knights. A mounted procession followed, dressed like the Hospitallers and including, in fourth place, carrying a banner marked 'Thomas Cook and Son', John Mason Cook, son of the founder of the travel firm. Both Cook and the Kaiser suffered from the curse of the Near East, attacks of dysentery, which killed Cook who died the following year at his home in Surrey. The Kaiser recovered. In the course of his visit Wilhelm inaugurated the German Lutheran Church of the Redeemer, a triumphalist structure overshadowing the Holy Sepulchre and commissioned a German hospice on the Mount of Olives, showing him and his consort in its chapel in company with German crusaders, including Barbarossa and Frederick II.

In Damascus he visited Saladin's mausoleum and saw his white marble sarcophagus which he promised to restore. He laid a laurel wreath of gilded wood with the inscription 'From one great Emperor to another' on Saladin's tomb.* At a gala dinner in Damascus he praised Saladin as one of the most chivalrous leaders in history and charmed his audience by saying that the sultan, Abdul-Hamid II, and the 300 million Muslims who revered his name should know that the German emperor was their friend for ever.

Punch made merry over the Kaiser seeking support in the East against Britain and France and yet having to use the leading British travel firm to organise the trip. In fact the visit and his almost pantomime performance, supporting both the crusaders and Saladin, had important effects when, in November 1914, the Turks entered the war on the German side.

The dictator Abdul-Hamid was a reformer with an interest in education, a major builder of schools, hospitals, docks and railways. However, a group of modernisers and secularisers formed a party reacting against the

---

* The wreath was confiscated by T. E. Lawrence at the end of the First World War and now lies in the Imperial War Museum in London.

Sultan's repression, called the Committee of Union and Progress, later known as the Young Turks. They ousted Abdul-Hamid in 1909 and brought back the constitution he had abrogated, but still in the end they were drawn into *jihad* and war. Enver Pasha, albeit a member of the Young Turks, was influenced by the past actions of the Kaiser and Abdul-Hamid and the special links with Germany then established. He was convinced Germany would win the war and its victory would best serve the Ottoman Empire. He made a secret agreement with Germany, and in November 1914 Mehmet V Rashid, the puppet caliph of the day, declared *jihad*. The entry of Turkey into the First World War against the Entente led to a vain attempt by the British to penetrate the Bosphorus with a naval force, losing capital ships to mines and to the botched land attack on Gallipoli. It led to the discrediting of Winston Churchill, who as First Lord of the Admiralty was closely associated with the great disaster and who also fatally delayed his potentially war-winning plans for mass production of tanks to break the deadlock on the Western Front.

In 1917 British campaigning against the Turks achieved success in the capture of Jerusalem. Allenby, a fine cavalry general transferred from the Western Front and an imaginative thinker about the Near East who worked with the War Cabinet, left no misunderstanding. One power, acting for the Entente, had defeated the Turks in battle and was not carrying out a crusade. In contrast to the Kaiser, the British general dismounted at the Jaffa Gate and entered on foot, at pains to avoid all British jingoism in announcements and flying no Union Jack. *Punch* published a cartoon showing Richard in full armour looking down at Jerusalem and saying, 'At last my dream come true'. It was a misinterpretation. Allenby included Muslims in his army and commanded an Egyptian Camel Corps.

Colonialism, Dictatorship and Abuse

In the 1850s two egos clashed over the Holy Sepulchre. Tsar Nicholas I of Russia and the French Emperor Napoleon III fought each other about custody and access to the Holy Places in Jerusalem. Their conflict was an abuse of the passionate wish of the medieval crusaders to recapture the

Sepulchre, for there was no true crisis about its possession in the mid-nineteenth century; it was one of the oddest wars in history, fought with remarkable incompetence on the Crimean peninsula, far from Jerusalem. Nicholas I loved war and uniforms, dreamed of recovering Constantinople and may even at one time have thought of capturing Jerusalem for Russian Orthodoxy. Moscow was, in the minds of many of his clergy and aristocrats, the Third Rome, heir to all the rights and claims of Byzantium. He sent an artist to Jerusalem to record just what the Sepulchre looked like, so that the seventeenth-century monastery south of Moscow, which deliberately imitated the layout of the Holy Places and had suffered fire, could have its substitute Sepulchre rebuilt like the original. He presided over a massive increase in Russian pilgrimages to Jerusalem, embracing all classes and including peasants in great numbers, who walked to Odessa and took the steamship, inundating the old city and the sacred sites and raising fears that the Russians were going to take over Jerusalem.

The President of the Republic, Bonaparte's nephew, made himself Emperor Napoleon III in 1852. A skilled operator, master of a controlled press, his aim was to overcome the ancient hostility between Britain and France by drawing Britain into alliance, effacing the humiliation inflicted on France through the failure of Napoleon's Russian campaign and rallying the nation to its former greatness in Europe: his interest, in short, lay firmly in the West and not in Jerusalem. But it mattered for his political purposes, because he knew that the Sepulchre and Catholic rights therein would rally to him all the Catholics who, though they cared for France, disliked the Revolution and Napoleon's atheism.

British attitudes were not necessarily favourable to Russia as a fellow Christian country. Preaching mattered: there was still an interest in Jerusalem and many a pulpit was devoted to the topic on purely religious grounds. Evangelicals such as Shaftesbury, made aware of the practices of Orthodox priests in Slav enclaves in the Ottoman Empire by reports of British merchants trading there, disliked the Orthodox more than the Turks, who, they felt, should be given time to reform on Tanzimat lines.

Palmerston was more belligerent: he saw the conflict over the Sepulchre as a stepping-stone towards dismembering the Russian Empire and eliminating the menace it represented to British interests in India. Britain sent an ultimatum to Russia in February 1854. Aberdeen, then Prime Minister, hoped military action would in the end not be necessary; however, Palmerston's view won the day. So Britain and France ended up fighting over the keys of the Sepulchre on behalf of the Ottoman sultan against the Christian tsar of Russia. Nicholas died of natural causes in 1855, and his successor, Alexander II, although he abandoned Nicholas's great schemes, maintained Russia's leading role at the Sepulchre and made peace in 1856. Many lives had been lost, and the Russian state in the aftermath engaged in large-scale ethnic cleansing, chasing out the Crimean Tartars – that is, the descendants of the Mongols, who had aided the attacks on the Russians and had not been protected from reprisals by the Peace – and forcing out Muslims from the Crimea. Russia prevailed; the French rejoiced and fêted Napoleon III; the British were disappointed.

Tsarist tradition was strongly anti-Semitic, and when Alexander II was assassinated in 1881 there was quite unjustified suspicion of Jewish responsibility. Pogroms followed on a great scale. The situation was made even worse by the libellous work *The Protocols of the Elders of Zion*, forged by a chief of secret police in the time of Nicholas II. Millions fled and, although most went to the USA, there was a great increase in Jewish immigration to Palestine. In anti-Semitic Vienna Theodor Herzl read the signs of the times and began to work for a major Jewish presence in Palestine and inevitably in Jerusalem, though he would have preferred Haifa: Zionism was born.

A paradoxical result of the publicity given to Jerusalem and its Holy Places by the war was a great increase in numbers of Western pilgrims and the slow transformation of a shabby Ottoman town into a more efficient pilgrim centre with hotels and banking. The sultan gave the Emperor Napoleon III Melisende's church of St Anne, which the French then renovated.

The Eastern Question, so long a thorny problem caused by the Ottoman decline, had a bloodstained outcome as the British errors at Gallipoli opened the way to a successful counter-attack by a Turkish officer, Mustafa Kemal, whose prestige propelled him into leadership as the Ottomans collapsed and then on to a decisive victory in the Greco-Turkish war of 1922.

Dhimmis in the Ottoman Empire were forced out of their homes and there was much suffering. Mustafa established himself as a reforming leader with the title Kemal Atatürk, transferred the capital from Istanbul to Ankara, abolished the veil for women, did away with the caliphate and created the modern state of Turkey.

Between 1915 and 1917 the British made contradictory promises to the French, the Arabs and the Jews under exigencies of war needs. After the failure at Gallipoli, easterners in the War Cabinet who believed the war could be won by knocking out Turkey, attacking Germany's soft flank and saving the dreadful losses on the Western Front turned to the possibilities of an Arab revolt to defeat the Turks. Young Turks had proved themselves to be far more formidable than the old Ottoman leadership. Jemal Pasha, their governor of Jerusalem, was a ferocious despot. Might this fearsome man capitalise on the *jihad* declared in 1914 and attack the British in Egypt? The British, determined to divert attention from Egypt, stimulated an Arab revolt. T. E. Lawrence, archaeologist, pioneer in the study of crusader castles and intelligence agent in Egypt, emerged as a guerrilla leader of great talent, a man who understood Bedouin and promoted a candidate for kingship in Faisal, son of the Sherif of Mecca. Allenby saw his gifts and backed him, using his fighters to meet numerical deficiencies in his own troops. In a great coup by his Arab camel force Lawrence took Aqaba and set about wrecking the Turkish railway line in Hijaz. Vague promises buoyed up Arab hopes.

In early January 1916 the British government sought to defuse hostility with France by a secret treaty. They were old enemies, pushed into a shotgun marriage in order to meet the menace of the Kaiser's Germany, and the prime minister, Lord Asquith, wished to eliminate tension. He remembered how the French had tried to challenge British power in the Sudan at Fashoda in 1898 and wanted to set clear boundaries to stop future trouble. Sir Mark Sykes, MP for Hull and an inveterate traveller in the Levant, convinced the Cabinet that he would put a limit on French ambitions by drawing a line on the Near Eastern map running from the 'e' of Acre to the 'k' of Kirkup. All land north of the line was to be a French sphere of influence, where they were free to colonise; all land to the south was to be in the British sphere. The other signatory was the French diplomat François Georges-Picot, strongly influenced by his father, an intransigent nationalist who had wished to establish French power in Asia and in Africa. The Sykes–Picot agreement did not stay secret for long. After the Revolution in Russia, the Bolsheviks discovered it in the Tsarist archives and promptly published it, showing that it confirmed the allegations of Abdul-Hamid II that Britain and France, despite their protestations, were just like the crusaders of the past, forcing themselves yet again on Muslims.

Meanwhile Lawrence, finding his attacks on the Turkish Hijaz railway not enough to damage his opponents, used explosives to wreck a railway hub at Derah, south of Damascus. It was an excellent tactic, but Derah was well north of the Sykes–Picot line and the attack was seen by the French as a breach of faith. Allenby went on after capturing Jerusalem to win the last cavalry battle in British history and defeated the Turks at Megiddo. It stimulated Lloyd George, who had succeeded Asquith in 1916, to think, irrespective of Sykes–Picot, that the British had done so much to defeat the Turks that they should have a major share of Near Eastern spoils to add to their empire. Lloyd George also played a major part in persuading his foreign secretary, Arthur Balfour, to write a formal letter to the British Zionist Lord Rothschild, giving Cabinet support for 'the establishment in Palestine of a national home for the Jewish people' with the caveat, 'it being clearly understood that nothing should be done which may prejudice the civil and religious rights of existing non-Jewish communities in Palestine'. This became known as the Balfour Declaration of November 1917. Lloyd George believed this high-minded statement would keep out the French and influence Jews in the United States in favour of Britain and the allies. The USA entered the war, and Germany was defeated.

Promises over future colonising to the French, promises to the Arabs of independence, promises of a home for the Jews had all been given by the British in the hope of reducing the loss of life and achieving victory. They could not all be kept. It was a witches' brew. Faisal, sidelined in peace negotiations, commented ruefully, 'Who did win the crusades?'

The Peace of Versailles rearranged most of the northern hemisphere.

In the West the peacemakers used Wilson's ideas of national self-determination as far as they were able. In the East there were mandates dividing the Ottoman Empire intended to prepare indigenous peoples for freedom and self-determination. Lloyd George took a British mandate under the League of Nations for Iraq and Palestine, and Clemenceau took a mandate for Syria and Lebanon. The mandate for Iraq gave the opportunity for the British to provide some sort of reward for Faisal. At first Clemenceau was happy, but he became furious as he realised that Sykes–Picot had not been observed. He appointed as ruler of Damascus an obdurate French general who expelled Lawrence's Arab rebels, exclaiming 'Saladin, we have returned'. French imperialism merely created a corrupt regime which favoured Christians over Muslims but was unable to displace the Druze, the supporters of the Fatimid caliph al-Hakim, who had ensconced themselves on a high plateau in the interior. The terrain, their sniping expertise, their faith and their belief in reincarnation gave them victory over French regular troops.

The British convinced themselves that the energy of incoming Zionists would make the desert bloom. This it did. But they also believed that the enhanced economic life which followed would benefit the Arabs and be welcomed by them. This was nonsense. Lord Dowding, of Battle of Britain fame, sent to Palestine to oversee peace, saw how Zionism was working in practice. Absentee Turkish landowners in Beirut demanded huge sums before they would sell their land to Jewish immigrants. Many Zionists, who had paid much in consequence, claimed all the lands for themselves and evicted Arab tenants who had worked the land over generations, offering no other employment. They grew angry with the British and the mandate. Dowding believed promises were not being honoured, and his sympathies lay with the Arabs. He was right, but oil was discovered in Iraq and the British were the more determined to hold Palestine because it provided an outlet to the sea for its exportation. The French became convinced that the British had been behind their troubles in Syria and Lebanon and, in their anger, supplied arms to Zionist terrorists. The mandate became impossible, as Zionist terrorists kidnapped British sergeants, hanged them and left their bodies on display, as well as killing civilians and soldiers by dynamiting British headquarters in the King David Hotel. The post-Second World War Labour government gave it up.

Arabs fled and the state of Israel was born in 1948. Swift recognition by President Truman was a major advantage but was inevitable. The impetus to immigrate after the Holocaust and world sympathy for the fate of the Jews created a great influx. Terror had had its effect. In wars that followed and that still follow, *jihad* has repeatedly been declared, using the term *intifada,* with great loss of life. In much hatred, one generous and statesmanlike action stands out and is too readily forgotten. Moshe Dayan, the Israeli general in the Six-Day War of 1967, the third Arab–Israeli war, achieved the triumph of his life with his troops when he took the Old City of Jerusalem from the Jordanians and captured the Temple Mount. The Rabbi who was chief chaplain to the Israeli army proposed blowing up the Dome of the Rock and the al-Aqsa mosque; Dayan rejected this, ordered the removal of the Israeli flag from the Dome and decreed that the Jews should not be allowed to pray on the site; it was to be allocated solely for worship by the Muslims. He was the one man who could have made this decision and it has, albeit narrowly, held force to this day.

Military problems have dominated the situation since Israel's founding days. The Yom Kippur War of 1973 came close to success, only being stymied by incompetence in Syria, and inevitably the very real pressure on security militarises both Jewish and Muslim sides. Christians within Israel are excluded from military service and so from a regular rite of passage for their age group: they appear as second-class citizens. Any mistake made in an apparently endless cycle of raids, bombings and attacks creates anti-Semitism in the outside world, especially as social media and television news bulletins capture devastation for all to see. The state is indeed a refuge for people persecuted by the Nazis, but its existence has tended to damage the position of Jews elsewhere in the world. A Muslim sense of failure over Israel has contributed to a more widespread malaise in modern Islam.

The Challenge of the West and the Islamic Response

Napoleon's dash to Egypt in 1798, his triumph and failure opened a new era in relations between Islam and the West. Napoleon's attack was pure opportunism, designed to conquer Egypt, put pressure on the British navy and open the way to successful invasion of England. He beat the Mamluks at the battle of the Pyramids but was in turn beaten by Nelson in his coup at Aboukir Bay, wrecking his fleet. The two battles made it plain that the West had established an overriding superiority in war. In science and industry Western powers also had the lead.

Egypt was the richest country in the Islamic world, yet it had been completely outpaced by the West; there followed an epoch of colonialism, in which Western powers took territory from the Muslims. Although there were resistance movements – *jihad* was preached, the British were troubled in India, the Kaiser seized opportunities in Turkey and General Gordon was overwhelmed by the inspired leader, the Mahdi, and his followers – all had no lasting effect. Mehmet Ali's reforms in Egypt and his army improvements were not enough. The Mahdi's forces were shattered at Omdurman; the British took a Protectorate over Egypt and advanced to the Sudan. It was all in grievous contrast to the early conquests under Muhammad and the great caliphs which had transformed the Near East and destroyed Byzantine power. The battles, Badr, the battle of the Trench, the great victory at Yarmuk and the dash of Khalid with his camels across the desert, the capture of Jerusalem and Abu Bakr's miles of conquest were part of the inheritance of Islam, well known to practising Muslims. The Ghaznavids, for example, were treacherous Arabs who fought with the Byzantines against the Muslim army; a reference to them is an insult in exchanges in the twenty-first century which is instantly understood. This has reinforced the loss of confidence among leaders, politicians, generals, religious leaders which is so striking a feature of Islam in the twentieth and twenty-first centuries. Awareness of Muslim weakness in contrast to the conquests of the past has produced and continues to produce a variety of responses and proposed reforms.

Responses to new challenges have been varied, even contradictory. Atatürk's focusing on one state, his own, Turkey – casting aside the

Ottoman capital Istanbul and replacing it with Ankara in the Anatolian heartland — deliberately secularised his country and abandoned any attempt at an Islamic unity; yet from 1945 his decision to substitute Turkish for Arabic in the call to prayer was overturned and the use of the veil for women has reappeared. The view has also been put forward that the divisions within Islam are too great to establish an effective *umma* and what is needed is a drive to Arab unity.

Pakistan, founded as a Muslim state in 1947 by Ali Jinnah, rejected the inter-religious ecumenical vision of Gandhi. The Sandhurst-trained general Ayyub Khan, after he seized power from the politicians in 1958, set about modifying the traditional status and treatment of women in his ordinance of 1961. He required a man to demonstrate before a court that he could treat his wives equally, as laid down in the Quran, and put obstacles in the way of unilateral divorce. It was a serious blow against traditional polygamy. But Ayyub Khan was forced out of office. In 1977 another soldier, Zia ul-Haq, led a coup and took Pakistan in a different direction, seeking to restore Islamic law, with amputation for theft, stoning for adultery, flogging for convictions for slander and made gradual moves to rid Pakistan of banking interest as un-Islamic — since interest payments were forbidden by Muhammad, aware of the wickedness of village moneylenders. The position of women deteriorated. The two soldiers, despite their differences, were both wrestling with the problem of Islamic law. How was it to be restored in Muslim societies, where the effects of colonial rule had been to remove *Sharia* altogether and replace it with codes of Western conquerors?

The Quranic ruling on inheritance laid down that a male child should receive double the portion of the females on the grounds that the male had greater financial responsibility. But what if society had changed and females (as is the case sometimes in Britain) had greater financial responsibility? The argument then was sometimes put forward that the Quranic ruling could be honourably modified in changed economic and social circumstances. This was, in effect, Mutazilism reborn and it struck against the belief that the Quran, uncreated, timeless and eternal, could never be subject to modification.

The Muslim Brotherhood, founded by an Egyptian schoolteacher, sought to revive the notion of an Islamic state and was progressively radi-calised by the effects of British rule in Palestine and resentment at the displacement of Arabs by Jewish immigrants. *Jihad,* it was felt, had fallen into neglect and should be preached against the Christian British oppres-sors and adherents of the Brotherhood should be willing to face personal martyrdom in the *jihad*. This comes close to recognition of the rightful-ness of suicide bombers. In tradition, *jihad* had to be preached by a legiti-mate authority and for specified reasons. Yet the grievous circumstances of the Islamic world, it was alleged, called for *jihad* to be revived; in effect, Islam had fallen back to *jahiliyya*, the state of ignorance before the coming of the Prophet and so *jihad* could and should be carried through by devout individuals without further authority. These were potent ideas and the Brotherhood showed its power when members assassinated Anwar Sadat for recognising the state of Israel. In our own day extremist Islamic move-ments have seized the 'sword-text', *sura* 9 verse 5: 'But when the forbidden months are past, then fight and slay the Pagans.' This was tempered only by the injunction to forgive them if they repent. It was seized on to abro-gate all the other much more moderate and peaceful *suras*, just as extremist Christian groups reject broadly based interpretation of Scripture in favour of arbitrary selection of key verses convenient to them.

In Bosnia, where the Muslim community, before the internecine war which broke up Yugoslavia, had benefited from Ottoman tolerance and was noted for its relaxed attitude to Islamic custom and *Sharia* law, the *hijab* has returned and travellers visiting Sarajevo have been startled to see its prevalence. In Egypt the influence of the Muslim Brotherhood has made the veil more and more customary. In northern Nigeria, a part of the country dominated by Islam, Boko Haram represents a radical Muslim alternative rejecting all Western influences, including voting in elections, secular education and the wearing of shirts and trousers. In Iran, Twelver Shiism, backed by the state, has hitherto retained its position, imposing harsh punishments on dissidents. In Britain a reaction against teenage binge-drinking has led some women, repelled by the abuse of alcohol and by promiscuity, to convert to Islam, finding protection in the headscarf and the known rejection of casual sex by Muslim women.

A Radical Survival in the East: Wahhabism

Wahhabism survived because of one man, Abd al-Aziz (1880–1953), known as Ibn Saud (an ancestral name taken up out of family respect), a master of traditional Bedouin desert warfare. As a child he survived the long civil war which came close to eliminating his dynasty; he then broke out of exile in Kuwait after his father's death and at the age of twenty-one led a tiny force to overwhelm the garrison placed in Riyadh by pro-Ottoman rivals. Then step by step he combined war with minimal bloodshed and generous hospitality to defeated enemies and created a coalition with tribal notables; in 1932 he became King of Saudi Arabia, an immense territory, with a Shiite regional minority, that came to embrace some agricultural land as well as desert, its wealth giving massive irrigation opportunities. The isolation of central Arabia in his formative years can hardly be exaggerated. Western powers were only interested in the coasts and currency hardly existed: Maria Theresa silver thalers were carried in camel saddlebags. Ibn Saud prevailed because he was imposing, especially in stature, on camel-back could outpace others and was a master of the sword and rifle. As a devout Wahhabi, he ruled an illiterate population with wives fully veiled and in seclusion, basing all on the Quran, hearing allcomers personally and making instant decisions to reward rightful appellants with gifts or to administer traditional punishments on the disobedient. With Wahhabi tradition came the maintaining of four wives and instant divorces, albeit with generous personal provision for the divorced and permission to remarry. Ibn Saud created an immense royal family, siring forty-five sons and over 200 daughters. A British connection was established early in his career due to individual British representatives, unmistakably alien in sun helmet and officer's uniform but with fluent Arabic and deep knowledge of Islam, commanding his respect. When he took Mecca and Medina, his discipline brought relief to pilgrims, long subject to robberies on their journey.

The discovery of oil in 1938 and the granting of concessions to the US oil company Aramco brought wealth and inevitable transformation, saddening him in old age. He could not adapt but his successors have and have avoided succession disputes of the kind which destroyed Ibn Saud's father, understanding that pious, observant Wahhabi rulers can manage quiet change and modernisation where Westernised, self-indulgent rulers cannot. The Saudi Arabian *ulama* are committed Wahhabis and impose traditional punishments of public beheadings, amputation and floggings; no ruler can afford to defy them. Yet vast changes have occurred, bringing prosperity, health provision and opportunities to a backward land and will in time go much further. True to Wahhabi principles, Ibn Saud has no known grave and the power of Wahhabism continued to be displayed when the king who died early in 2015, one of the richest men in the world, was given no tomb. Western observers have argued that the contradictions within Saudi Arabia will destroy the kingdom: they may well have misunderstood the shrewdness of the Saudis.

No clear-cut answer can be given on links between Saudi Arabia and modern *jihadis*. An illiterate stonemason built up a fortune through the building boom based on oil revenues and his funds went to support al-Qaeda. Individuals have given resources to anti-Western movements while the official policy of the government is to maintain correct, peaceful relations with the West and welcome Western expertise. Christian services are permitted in the embassy premises and, as across the world, there remains a passive force of families desiring peace and reconciliation and looking to commerce to heal wounds. Wahhabis are an extreme wing of Sunnism and remain most hostile of all to the Shiites of Iran. This deep division is the hardest to heal within the modern world.

An Eccentric Survival: The Hospitallers

In 1798 Napoleon seized Malta. Under the Grand Master Ferdinand von Holpesch, a vapid diplomat, the Order succumbed easily and was forced to hand over a massive treasure in silver and gold which he took to Egypt. It now lies under the shallows of Aboukir Bay, together with the remains of Napoleon's flagship, *L'Orient*, blown up by Nelson. Napoleon gave the islanders a republican constitution but they found the occupiers left behind by the emperor so rapacious that they rose in rebellion. Fifty of the Knights accepted Napoleon's offer of a place in his army but 150 declined and left, facing penury in consequence. Some fled to Russia and, once there, voted to depose Holpesch and elect in his place the deranged Tsar Paul I – who was in any case ineligible both as a married man and as a member of the Russian Orthodox Church. Years of confusion thereafter, nationalist conflicts and decades without a recognised Grand Master made it most likely that the French Revolution and its bastard child Napoleon would succeed not only in forcing the Knights out of Malta but in ending their existence. Yet an improbable series of events in the nineteenth and twentieth centuries enabled the order to survive and exercise a function in the twenty-first century.

Protestant Knights of St John, children of the Reformation in Germany, had remained in contact with the traditional Knights and a similar imitation Order supported by Anglicans, romantic enthusiasts and eccentrics emerged in Britain. French Knights encouraged them, wishing to enlist their support in an attack, with the backing of the Greeks, on the Ottomans in Rhodes (Turkish since 1523), which, it was thought, could become a substitute for Malta. These British Knights favoured the military action of the Hospitallers and were inclined to look down on their other activity of care of the sick. Some improbable leaders functioned at various times – a fraudster, a bogus aristocrat and a supplier of accoutrements to the British army.

The most attractive of them all was Sir Richard Hillary, who took up the cause of the Knights long after the Rhodes scheme had foundered. Hillary, once an equerry to the Duke of Sussex, had founded an organisation on the Isle of Man for rescuing victims of shipwreck, which evolved into the RNLI. Late in life and in ill health because of his personal efforts rescuing victims, he thought of the Knights of St John landing again in the Holy Land and acting as guarantors in a scheme to make it Christian. He was disturbed by an episode in which the Royal Navy played a part in suppressing rebellions against the Ottomans, at that time British allies, and subsequently handing back Beirut and Acre to the sultan. Why, he mused, should the sultan continue to rule in the Holy Land? Could it be returned peacefully into Christian hands, paying rent to the sultan and allowing both Muslims and Christians to enjoy the fruits of commerce? Christian nations might quarrel over who should take the leadership and the revived

Order of St John would be better placed to do so, having a high repute and being a supra-national organisation. Hillary was still canvassing for his scheme when he died in 1847. The Order had captured his imagination far back in time, when as an observer he had attended the inauguration of Holpesch as Grand Master in 1797, and the magnificence of the occasion, the attendance of aristocrats and the splendid uniforms had greatly moved him. Echoes and memories of Hospitaller life in its heyday continued to hold sway in Britain.

In 1858 the Catholic Order finally repudiated the British Knights, and they mutated into a chivalric order, bearing the title of the Venerable Order of the Hospital of St John of Jerusalem in England, inaugurated under the British Crown and given a charter in 1888, adding to the title Grand Priory; they held meetings, sponsored charities and finally acquired Edward, Prince of Wales, the future Edward VII, as Grand Prior. At a memorable costumed ball held by the Duchess of Devonshire in 1897 on the occasion of the Diamond Jubilee of Queen Victoria he appeared in the uniform of a Knight of the traditional past. In the twenty-first century Queen Victoria's chivalric order remains in friendly contact with the traditional Catholic order in Rome.

The romance of crusading and the repute of the Hospitallers saw the launch of the St John Ambulance Brigade, an offshoot of Queen Victoria's order, with a uniform bearing the Maltese cross of the traditional Order. It had success probably quite unforeseen at its inauguration in 1877 and spread across the British Empire, its members a familiar and reassuring presence on public occasions in Britain to this day. Its prime original purpose was to provide emergency first aid in Victorian factories and on the railways, where the absence of adequate safety devices and the habitual overworking of employees led to many accidents. It was an example of the loose use of crusading, giving romance to medical work, and justly recalled the healing work of the Order, well known in its heyday for its generosity in tending all-comers, Muslim or Christian, in its hospital in Jerusalem.

Meanwhile the traditional order began to revive, acquiring a hospital in Rome, establishing once again a novitiate and caring for the wounded in Prussian wars – beginning with the campaign against Denmark in 1864 and continuing in the campaigns of 1866 and 1870 under the influence of Catholic noblemen. In 1879 Pope Leo IX gave recognition to a Grand Master, the first to be accepted by the papacy for many years. He also listened to a proposal by Archbishop Lavigerie of Algeria to revive a fighting function for Knights under vows. At first the archbishop had hoped to interest the traditional Order of St John in returning to their military past but he was politely rejected by the Grand Master, who preferred it to continue with its work with the wounded. In place of this Lavigerie suggested grafting on to his existing missionary orders, the White Fathers and White Sisters, founded by him in 1868 and 1869 respectively, a military wing to fight the slave trade in Africa.

Lavigerie had much in common with Michaud, reacting against anticlerical parents who refused to support him in his seminary education. Pope Leo regarded him with great affection and was sympathetic to his scheme for fighters to wear uniforms, white with red crosses, and protect his missionaries. Anger at the slave trade and the abuse of African labour was widespread, and Lavigerie had initial support not only from Cardinal Manning in England but also from the Anglo-Catholic University Mission to Central Africa. It foundered, for, sympathetic as all these were, they felt that the use of arms was the function of governments; moreover, Lavigerie became aware that Leopold II of Belgium, a vicious abuser of African labour, was planning to take over his scheme. Then, learning of a scheme for France to acquire a colony in north-west Africa, he tried to set up his warriors in the Sahara desert. That failed too. He had abandoned his Institut des Frères Armées just before his death in 1892. His missionary order, however, lived on and has to this day a high reputation for devotion to their cause and understanding the peoples whom they seek to convert. Melisende's church of St Anne is their headquarters church; repaired by the French and existing in unpolluted air, it stands as an example of a Gothic church shining white, as English cathedrals would once have looked, and stirs the imagination because of its extraordinary history, passing from a church built for crusaders and dedicated to using arms against Muslims to being one of Saladin's *madrasas* and ending as a church for a modern order dedicated to peaceful missionary work.

Pope Leo's sympathy buoyed up the traditional order, which has survived to the present, consisting of little more than a platoon of celibate knights of high aristocratic lineage and wealth, supporting themselves for their charitable work and, while retaining their centre in Rome, making use of the Fort Sant'Angelo in Malta. They stand as a bulwark of tradition, using Latin for Lauds and Vespers, never compromising in their determination to remain a sovereign order with its Knights of Justice and their insistence on high aristocratic descent and their own Cardinal Protector. They narrowly escaped centralising endeavours under Pope Pius XII and rejected Eva Peron's attempt to pay her way into their ranks. Their achievement is a surprising one. It lies in imparting romance to fundraising and charitable work while associating with the celibate Knights of Malta a class of Knights of Obedience and Donats of Justice who, although married, follow the spiritual direction of the Order. Below that stands a mass of National Associations linked to the Order and including Knights and Dames, ranks conferred on married associates who show great generosity in giving to charitable works.

In all, the nineteenth century saw a culture of using crusading and *jihadi* history, whether positive or negative, as a means to galvanise support and justify present actions by looking at the past. One part of the Order of St John's activities, the care of the sick, has flourished, while its military and maritime work has disappeared. In both the Venerable Order of St John in Britain and the traditional Catholic Order and its Associations, the romance of crusading, so often arbitrarily used and misused in the nineteenth and twentieth centuries, has lived on to inspire much good work for the benefit of humanity.

12
REFLECTIONS

Crusade mounted by Christians in order to recover and reoccupy Jerusalem was an episode in Western European history, very influential in its time, long-lasting and a force for change, but now dead. Today in scholarly circles, popular writing and the media there is a widespread tendency to look askance at the whole crusading movement, the injustices it brought with it and the damage it inflicted on Judaism, on Byzantium and, above all, on the Islamic world.

By contrast, *jihad* understood as holy war in the defence of Islam still lives. It arouses many passions and is open to fierce disputes and has been used as a reason for warfare, not only against those seen as invaders but also against fellow Muslims who are seen as heretics. It has had an extraordinarily varied history.

In both cases the call to crusade or *jihad* as armed conflict has galvanised men into achieving extraordinary feats on the battlefield against overwhelming odds. One only has to think about the Muslim success at Yarmuk or the Christian capture of Jerusalem, where the forces were all but written off by their opponents but religious zeal and the conviction of the rightful nature of their mission tipped the balance in their favour.

Preoccupation with the evils of crusading has blurred the vision of modern analysts and led them to be less than objective in assessing the history of Western Christianity and of Islam. It has led, for example, to a failure to convey to the reading public the massacres of Muslims by Muslims in the bloodstained eleventh century. Crusades had no monopoly of atrocities. This discrepancy may be due to the fact that historians see the First Crusade as a finite event which can be studied, whereas Muslim atrocities do not fit into any easy time-scale. The history departments of modern Muslim universities have naturally been preoccupied with the events of the First Crusade and its aftermath but have not been investigating what was happening independently of these events in the Muslim world. Two distinguished modern authorities, British and French, have regretted the absence of translations of Muslim sources by Islamic scholars working within the epoch of the crusades. Study of this side of the hill at present rests on much too narrow a base and it is generally felt there may well have been distortions. Popular Muslim writing has taken up Abdul-Hamid II's ingenious device for saving his empire and is stuck with the idea that Western powers are crusaders all over again. Unable to make the distinctions necessary for true history writing, they pander to crudely nationalist and religious passions. Hence objective historical writing about the Islamic past, particularly in the time of the crusades, can be difficult. Readers deserve better of their Muslim historians.

As compensation for the very real evils of the crusading movement, Western writers have been inclined to exaggerate Muslim achievement. A case in point is the belief that Islamic medicine was superior to that of the West. It is quite untrue, yet so long believed. Battlefield surgeons on the two sides had an expertise that was of equal standard. Surgeons were of low status, artisans without academic training, but they developed practical skill in amputations and, on the Western side and no doubt the Eastern too, a pragmatic ability to check infections. Physicians were a different matter. Both East and West were trained in the Hippocratic tradition of the elements and the balance of the four humours. They were expensive to employ and it is known that Western aristocrats and kings had Muslim physicians, but it is equally true that Eastern caliphs similarly employed Christians and Jews. Leaders who could afford physicians were entirely pragmatic and were happy to use talent from any tradition. The acceptance of the belief that Islam had superiority in medicine long held sway because of an assumption that the 'mysterious East' had powers which the West had not. It has a whiff of Scott's *Talisman*.

The debt the West owed to Islamic scholars, largely in Spain, came through their knowledge of scientific and philosophical classical learning which had been completely lost in Western Europe after the destruction wrought by the Germanic invasions. Here is an example of the peaceful contact between the two worlds which went on despite the aggression of crusading and *jihad* and which has certainly been underestimated.

Commentators have been backward in recognising benefits brought to the West during the crusade epoch. Those who went on the First Crusade had scant knowledge of their antagonists and were little inclined to learn more: the chaplain who wrote the *Gesta Francorum* was interested in Seljuq methods of warfare but otherwise remarkably incurious. Similarly in Islam. The First Crusade for the Muslim world was just thought of initially as another attack, to be dealt with like those made by fellow Muslims, and which could be easily contained. Crusading over the years broadened horizons in the West. Shared experience of prolonged danger in alien territory brought men from different cultures and backgrounds into contact, carried them out of the closed world of the *mouvances* and its petty battles and began to create a new sense of Christendom. Settlers learned about Muslim personalities and their quarrels, ethnic and religious divisions, because such knowledge was crucial to their survival: they knew they had to have allies and exploit enemy differences in order to survive. Such working knowledge did nothing to dissipate the prejudice overall about Muslim belief, but it did not prevent individuals establishing working relationships and common interests in trade, luxury goods and working the land. Similarly in the Muslim world there were those who were keen to escape oppressive rulers and who sought a sense of security and protection – a haven where trade could be carried out peacefully. Hospitallers in their care of the sick, opened their facilities to Muslims on equal terms and these were used.

The West faced a challenge in the crusading epoch. Driven by expansion into unknown territory, coming into contact with peoples totally unknown and dependent on unfamiliar territory for survival, the crusaders

travelled hundreds of miles to a destination many had only heard about
– initially, that of Jerusalem. Crusading brought broader knowledge and
some acquisitions, incorporating pagan east Germany and claiming back
the Iberian peninsula for the Christian West; the search for a counterweight to Muslim power brought knowledge of the Mongol heartland and
of a world religion, Buddhism, hitherto unheard of; a once hemmed-in
society was given a prolonged geography lesson. Inevitably the large
numbers who went on crusade meant that, despite heavy losses, many survived and returned home to tell the tale and stimulate interest. Warfare,
particularly under the auspices of the Hospitallers, contributed to Western
advances in shipbuilding, the use of the broadside and weaponry and the
making of ocean-going vessels, which brought the West into a position of
superiority in the Eastern spice trade and an ability to look for new markets
in the New World. The East was a forcing-ground for techniques in land
warfare and produced some of the greatest castles ever built. The conversion of Muslims played no part in the First Crusade but gained ground as
public opinion in the West became aware of the immensity of the task of
recovering Jerusalem after its fall to Saladin in 1187. It was, however, never
completely dissociated from the use of force. A great canonist, Innocent
IV, stimulated by the contact with alien peoples and religions brought
about by the crusading movement, made decisions about the right of
Christian rulers in cases where a Christian right to preach was refused, to
compel alien rulers to allow their people to listen. This decision was abused
by the conquerors of Mexico and Peru in the sixteenth century to justify
wholesale plunder and forced conversions. It was one of the worst effects
of crusading, as B. Z. Kedar has well reminded us.

A quite unexpected by-product of crusading lay in the field of finance.
The immense volume of crusading taxation increased international liquid-
ity, turned the Templars and Hospitallers into bankers and made the papacy
into a financial power – albeit not always to its long-term advantage.
However, financially, as far as Muslims were concerned, poverty was
important. Wealth could be and was acquired, but personal wealth was not
seen by the devout as a legitimate by-product of *jihad*. The powerful, it was
thought, should be ready to spend generously for poor fellow-religionists

and for the good of Islam. Neglect of this has led to many inner conflicts and the formation of new, radical Islamic groups.

The crusading movement was unequivocally disastrous for Judaism, from the earliest whispers of an expedition to free Jerusalem, as chroniclers' speculations issued in pogroms; anti-Semitism continued with the exploitation of Jewish moneylenders by Godfrey of Bouillon and forced baptisms associated with the People's Crusade. Riots at the coronation of Richard Lionheart issued in attacks on Jews and the tragic episode of betrayal and murder in York. The association between warfare to recover Jerusalem from the enemies of Christ and attacks on Jews, however illogical, long had its effect. Innocent III's decree requiring them to wear the yellow star was echoed by Nazi legislation. Edward I of England was distinguished for his commitment to crusading and it may not be an accident that he expelled Jews.

The belief that *jihad*, striving in the path of God, meant combat and that all able-bodied males had a duty to fight at caliphal command prevailed against the dissident views of individual scholars emphasising peaceful striving, perseverance in prayer and the struggle against evil passions in the soul.

But the errors of Abbasid caliphs and the disorders within the Islamic world created by self-seeking *atabegs* came to occupy centre stage. Warlike *jihad* faded. Only the coming of the crusaders brought it back, and it did so slowly. Even the massacre in Jerusalem in July 1099 had no immediate impact. Western settlers established Crusader States displacing Muslim rulers and Templars built their stables onto the al-Aqsa mosque with impunity. Only the abortive siege of Damascus by the immense army of the Second Crusade changed the attitudes of rank and file Muslims. As the army threatened, crowds in the Great Mosque threw ashes over their heads in repentance for the sins which they believed had allowed crusaders to flourish. Passions were excited by the iconic bloodstained Quran of Caliph Uthman, and scholars rode out to martyrdom under the hooves of the crusaders' horses. Thereafter, combat *jihad* prevailed and carried Muslims forward to recapture Jerusalem under Nur al-Din and Saladin.

Although *jihad* faltered as the heirs of Saladin fell to quarrelling after his death, reaction against the intervention of the Mongols reunited the Muslim world and, after the critical battle of Ain Jalud in 1260, brought to power the most gifted and ferocious general the Muslims ever had, Sultan Baybars. His Mamluk slave-soldiers, devoted to holy war, dominated battlefields, culminating in the capture of the last Christian stronghold of Acre in 1291 by one of Baybars's successors.

Later Ottoman Turks, supplanting the Mamluks as standard bearers of holy war *jihad*, developed their own slave-soldiers, the Janissaries, as devoted to military life and to Islam as the Mamluks had been, and used their heroic dedication to capture Constantinople from the Byzantine Christians and build the greatest empire the Muslim world had ever seen.

The demands of war against the crusaders, the Mongols and the Byzantines militarised Islam. This militarisation brought victories against their non-Muslim enemies but also acted as an armour plate for them against rivals in the Islamic world. It favoured autocracy and worked against the play of discussion, counsel and consent found in the West which could have served, however imperfectly, to check trends to despotic rule.

Crusade and *jihad* were twins and the one reacted on the other, raising the importance of Jerusalem as a goal of pilgrimage for Muslims and Christians alike, making a small parcel of land that was once Herod's Temple into an object that was of the highest importance to all three monotheist religions.

One important difference between Islam and the West lay in Gregory VII's insistence that the aims of the Church and of secular leaders were different and that the Church must be set free. Thereafter Western rulers had to reckon with an independent force which in debates, conflicts and manoeuvres over the centuries acted as a check on their authority. This separation of powers never existed in the East. There the tradition of Muhammad was to combine religious, political and military power, a tradition handed on to the great caliphs of the age of conquest and into the time of the hereditary caliphates. With the decline of the Abbasids' power came an alteration: secular powers began to manipulate caliphs to their advantage, even in later centuries appointing young candidates or men of straw to suit their convenience. But the central fact remained: there was no check in the Islamic world of the kind that existed in the West against autocracy through the claims to independent authority of popes, archbishops and bishops.

Discussion in the West led to the assertion of secular rights in Magna Carta, which rallied the baronage to fend off the invasion headed by a French prince and took on new vitality in the seventeenth century as a focus against the Divine Right of Kings, later enshrined in the Bill of Rights both in seventeenth-century Britain and in eighteenth-century America, while in the fourteenth century the financing of war gave bargaining power to the House of Commons. Similarly in Europe of the sixteenth century, the Reformed religion of Luther and Calvin was used by states as a rallying point to shake off the dominance exercised by the Holy Roman Empire under Habsburg leadership. Nothing of this kind diminished autocracy in Islam and in the late stages of Ottoman history the rise of the power of the harem was yet another force in favour of arbitrary despotism.

The past exerts its sway both to bane and to benefit. The term crusade in the West has passed into common currency as a way of describing any selfless determined movement to uproot an evil; in this way the United States, for example, has seen a movement by teetotallers to outlaw alcohol, called the Crusade for Temperance. In the Near East it has a poisonous resonance, which many Westerners have not understood. President Bush made a profound error when he described the actions taken against terrorism in the struggle against the *jihadis* following the attack on the Twin Towers in New York in 2001 as a crusade. Ambassadors of western nations in the Near East, well aware of the assumptions of the governments with which they deal and of the complexities of Muslim history, have too often been disregarded by both Britain and the United States.

The continued existence of the strand of scholarship emphasising the peaceable interpretation of striving in the path of God was vividly demonstrated by the response of distinguished Muslim scholars to the attack on the Twin Towers. Resident in different parts of the Muslim world and adducing slightly different arguments, they were nonetheless united in their utter repudiation of this act of terrorism as incompatible with the principles of Islam.

Ali Juma, professor at the al-Azhar University in Cairo, believed that there were criteria for making war in the Quran, but they were strictly limited and certainly not met by the Twin Towers episode. He could see a possible need for the use of force to preserve the environment, to remove tyrants and to serve the common good. He does not believe that the great conquests of the early centuries were responsible for conversions to Islamic belief, which took place only slowly, and adduces the case of China, where there were no Islamic conquests but many conversions. Revelation in *sura* 21 107, envisaged the Messenger of God bringing with him the rule of mercy, and *sura* 8 61, urged believers to make peace whenever their enemies showed a wish to do so.

Jawdat Said, a Syrian scholar resident in the Golan Heights, by contrast wrote as an avowed pacifist, adducing the story of the sons of Adam in one of the *hadiths* and the attitudes there inculcated as proof that the Prophet would reject violence, even when used in self-defence. Violence, he believed, was a 'disease' in the modern world. He accepted the existence of bellicose verses in the Quran but believed they could have no weight in the modern world, in the absence of any authority which could legitimately issue a command to the faithful. *Sura* 22 256 – 'let there be no compulsion in religion' – was a vital text.

Wahiduddin Khan, president of the Islamic Institute in New Delhi, believes that in Islam war can only be allowed in exceptional circumstances. He notes that warfare was a way of life in the pre-modern age. Now, however, conflict is to be obviated by peaceful means. *Sharia* law was not to be held as rigidly sacrosanct but should be adapted to meet modern needs. Commands to fight in the Quran related to particular circumstances and could have no validity today. Peaceful activism would bring about change, and would automatically bring in its wake needful political and social reforms. In *sura* 10 25, 'God calls to the Home of Peace', and *sura* 41 33–4, declares that 'good and evil deeds are not alike' and urges the faithful to 'repel evil with good', leading to the result that 'he who is your enemy will become your friend'. Suicide terrorism is condemned by Wahiduddin Khan: 'we may become martyrs but must not seek martyrdom.'

Muhammed Fathullah Güllen, a Turkish scholar now living in Pennsylvania, is a Sufi and attaches importance to the inner growth of the dedicated individual, 'sieved' by Sufi practices, humility and patient forbearance in good times and bad. He cannot exclude warfare, the lesser *jihad*. The armed struggle of the Prophet he sees, just as the Indian scholar Whaddudin Khan did, as required by special circumstances. The defence of honour, of children and the like may require the use of force, but the major stress of his exposition lies on peaceful activism, the battle with evil desires and on the revival of a holistic Islamic education with respect for life and creation. He rejects terrorism out of hand, as the work of a tiny minority of opportunists who have no grasp of Islamic principles. Doing good to others is, he believes, the fundamental Muslim principle.

It is a tragedy that the response of such Islamic scholars to the attack on the Twin Towers has been given so little publicity.

The Muslim world continues to suffer from corrupt and dictatorial leadership. The struggles in the Middle Ages for a caliphate doing justice have echoes in modern times. Now as then anger is caused by disregard of the Prophet's insistence on the need to surrender wealth and deploy it for the relief of the poor and the cause of Islam in the world. The spectacle of elite cadres heaping up wealth and rewarding relatives may lead to a sharp reaction, as is the case with Boko Haram in Nigeria who blame the West for their problems and the distortions in other people's lives, reacting so profoundly as to dismiss any form of Western clothes.

The words crusade and *jihad* have continued to have immense potency. The Young Turks sought victory against the western Great Powers and manipulated *jihad* for their own political purposes by making their caliph declare *jihad* in 1914. To a reading Western public, 'Who did win the crusades?' was emotive, but Abdul-Hamid II was not fair to the medieval crusaders when he likened the nineteenth century situation to the past. The First Crusade sought to recover Jerusalem. It was a religious objective. Although some, such as Baldwin the Conqueror, sought land, the vast majority came to take Jerusalem and then returned home. The colonial powers in the nineteenth and twentieth centuries were concerned with territorial expansion and political influence and distorted the past to justify political expansion. The Bolshevik publication of the Sykes–Picot agreement was designed by them to show that the capitalist world was corrupt and that the Marxist approach was infinitely better. There was humbug in both the British and the French use of their League of Nations mandates to serve their colonising purposes and try to make up for the grievous personal and financial losses both had suffered in the First World War.

One strand of opinion within embattled Israel has observed that the claim of the state of Israel to be the only truly democratic state in the Near East cannot hold if the Arab citizens within Israel keep the vote, as democracy requires, for the greater fertility of Arab households is bound over time to alter the population balance to the detriment of the Jews. Logic in this argument imposes a two-state solution, with independence for an Arab state. No doubt *jihad/intifada* is so well established that it would certainly not die away at once but the only alternative involves an Israeli government resorting to precisely the kind of racialism lying behind anti-Semitism over many years – only in reverse.

The misunderstanding between West and East has always had consequences. There have been incidents where a clash of cultures has caused problems. Only those in the West who have studied Islamic society can begin to understand the complex nature of Islam and its adherents, with wide cultural differences and diversities of belief, exacerbated by the strains on simple societies of sudden wealth produced by the discovery of oil. Muslims may have problems in understanding divisions in belief and practice within Christianity. Crudely to classify Christians as crusaders or Muslims as *jihadis* is unjustified.

A proof of the extraordinary range of belief and practice in contemporary Islam lies in the singular case of the Ismaili adherence of the Aga Khan, who in 1818 broke on personal grounds with his superior, who had given him this Persian pet name of honour, moved away from Iran and eventually settled in India. He used the inherited powers of the Fatimid imamate to attract a host of followers, some 15 million at present scattered across more than twenty-five countries, who accept his beneficent doctrinal decisions. The Nizaris under the Aga Khans supported British rule in India, were peace-loving and occupied a position of honour in international affairs, one of them presiding over the League of Nations. Designation, the Shiite *nass*, has been used by them to nominate successors, albeit broadly in a hereditary line. Within Ismaili range of doctrines lay exotic Gnostic beliefs but in modern times they probably matter much less than the links of personal solidarity, their meeting places (not in mosques) and their musical inheritance. Faithful adherence to the Quran in their case has led to tolerance of other beliefs and a rejection of polygamy and under-age marriage. At present the holder of office, Karim Aga Khan IV (born 1936), transferred the centre of Nizari Ismailis to London and combines charitable, tolerant activities with a genial love of racing. Tithes paid by followers provide a powerful financial base for charitable works.

The cross carries implications for Muslims. A modern practising Muslim with Christian friends and much knowledge of Christianity likes to say her prayers in Christian churches in England but finds the sight of crosses disturbing because they remind her of the wars carried out by Western armies under this symbol. In Turkey, the rejection of veil, scarf and *hijab* through the secularisation policies of Atatürk was welcomed by women who saw these restrictions in public dress as symbols of subjection and have spoken with sorrow of their reactions to a reversion to traditional practice. In France, too, outlawing this symbol of Islamic faith has caused problems, with defiance of the state seen in schools and elsewhere. The struggle for women's education, so gallantly carried on against obscurantism in Pakistan and leading to the award of a Nobel Prize, is another facet of a major, worldwide effort. On the other hand, Islamic revival has brought fruit of an unexpected kind in business as the practice of Islamic virtue, as followed most notably by Saladin after his personal conversion, the bonds of honesty and reliability in all dealings has brought rewards for a class of Anatolian Tigers who have built up international companies on the strength of their care and trustworthiness, bringing much needed economic growth and employment to their country.

The failure of an Iraqi government to sustain co-operation between Sunni and Shiite has given opportunity for an adventurer taking the name of Caliph Abu Bakr to preach *jihad*, call for an Islamic empire and assemble an army guilty of atrocities on a wide scale against their fellow Muslims, Shiites and Kurds as well as Yazidis and Christians. It is not Quranic, neither is the practice of suicide terrorism. Suicide is condemned in the Quran unequivocally. There is a clear distinction between the soldier who fights bravely for a good cause, takes risks and then suffers death and the suicide terrorist who deliberately destroys his life to detonate a bomb. Suicide terrorism seems to have originated in Saddam Hussein's Iran–Iraq war, ostensibly a Sunni–Shiite conflict, when a thirteen-year-old Shiite blew himself up with grenades to stop an enemy advance. It resurrects harshnesses of the seventh and eighth centuries, neglects moments of diplomacy and mercy in the life of the Prophet and his insistence on the respect due to the Peoples of the Book, Christians and Jews. The familiar doctrine of the continuance of crusading and the need for Muslims to fight against it has been used to condemn Kurds on the strange grounds that they are instruments of the West.

Anger against Shiites was, however, a starting-point for this conflict, and a seedbed for the trouble lay in the conviction of moderate Sunnis that they were being put at a heavy disadvantage by Shiite manoeuvring. A very long-lasting dispute, with rival narratives of cruelties and deceptions, inevitably comes to have a life of its own, as the experience of disputes and warfare in Ireland will recall to British readers, although the seeds of the Sunni–Shiite conflict go back to the seventh century while the conflict within Ireland goes back only to the sixteenth. And yet those who despair of any end to this conflict recurring, and reviving a grievous wound in Islam, have underestimated the possibilities of healing and compromise stemming from within the Muslim world. Such possibilities benefit from the extreme difficulties of all modern dictatorships in suppressing information appearing on the internet and on social media, such as Facebook. In Iran modern communications may yet work against the dictatorship of scholars and Ayatollahs attempting to impose their understanding of Twelver Shiism and their version of Islamic law on a young, growing population. This new generation, aware of other possibilities of democracy without crude Western hedonism and of fulfilling their faith in ways not envisaged by religious police, are able to communicate in a manner inconceivable even in the nineteenth century. Dishearteningly, as sophisticated propaganda from Isil reaches out to Muslims in Britain, America and Europe, it obscures its true nature and leads teenagers to join, believing that they are fulfilling their faith by becoming *jihadis*.

Islam, past and present, offers precedents for healing. Nur al-Din himself, wishing to draw believers together to expel crusaders from the *sahil*, espoused an ecumenical Sunnism with openings for some Shiites. There are modern-day members of the Sunni majority who take pride in being able to work with Shiites and stress their common links in belief. The Naqshbandi order of Sufis has had an extraordinary success in bridging the gulf between Islam and the West under the leadership of the late Sufi scholar and preacher Nizam al-Haqqani, widely travelled and holding views which leave behind the crudities of Shiite–Sunni conflict. British Muslims, at risk to themselves, have rejected the threats of *jihadis* and whole communities have repudiated assassinations and mendacious propaganda.

Scholarship can bridge gaps and Britain, because of its imperialist experience and the knowledge which flowed from it, has nurtured a body of respected investigators at home in dialogue with their opposite numbers. The challenge to Christianity presented by the Enlightenment – which believed that more than a century had elapsed between the writing of the Gospels and the events they described, and that they consequently included a body of myths and inventions – has been met by a line of scholars working to establish the time-scale of writing and the means of transmission of texts. By contrast, the text of the Quran awaits deeper analysis. Hugh Kennedy has given good grounds for accepting the main lines of the classic life of Muhammad by ibn Ishaq against many sceptics; scholars, perhaps given confidence by this, need to go back to clarify the obscurities of words in the Quran. The talent is there to do it.

The late Fathi Osman, once a member of the Muslim Brotherhood, the assassins of President Sadat of Egypt, believed that hatred was the child of misinformation and that the Islamic world and the West had come to live in fear and dislike of each other because they knew far too little about their respective beliefs and problems. In a lifetime of study he has moved from the Brotherhood to ecumenical contacts, reorganising narrowly conventional Islamic courses. Dictatorship, he came to see, bred terrorism. If Muslims were free to practise democracy and discuss issues, they would not need to turn to the gun to make their views prevail. He asked his fellow believers to re-examine *jihad* and replace it with *ijtihad*. Both words mean struggle, but *ijtihad* refers to intellectual struggle, leading to reinterpretation. He has called for a more profound study of the Quran, where vague passages give vantage points for leaders wishing to twist verses for their own ends. His masterwork of 1,000 pages, called *Concepts of the Quran*, has replaced analysis *sura* by *sura* with an examination of issues such as *jihad* in the light of the sacred writing as a whole. The human mind opens Scripture, he taught, and illuminates it; to refuse rational analysis is to back into a closed and stagnant world. Osman's honesty and lack of any political connections or desire for reward have protected him from obloquy and such dedication has a powerful potential for the future.

GUIDE TO FURTHER
READING

Christianity and Crusading

Background

B. Hamilton, *Religion in the Medieval West* (2nd edn, London, 2003), especially valuable for popular religion and attitude to relics.

M. Barber, *The Two Cities: Medieval Europe, 1050–1320* (2nd edn, Abingdon, 2008), a detailed exposition on all aspects of medieval life.

H. E. J. Cowdrey, 'Pope Gregory VII', *Headstart History* (1991), pp. 23–36, for the acknowledged master of his elusive subject.

Crusades

C. J. Tyerman, *The Invention of the Crusades* (London, 1998), is polemical and helpful on historiography. His *God's War: A New History of the Crusades* (London, 2006) is an encyclopaedic reference book, covering the crusades thoroughly with an interest in political aspects; use for facts and for its bibliography.

J. Riley-Smith (ed.), *The Atlas of the Crusades* (London, 1991).

S. Runciman, *A History of the Crusades*, vols I–III (Cambridge 1951–4), is outdated but still elegant and attractive; read it for pleasure but be sure to go on to other books.

T. Asbridge, *The Crusades: The War for the Holy Land* (London, 2010). A crisp account especially helpful on Nur al-Din, with a passionate plea for leaving crusade and *jihad* in the Middle Ages, where they 'belong'.

J. Phillips, *Holy Warriors: A Modern History of the Crusades* (London, 2009). This is by the expert on the Fourth Crusade, with some unusual points, and is helpful on Melisende.

J. Riley-Smith, *The Crusades: A Short History* (London, 1990). A detailed, comprehensive account to be dipped into for reference. The author is illuminating on the relation between just war and holy war.

Richard Lionheart

J. Gillingham, *Richard I* (New Haven, CT, and London, 1999), is the definitive work. On no account read his first biography, utterly superseded by his own later book.

J. Flori, *Richard the Lionheart, King and Knight* (Edinburgh, 1999), is valuable for ideas. The author has a Gallic relish in correcting Gillingham, and is mostly wrong, but right on Richard's dramatic confession in Messina.

D. D. R. Owen, *The Legend of Roland: A Pageant of the Middle Ages* (London and New York, 1973). Stories which inspired the young Richard. The illustrations are excellent.

Military Orders

H. Nicholson, *The Knights Hospitallers* (Woodbridge, 2001), is clear and readable, more lenient to Philip the Fair than the present writer. See also Nicholson's companion work, *The Knights Templar* (Botley, 2003).

M. Barber, *The Trial of the Templars* (Cambridge, 1978), clarifies all the smears.

G. Napier, *A to Z of the Knights Templar* (Stroud, 2008), is a reference work on crusades as well as Templars, and especially good on the modern lunatic fringe. A revised edition should correct factual errors.

H. J. A. Sire, *The Knights of Malta* (New Haven, CT, and London, 1994), is detailed and full of enthusiasm, with the best account of the great sieges.

R. D. Smith and K. Devries, *Rhodes Besieged: A New History* (Stroud, 2011), although a detailed academic book, is excellent for developments in siege warfare and cannon.

Chronicles

E. Hallam (ed.), *Chronicles of the Crusades* (Godalming, 1989), is wide-ranging, with illustrations.

Joinville, *The Life of St Louis,* ed. B. Radice and R. Baldick, trans. M. R. B. Shaw (Harmondsworth, 1970). This is by the companion of St Louis and contains the most vivid account of what crusading felt like.

A. Wolff, *How Many Miles to Babylon: Travels and Adventures of Egypt and beyond from 1300 to 1640* (Liverpool, 2003), is gripping on Venetian maltreatment of pilgrims, the problems of the *hajj* and life under the Ottomans.

R. Allen (ed.), *Eastward Bound: Travel and Travellers, 1050–1550* (Manchester, 2004). Pilgrims, Islamic travellers, crusading plans, with analysis.

J. and L. Riley-Smith, *The Crusades: Idea and Reality, 1095–1274* (London, 1981). This has some varied and interesting extracts.

Modern Times

T. S. R. Boase, *Castles and Churches of the Crusading Kingdom* (London, New York, 1967), is moving and evocative, with colour photographs and drawings old and new, taking his story into the twentieth century.

J. Riley-Smith, *The Crusades, Christianity and Islam* (New York and Chichester, 2008). A volume of lectures, sometimes surprising, especially on Leo XIII.

J. Milton, R. Steinberg and S. Lewis (eds), (Milton for Byzantium, Lewis for the Turks), *The Rise and Fall of Empires: Religion at the Crossroads* (London, 1980). This outlines Byzantine history from Constantine to the fall of Constantinople in 1453, linking it to Turkish history from the Seljuqs to Atatürk and the abolition of the caliphate. It has unusually fine illustrations; see especially pp. 22–3, for the decline of the Byzantine Empire, and pp. 36–7, for the relics of Muhammad and the Night Journey.

Oxford Dictionary of National Biography has an excellent piece on Allenby, based on the biography written by his chief of staff, Wavell.

Islam

Background

The Quran, trans. N. J. Dawood (Harmondsworth, rev. edn, 1972), who sees the work as a literary masterpiece and tries to do justice to its majestic Arabic with a free-flowing translation.*

The Holy Qur'an, trans. Abdullah Yusuf Ali (Birmingham, 1934; repr. 2000) is set out like the Authorised Version of the Bible, with Arabic, translation and commentary on each page and, like the Gideon Bible, an injunction to read a little each day.

M. S. Gordon, *Understanding Islam* (London, 2002), is a short, sympathetic analysis; illustrated.

A. J. Silverstein, *Islamic History: A Very Short Introduction* (Oxford, 2010), consists of reflections by a historian of Jewish background, examining sources critically and reviewing the history of the caliphate.

C. Hillenbrand, *Islam: A New Historical Introduction* (London, 2015), is a work of distinction, crystallising many years of study, providing chapters on varied themes and relating them to current issues. The selective use of Arabic in the chapter on the Quran is especially illuminating. Behind it lies a passion for dissipating misinformation and a plea for movement on the storm point of Palestine, which radicalises so many moderate Muslims. It is best read slowly and reflectively.

M. Ruthven with A. Nanji, *Historical Atlas of the Islamic World* (Oxford, 2004). A wide-ranging survey, including modern disputes and Islamic art; use for the Seljuqs.

O. Grabar, *The Dome of the Rock* (Cambridge, MA, 2006), is a scholarly reconstruction with excellent illustrations.

B. Rogerson, *The Heirs of Muhammad* (New York, 2006). A narrative, with good diagrams and analysis.

S. O'Shea, *Sea of Faith, Islam and Christianity in the Medieval Mediterranean World* (London, 2006), provides vivid battle analyses by a writer with a fine eye for terrain; has the best account of Yarmuk.

---

*I am indebted for this to Badgers Books, a sadly rare example of an old-style browsing bookshop, at 8–10 Gratwicke Road, Worthing, West Sussex, BN11 4BH (Tel. 01903 211816); http://www.badgers-books.co.uk.

P. Partner, *God of Battles, Holy Wars of Christianity and Islam* (London, 1997), is unusually wide-ranging, carrying his story from the ancient Near East to the 1990s with much wisdom.

J. L. Exposito (ed.), *The Oxford History of Islam* (Oxford, 1999).

P. M. Cobb, *Usama ibn Munqidh, Warrior Poet of the Age of the Crusades* (Oxford, 2006). A reconstruction of the life of the greatest eleventh-century Arabic poet, revealing the Arab notion of a gentleman and Usama's murky political history; has implications for the role of women.

A. Malouf (ed.), *The Crusades through Arab Eyes* (London, 1984). Chronicle extracts, with commentary.

H. Kennedy, *The Court of the Caliphs: The Rise and Fall of Islam's Greatest Dynasty* (London, 2004), is a flowing, large-scale and amusing narrative of the history of the Abbasids, to be read casually, with attention to photos of Merv, Samarra and the Zagros mountains and the plan of Baghdad.

L. Singer (ed.), *The Minbar of Saladin* (London, 2008), describes re-creating the *minbar* in the al-Aqsa mosque, destroyed in 1969. It has gripping illustrations on classic craftsmanship and links to HRH the Prince of Wales's School of Traditional Arts.

HRH, The Prince of Wales, *A Sense of the Sacred: Building Bridges Between Islam and the West* (online article: http://www. sacredweb. com/online_ articles/sw13_hrh. html).

Saladin

M. C. Lyons and D. Jackson, *Saladin: The Politics of Holy War* (Cambridge, 1984), is still the classic work for Saladin. It stresses the fluidity of the Islamic world in this epoch, which gave unusual chances to Saladin.

A. -M. Eddé, *Saladin* (Cambridge, MA, and London, 2011), gives a full account of the Islamic world and is excellent to browse in, but decides against giving a chronological analysis, which the present writer believes is possible. There is good evidence for a personal conversion following illness in the winter of 1186–7 affecting his subsequent actions, especially in relation to the caliph. Eddé puts paid to the uniformly pejorative view of Saladin of A. S. Ehrenkreuz in 1972.

G. Hindley, *Saladin: Hero of Islam* ([2007] Barnsley, 2010), covers the military aspects.

Modern Times

D. W. Brown, *A New Introduction to Islam* (2nd edn, Chichester, 2009), is a masterly account, covering pre-Islamic Arabia, Muhammad, history, law and doctrine. This is much the best book for an inquirer because of the author's early life in Pakistan and the first-class indexing. See especially the origins of Shiism, the coffee controversy and the implications of feminism. The present writer has not followed him on the hypotheses on early Islamic history of Patricia Crone and John Wasborough.

C. Hillenbrand, *The Crusades: Islamic Perspectives* (Edinburgh, 1999), is essential for Mamluks and their art, but also to be read for general attitudes to crusaders among Muslims. The book is full of splendid, varied illustrations.

H. Kennedy, *The Great Arab Conquests: How the Spread of Islam Changed the World We Live in* (London, 2007). I have made great use of this book. The end-paper on the limit of Muslim rule in 750 is a most convenient way of surveying the area of early conquests. Only in Portugal and Spain were the conquests reversed.

J. Freely, *The Grand Turk Sultan Mehmet II: Conqueror of Constantinople and Master in Empire* (New York, 2009). Use for a general account of the sultanate as well as Mehmet: he takes the story down to the death of Suleiman the Magnificent.

D. A. Howarth, *The Desert King: A Life of Ibn Saud* (London, 1964), is a vivid account of Wahhabism and the creator of Saudi Arabia. *The Kingdom of Saudi Arabia* (London, 2011), with no single editor, issued by Stacey International, describes the modern kingdom, with vivid illustrations; see pp. 33–4 for Ibn Saud's camel force, led by him in action in 1913.

M. Bonner, *Jihad in Islamic History: Doctrines and Practice* (Woodstock, 2006). The emphasis on the flexibility of the concept, the weaving together of jurists' definitions and practice of *jihad* in history are most illuminating.

L. W. Adamec, *Islam: A Historical Companion* (2nd edn, Stroud, 2007). Very good quality, especially for snappy consultation. Useful on Wahhabism.

Recent Events and Western Responses

R. S. Lieken, *Europe's Angry Muslims. The Revolt of the Second Generation* (Oxford and New York, 2012), focuses on France, Britain and Germany, and actions and responses in those countries. Leiken provides first-class reporting and pleads for cool analysis.

M. Siddique, *Christians, Muslims and Jews* (New Haven, CT, and London, 2013), is a moving personal account of the author's encounters as a practising Muslim with monotheists of other faiths, above all Christians. Her work is distinguished by a determination to do justice through quotation and analysis to the variety of viewpoints now extant. She is strikingly up-to-date.

F. Mernissi, *Islam and Democracy: Fears of the Modern World* (Cambridge, MA, 2002), has comments, often scathing, on the mutual misunderstanding of Islam and the United States, and on the baleful effect of oppressive economic regimes. A final chapter describes women's rights and hopes.

D. W. Brown, *A New Introduction to Islam* (Malden, MA, and Oxford, 2009), already cited, has a penetrating survey of Islam in the twenty-first century, pp. 282–98. Although sympathetic, the author points out the flaws in Mernissi's feminist plea, p. 295.

Judaism

S. Sebag Montefiore, *Jerusalem: The Biography* (London, 2011), is a gripping account by a member of a Liberal Jewish synagogue who lived in the city as a boy, taking his story from David to Moshe Dayan. See his observations on the crucifixions of Jews and modern-day 'indifferentism'. He is illuminating on T. E. Lawrence.

H. Shanks, *Jerusalem's Temple Mount from Solomon to the Golden Dome* (New York and London, 2009), concentrates on the Jewish Temple but has much on Christian and Muslim sites. Note Heraclius's coin, p. 59.

GLOSSARY

Abbasid caliphate	Sunni hereditary caliphate, named after Muhammad's uncle al-Abbas; its capital became Baghdad.
adab	Characteristics of an Arab gentleman.
Alid	Descendant of Ali and Fatima or supporter of Ali's cause.
allods	Tracts of territory in the German Empire held in virtual independence of the emperor.
Anatolia/Asia Minor	Approximately modern Turkey.
apostasy	Abandonment of beliefs. Term applied to expeditions directed by Caliph Abu Bakr to recall Arabs to the Faith.
appanage	A dependent territory created, for example, for a younger child, which gradually diminishes the stock of land and income from land available to the sovereign; avoided by the early caliphs providing money pensions for superannuated warriors.
Aramaeans	Farmers from lands between the Tigris and Euphrates, oppressed by the Sassanians.
Aramaic	Semitic language spoken by Christ.

Armenians	Inhabitants of a kingdom converted to Christianity early in the fourth century who developed their own script to translate the Bible and declined to accept Byzantine doctrinal authority.
arnaldia	*see* murrain.
arquebusiers	Firearm-wielding soldiers, marksmen.
Artuqids	Heirs to Artuq I, Seljuq governor of Jerusalem, removed in August 1098, also known as Ortoqids.
Assassins	Extremist Shiites angered at the corruption of the Fatimid caliphate in Cairo and hostile to Sunnis, based in the inaccessible Elburz mountains. They used murder to eliminate individuals.
atabeg	Ostensibly a guardian of a young heir; in fact, *atabegs* were contenders for power in the twelfth century.
Ayyubids	Descendants of Saladin.
bahriyya	An elite force of slave soldiers kept on the island in the Nile, Bahr al-Nil.
bailli	Another name for seneschal.
batin	The deeper meaning of the Quran, which could be elucidated by the Ismaili Shiites.
Berbers	Inhabitants of North African mountains used as troops for the Fatimid caliphate.
bila kaif	'Without speculation'.
Buyids	Opportunist, loosely Shiite warriors from the Iranian mountains, dominating Abbasid caliphs.
Byzantium	Ancient title of the strategic site taken by the Emperor Constantine and named Constantinople; it became half of the Roman Empire, Greek Orthodox Christian in belief; above all, a naval power.
caliph	A leader of Islam, a successor to Muhammad; Sunnis gave the caliph the title Commander of the Faithful.

carapace	A hard outer shell.
castellan	Governor or keeper of a castle.
cenacle	The room traditionally believed in Christianity to be the room where the Last Supper was held.
Circassians	Soldiers recruited from the Western Caucasus by the Ottomans.
Companions	Adherents of Muhammad in Mecca who fled for safety to Medina and were subsequently known as the Emigrants.
concomitant	Occurring simultaneously.
Coptic Monophysites	Egyptian Christians, believers that Christ had one nature; condemned as heretics by the Byzantine Church.
couched spears	Spears carried by cavalry to thrust at the enemy, a sophisticated technique used by Bohemond in ambushing Ridwan at Antioch.
dais	Fatimid missionaries.
dhimmis	Peoples of the Book, Christians and Jews.
dirhams	Silver coinage of Muslims.
diwan	System of pensioning warriors devised by Caliph Umar.
dower	Dowry given to a husband on marriage; an endowment.
Druze	Followers of the Fatimid caliph al-Hakim.
ecumenism	A movement seeking unity among different branches of the Christian Church.
Emigrants	*see* Companions.
encyclical	A formal pronouncement by a pope.
excommunication	An institutional act of religious censure used to deprive, suspend or limit membership in a religious community or to restrict certain rights within it: in particular, reception of the sacraments.
Faisal I	Protégé of T. E. Lawrence who was made king of Iraq in a kingdom made by the British.

Fatimid	Dynasty of Shiite caliphs holding power in Egypt, named after Fatima, Muhammad's daughter.
furusiyya	Military guides to cavalry techniques and the use of horses.
Ghadir Khumm	Oasis between Mecca and Medina where Shiites believe that Muhammad conferred spiritual powers on Ali, his son-in-law.
ghazi	A Muslim fighter against non-Muslims.
Ghazznavid dynasty	Arabs who supported Byzantium, thought of as traitors by Islamic armies fighting Byzantium.
Great Schism	The split between the Roman and Avignonese claimants to the Papacy, 1378–1417.
Gregorian Reform	A tradition created by Pope Gregory VII, insisting on the independence of the Church and seeking to end practices of buying and selling ecclesiastical offices and the priesthood passing from father to son.
hadith	A collection of sayings and actions attributed to Muhammad, used in the Sunni tradition to support customs and beliefs.
Hanbalism	The belief that the Quran was uncreated and not susceptible to any modification, associated with the scholar Ahmed ibn Hanbal.
hagiography	Lives of saints.
hajj	Pilgrimage to Mecca.
Hamasah of Abu Tamman	Classic collection of Arabic poems known by heart by Saladin.
haram	Pagan sanctuary.
Hashemites	A lesser clan of the Quraysh to which Muhammad belonged; contemporary rulers of Jordan.
Helpers	Converts to Muslim teaching in Medina.
hijab	Headscarf.

hijra	Muhammad's flight from Mecca to Medina in 622; starting point for the Islamic calendar.
Hira	Capital of the ancient kingdom of Southern Iraq.
Ibn Saud	Arab desert leader who revived Wahhabism and became king of Saudi Arabia in 1932; the name was assumed in honour of a predecessor.
Ilkhanate	A breakaway state of the Mongol Empire, established in the thirteenth century and ruled by the Mongol House of Hulegu, the grandson of Ghengiz Khan, which converted to Islam. It was established in the thirteenth century and was based primarily in Iran and neighbouring territories.
imam	A preacher leading prayers; for Ismaili Shiites, an infallible guide to doctrine.
Ismaili	Shiite Muslims who believed that Ismail, the seventh imam, had rightly taken prophetic authority; this tradition founded the Fatimid dynasty in Egypt.
jahiliyya	Time of ignorance in Arabia before the coming of the Prophet.
jama-l Sunnism	A movement launched by Nur al-Din to unite rival schools of Sunni jurists and moderate Shiites in the interests of destroying Fatimid heresy.
Janissaries	Slave soldiers recruited from Christian children in the Balkans by Ottomans.
jihad	Striving against evil in the soul or striving in war against the enemies of the Faith.
jinn	Spiritual beings created from fire, capable of assuming various shapes.
jizya	Head tax paid by Christians and Jews under Muslim rule.
Kaba	The shrine in Mecca, object of the pilgrimage of the *hajj*, incorporating the black stone, believed to have been bestowed on Abraham by the Archangel Gabriel.

Karbala	Site of the martyrdom of the Shiite al-Husayn in 680.
khanqah	Training place for Sufis.
Khurasanis	A body of soldiers faithful to the Abbasid Caliph al-Mansur, kept as a garrison in Baghdad.
khutba	Prayer for a ruler, solemnly pronounced on the occasion of Friday prayers.
kiswa	Veil covering the temple of the *Kaba*.
Kufic	Ornamental calligraphy of the Quran, whose beauty, in the judgement of Nur al-Din, obscured meaning.
laity	Members of the Church distinguished from the priesthood.
madrasa	Training college for Sunni scholars and *qadis*.
Mahgrib	North-western Africa, source of a simple administrative Arabic script adopted for the Quran under Nur al-Din's influence.
Mamluk	Slave soldier, also ruling dynasty in Egypt.
mangonel	A throwing machine.
manumitting	Releasing from slavery.
mawali	New converts to the faith in the epoch of the Umayyads who ceased to pay the *jizya*.
Melkites	Arab-speaking churchmen with patriarchates; a Melkite Patriarch was responsible for the miracle of the Holy Fire.
mihrab	Niche in a mosque showing the direction of Mecca.
minbar	Pulpit in a mosque.
minha	Authority devised to search out and intimidate those who declined to accept Mutazilism.
monotheism	Form of belief in one God.
monothelitism	A form of Trinitarian doctrine designed to compromise between competing interpretations; imposed on the Byzantine Empire by Emperor Heraclius.

mouvance	A circle of landholding, the centre point in anarchic fighting between rivals in the lands of the western Franks.
muezzin	Call to prayer.
mujahidin	Zealots of armed *jihad* against enemies of Islam.
mulukhiyya	Flavouring for soups in Egypt, condemned by Caliph al-Hakim.
muqarnas	Vaulting, adopted to illustrate eleventh-century Abbasid orthodoxy on the utter dependence of the universe on God.
murrain	Infectious disease affecting cattle and sheep (similar to *arnaldia*).
Mutazilism	Rationalist teaching developed by the Abbasid Caliph al-Mamun in the ninth century, arguing that the Quran was created and could rightly be interpreted by caliphs on matters not settled in the Quran.
naphtha	Deadly inflammable fluid developed by the Byzantines.
nass	Shiite doctrine whereby imams of this persuasion could decide on rightful succession.
Nestorians	Dissidents from the Byzantine Church's definition of the two natures of Christ, human and divine, associated with Nestorius, Bishop of Constantinople.
nicolaitism	Hereditary priesthood.
niqab	Also known as *burka*: a veil of a Muslim woman, covering the head and face.
Occitan	A romance language spoken in southern France, Italy's Occitan Valleys, Monaco and Spain's Val d'Aran.
Omar	*see* Umar.
Ortoqids	*see* Artuqids.
Osman	Founder of the Ottoman dynasty, whose sword was carried by Ottoman caliphs.

Ottomans	Muslim dynasty evolving from Turkish war bands in Anatolia who seized Constantinople in 1453 and created the largest Muslim empire in history.
Outremer	The Crusader States.
panegyrist	A eulogist or public speaker who uses verse to give high praise to a person or thing.
passagium particulare	A deliberately small-scale and highly professional expedition.
pogroms	Persecutions of Jews (latterly, specifically by Tsarist Russia).
Procession of the Holy Spirit	Trinitarian doctrine dividing the Greek and Latin Churches: for the Greeks, the Holy Spirit proceeds from the Father through the Son; for the Latins it proceeds from the Father and the Son.
qadis	Islamic judges.
Qarmatians	Fighting Shiites active in the late ninth and tenth centuries who formed a mini-state.
qibla	Direction of prayer.
qumiz	Fermented mare's milk.
Quraysh	Ruling aristocracy of Mecca.
ridda	Muslim crime of apostasy, for which there are severe penalties.
Rightly Guided	A term used by Muslims for the first four caliphs: Abu Bakr, Umar, Uthman and Ali.
sahil	Coastal strip of the Holy Land.
Sassanians	Dynasty ruling Persia, whose state religion was Zoroastrianism.
Seljuq Turks	Nomads from the Russian steppe driven into settled Islamic lands by famine, converted to Sunnism.

seneschal	An officer in the household of important Western nobles usually in charge of domestic arrangements and administration.
Shafites	School of Sunni jurists named after Muhammad ibn Idris al-Shafi (767–820) supported by Saladin, who built a tomb for him in Cairo.
shahada	An Islamic creed declaring belief in the oneness of God and the acceptance of Muhammad as God's prophet.
shahid	Martyr or witness.
shura	Examination of the suitability of a caliph.
simony	Buying or selling of a bishopric or other ecclesiastical office.
siyar	An elaborate system of public and private international law which emphasised human rights regardless of religious affiliation created in the eighth century.
sufi	An Islamic mystic, title derived from the Arabic for wool, *suf*.
Sultan	Title conferred on Seljuq Turks by Abbasid caliphs in the eleventh century, acknowledging their military power while retaining their own spiritual authority.
sura	Chapter of the Quran.
Syriac	Aramaic dialect of Syria.
Tafsir	Commentaries on the Quran.
Tafurs	Cannibal extremists in the crusader force on the First Crusade.
Tanzimat	Secularising movement within the late Ottoman Empire, aiming to preserve it by modernising.
taqiyya (quietism)	Doctrine developed by the Shiite scholar Muhammad al-Baqr enabling Shiite supporters to conceal their beliefs.

Thagafi	Member of the family inhabiting Taif, a wealthy hill town used by Meccans as a relief from summer heat.
trebuchet	Counter-weight throwing machine, potentially more powerful than the mangonel.
Trinitarian	Christian doctrine of the Holy Trinity: Father, Son and Holy Spirit.
Turcopoles	Muslims enlisted for pay under crusader settlers.
Twelver Shiism	Believers that an infallible imam, occulted by God, will come back to usher in the end of the world, a doctrine held by the leadership in contemporary Iran.
ulama	Body of Islamic scholars.
Umar (also known as Omar)	Second caliph and conqueror of Jerusalem.
Umayyads	Hereditary dynasty founded by Muawiya which made Damascus its capital.
umma	Muslim community, established in Medina; later used as a term for Muslims throughout the world.
Visigoths	Western Goths, a barbarian people settled in southern France and Spain who accepted Christianity.
vizier	Chief representative and adviser of the caliph.
Wahhabis	Named after the eighteenth-century scholar Muhammad ibn Abd al-Wahhab, who preached a puritanical form of Islam based rigidly on the Quran, rejecting Sufism, all forms of intercession, saint cults and shrines, and believing in the duty of the state to enforce doctrine and suppress vice.

ILLUSTRATION CREDITS

Colour

1   The Church of the Holy Sepulchre, Jerusalem. Photo: © Sonia Halliday Photo Library
2   The *Kaba* (cube) the House of God, Mecca. Photo: © Sufi/shutterstock
3   Ali and Muhammad destroying the Idols. Photo: © The Trustees of the Chester Beatty Library, Dublin
4   Muhammad being defended by Abu Bakr. From the Spencer Collection, the *New York Public Library Digital Collections*
5   The Night Journey of the Prophet. Reproduced with kind permission of Desmond Stewart, *Mecca* (The Reader's Digest Association, Ltd., 1980)
6   The Dome of the Rock, Jerusalem. Photo: © akg-images/Bildarchiv Steffens
7   The *minbar* of Nur al-Din. From Carole Hillenbrand, *The Crusades, Islamic Perspectives* (Edinburgh University Press, 1999), with permission of the author
8   The Janissaries on ceremonial parade at the court of Sultan Selim III, Istanbul, late eighteenth century. Photo: ReinhardDirscherl/WaterFrame/Getty Images
9   Prince Zizim is feasted by the Knights of Rhodes. Bibliothèque Nationale, Paris. Caoursin MS Lat. 6067
10   King Louis Philippe of France. Photo: Winterhalter/National Museum of Versailles/Mary Evans/BeBa/Iberfoto

11 Kaiser Wilhelm II. Photo: © Robert Hunt Library/Mary Evans
12 Sultan Abdul-Hamid II. Unattributed design in *Le Petit Journal*, 21 February 1897/Mary Evans
13 The statue of Saladin in Damascus with sculptor Abdallah al-Sayed. From Hillenbrand, *The Crusades, Islamic Perspectives*

Black and White

1 Statue from Belval abbey church, Lorraine. From Wolfgang Müller-Wiener, *Castles of the Crusaders* (Thames and Hudson, 1966). Photo by A. F. Kersting
2 The fragment of a tower in the Turkish township of Antakya. From Müller-Wiener, *Castles of the Crusaders*
3 Krak des Chevaliers, in the Nusairi mountains. From Müller-Wiener, *Castles of the Crusaders*
4 Krak des Chevaliers (plan). From Müller-Wiener, *Castles of the Crusaders*
5 The castle and garrison town of Kerak. From Müller-Wiener, *Castles of the Crusaders*
6 The Citadel at Aleppo. From Müller-Wiener, *Castles of the Crusaders*
7 The Citadel (plan). From Hillenbrand, *The Crusades, Islamic Perspectives*
8 Masyaf, Syria. From Müller-Wiener, *Castles of the Crusaders*
9 The Horns of Hattin, Israel. From Michael Haag *The Tragedy of the Templars* (Profile Books, 2012), with permission of the author
10 Sahyun, Syria. From Müller-Wiener, *Castles of the Crusaders*
11 The Ablution Tower on the Haram. Reproduced with kind permission of J. M. Landay, *Dome of the Rock Three Faiths of Jerusalem* (The Reader's Digest Association Ltd., 1980)
12 The Latin cathedral dedicated to St Antony, Famagusta, Cyprus. From Müller-Wiener, *Castles of the Crusaders*
13 Bodrum – an engraved slab, 1472, showing the arms of the Grand Master. From Müller-Wiener, *Castles of the Crusaders*
14 King Ibn Saud. Picture dated to 1927, source unknown, Wikicommons.
15 Sultan Atrash, Druze Leader. Photo: ©Pictures from History/Bridgeman Images
16 Sir Mark Sykes, MP for Hull. Photo: ©Getty Images

17 F. Georges-Picot, French Colonialist. From: James Barr, *A Line in the Sand, Britain, France and the Struggle for Mastery of the Middle East* (Simon and Schuster UK Ltd., 2001)

While every effort has been made to contact copyright-holders of illustrations, the author and publishers would be grateful for information about any illustrations where they have been unable to trace them, and would be glad to make amendments in further editions.

ACKNOWLEDGEMENTS

My thanks are due to Dr C. Lohmer of the Monumenta Germaniae Historica who has been an unfailing source of references. Professor C. Hillenbrand of Edinburgh answered bibliographical queries. Professor J. France of Swansea sent copies of his articles and has been a major influence on my account of the First Crusade. Professor P. Herde of Würzburg has answered queries, as has Professor M. Barber of Reading. The staff at London Library have shown me great kindness, Readers Digest of New York deserve a special mention for their kindness over photographs, the Thomas Cook archive was unstinting with information and I am much indebted to the secretarial skills of Pauline James especially in electronic crises.

I owe more than I can say to the computer skills and understanding of adult education of my friend and former student Alison Webb and, as always, to my wife's patience, co-operative work and logical sense.

INDEX